NEW WORLD HEGEMONY

IN THE

MALAY WORLD

Geoffrey C. Gunn

The Red Sea Press, Inc.

Publishers & Distributors of Third World Books

11-D Princess Road
Lawrenceville, NJ 08648

RSP

P. O. Box 48
Asmara, ERITREA

The Red Sea Press, Inc.

Publishers & Distributors of Third World Books

11-D Princess Road   **RSP**   P. O. Box 48
Lawrenceville, NJ 08648   Asmara, ERITREA

Copyright © 2000 Geoffrey C. Gunn

First Printing 2000

Cover Design: Debbie Hird

Library of Congress Catalog-in-Publication Data

Gunn, Geoffrey C.
    New world hegemony in the Malay world / Geoffrey Gunn.
        p.   cm.
    Includes bilbliographical references and index.
    ISBN 1-56902-134-1 (hb) — ISBN 1-56902-135-X (pb)
      1. Indonesia--Politics and government--20th century. 2. Malaysia--
Politics and government. 3. Brunei--Politcs and government.
    4. Timor Timur (Indonesia)--Poltics and government. I. Title.

DS644.G86 2000
959.803--dc21

                                              99-059269

Contents

Preface

To the surprise of many the much vaunted "Asian economic miracle" took a nose dive in 1998, sending stock exchanges and currencies into disarray, sinking the new middle classes, drastically raising unemployment and poverty levels and throwing grave doubts upon the authoritarian "Asian value" model of development. While the debate over the globalizing effects of currency movements rages on, no longer could the debilitating mix of military-led dictatorship, one-party dominant authoritarianism, and the region's signature crony capitalism style of business be shielded from the rising wrath of new emergent forces, especially around the slogan of *reformasi*.

Nowhere has the challenge to military-led dictatorship been as stormy, and nowhere have the stakes been so high as in the sprawling tropical archipelagic nation, Indonesia, also the world's fourth most populous country. Just as the dramatic resignation of Indonesian President General Suharto in May 1998 signalled the climax of a nation-wide "people's power" movement, so the peoples of East Timor, the former Portuguese colony brutally annexed by the dictatorship in 1975, upped the ante in their own struggle for self-determination, seizing upon the slogan "no democracy in Indonesia without freedom for East Timor."

So, in taking the "Malay world" or the world of the Malay-speaking countries of Indonesia, Malaysia, and Brunei Darussalam as paradigmatic of debates on democracy versus authoritarianism in the postcolonial world, this book also adumbrates the East Timor case as emblematic of the universal question of social justice and human rights which engage all human beings. Complex fractured societies at the juncture of three imperialisms, Dutch, British, and Portuguese, the major ecological, political, and economic crises of the late twentieth century remind us that the boundaries of colonialism and the writ of dictators are nowhere immutable when it comes to questions of freedom, autonomy, and self-determination.

Introduction

Beginning January 1998, foreign embassies in the Indonesian capital of Jakarta began to draw up contingency plans for the evacuation of their civilians. By April, ships of the U.S. Pacific fleet were positioned on "vacation" off the Indonesian holiday island of Bali. By May, as economic meltdown in the world's fourth-most populous country fanned popular dissent, the U.S. moved three ships and 3,000 Okinawa-based marines to the Java Sea area. In an unprecedented action, the Tokyo government ordered Maritime Defense Force ships positioned off Java ready to handle the contingency of a mass seaborne evacuation of its substantial Japanese civilian and business community. Was this the long-expected bloody demise of the now tottering Indonesian New Order of General Suharto? Were the events unfolding in some way manageable? As the personification of Indonesia's "economic miracle," turned wreck in the throes of the great Asian economic and financial crisis of 1997-99, was the aging dictator now dispensable?

As key supporting formateur, major military backer, and, along with Japan, leading economic prop of the Indonesian New Order regime of General-President Suharto since its establishment in 1965-66, the U.S. reaction was crucial at this juncture. Critically, on 17 March, U.S. journalist Allan Nairn in Jakarta exposed continued military training of Indonesian Kopassus Red Beret units under the Pentagon's Joint Combined Exchange and Training (JCET) program (36 exercises since 1992), unknown even to U.S. Congress and in circumvention of an earlier announced cutoff.[1] On 7 May, an articulate young Indonesian pro-democracy activist, Pius Lustrilanang, offered graphic testimony to a U.S. Congressional hearing as to his kidnapping and month-long illegal detention by a military unit in Java, part of a wave of disappearances of pro-democracy

activists perpetrated between May 1997 and March 1998. In a
major prelude to change amidst a subsequent outcry in Congress
supported by key Indonesian opposition figure, Megawati
Sukarnoputri, daughter of Indonesia's first President, Sukarno,
the Pentagon suspended its highly compromised military training
program.

Until appointed in March 1998 to head Kostrad (Army
Strategic Reserve), the strategic force that guards Jakarta, the
6,250-man Koppasus had been headed by Major-General
Prabowo Subianto, Suharto's son-in law. In 1965-66, Kopassus,
then known as RPKAD, and headed by Colonel Sarwo Edhie,
spearheaded the Suharto countercoup against the Republic of
Indonesia's first president, the charismatic Sukarno, leading to
hundreds of thousands of deaths across the sprawling
archipelago. Using U.S.-supplied armor, Koppasus also led the
invasion of the former Portuguese colony of East Timor in
December 1975.

On 9 May 1998, following weeks of student protest, Suharto
bravely flew off to Egypt to attend a G-15 summit, heading off a
domestic political storm and mounting criticism over his decision
in following an IMF demand to drop subsidies on key
commodities. In his absence (12 May), six students of the elite
Trisakti University were shot dead by security forces, igniting a
firestorm of nationwide campus protests. Just as Forum Kota
(City Forum), a cross-campus coalition, took a leading role in
coordinating the mobilizations, so we should not ignore the
broader intellectual role of new electronic media (Internet) in
disseminating information, an activity deployed with effect by
PIJAR (Pusat Informasi dan Jaringan Aksi untuk Reformasi), a
student action group founded in 1989. Together, the call for
reformasi and the end to collusion, corruption, and nepotism
(KKN), including the Suharto family wealth, became the adopted
slogans of the student movement and the mass mobilizations,
although the question of a student-urban poor alliance was
subject of a major debate within Forum Kota on 14 May.

Many doubted the 77-year-old dictator would return,
however. Continuing, on 13 and 14 May, riots engulfed Jakarta,
leaving thousands of buildings torched and 1,200 dead. Darker

acts of rape and ethnocide were committed in Jakarta's China-town as well as in such other cities as Solo, Bandung, and Medan. Meanwhile, tens of thousands of expatriates along with ethnic Chinese scrambled to evacuate the burning city of Jakarta, becoming signature headlines 'round the world. Yet Suharto returned, badly underestimating the depth of domestic opposition, a reference to the broad coalition of student protesters, intellectuals, and opposition figures, as symbolized by the spectacular mass student occupation of the parliament building.

On 21 May, to the surprise of many, including his deputy and long-term protege, the civilian technocrat, B.J. Habibie, Suharto announced his resignation, simultaneously swearing-in Habibie, as third President of the Republic, and heading off the looming scenario of military coup. In this elite transfer of power, the role of the recently appointed Defense Minister and Commander of Angkatan Bersenjata Republik Indonesia (ABRI)/Tentara National Indonesia (TNI) or Indonesian armed forces, General Wiranto, was undoubtedly decisive, if not determinate. First, Wiranto distinguished himself by eschewing the violence typically associated with ABRI crowd control and by tolerating the student protests. Second, the military supremo evinced a high degree of consultation with Suharto in the lead up to his resignation and the transition of power, visiting the President three times on 22 May and again on the 26th, emerging, in the pact, as the dictator turned erstwhile shadow shogun's sworn physical guarantor.

Few Indonesia watchers predicted the method and timing of Suharto's resignation, although it became increasingly clear that Suharto's options were narrowed with the defection of key ministers, among them Ginanjar Kartasmita, Japanese-trained economist, International Monetary Fund (IMF) darling, and Minister for Economy and Finance, along with Parliament speaker Harmoko. At the end of the day, Suharto was snubbed by Muslim leaders and abandoned by business cronies who had fled the country. Habibie, as head of the Islamic Association of Intelectuals (MUIS), was more acceptable to that quarter.

Less well known at the time, or less reported, was the orchestrated character of the riots, blamed by some upon Suharto

viii *Introduction*

to justify a return to law and order and, more realistically, to intra-military manoeuvring in Jakarta. On the evening following Suharto's resignation, Kostrad units under Colonel Prabowo Subianto who had earlier that day been stripped by Wiranto of his position as head of Kostrad, staged a show of force in Jakarta, more theatre than attempted coup, but according to script? In any case the "treason" confirmed Wiranto's position. Wiranto's victory and Prabowo's swift fall from grace might not have been an entirely internalist military affair but had all the hallmarks of a Fort Bragg-scripted scenario to ensure an "acceptable" transition. There is no question that the U.S. played the Prabowo card when it suited them, and when it seemed he was acting in defense of Suharto and "stability," but equally obvious that the U.S. precipitously dropped its client of 32 years, when cornered in Congress and, especially, faced with an anarchic outcome on the streets of Jakarta. At the end of the day, Prabowo was a liability to Suharto, his albatross.

Australian pro-democracy activist and political analyst Max Lane has argued that it was actually fear of grassroots political unrest and political power that panicked the regime leading to Suharto's resignation. Such an estimation becomes highly credible in view of the rise of mass protest and the challenge mounted to the Suharto strategy of depoliticization and the "floating mass" brought down in 1971. While, over the years, the regime had been highly successful in cowing the media, the unions, and the students, especially through the use of subversion laws, the bloody military-led crackdown on the headquarters of Megawati's PDI-Perjuangan (Struggle) Party in July 1996 and ensuing riots in downtown Jakarta signalled a dangerous collision course between the policy of the iron fist and unrest brewing at the grassroots. In the event, street and worker protests, bringing out racialist elements but also the urban poor, continued on both an organized and unorganized basis, with a million people on the streets in Jakarta prior to the May 1997 general elections.[2]

While Suharto's transfer of the levers of power to Habibie can be seen as the consummate act of the so-called "May revolution," it was also an anticlimactic end to 32 years of personalistic dictatorship. Demonstrably not the end of the New

Order, the new Habibie cabinet comprised not a few Suharto holdovers. Moreover, as mass student-led demonstrations in Jakarta in mid-November 1998 questioned with increasing clamor, was this a constitutional transfer of power? After all, Habibie had been earlier appointed, not elected, Vice President by the Suharto/Golkar/ military-dominated Assembly. As well, was the new parliament then convening either valid or representative? And was Habibie a transitional figure or harboring personal ambitions to be elected in future elections? Overriding such questions was the larger issue as to the armed forces withdrawing from its so-called *dwi-fungsi* or dual function role, inter alia legitimizing its role in politics and society, and returning to the barracks as a professional force, in any case an option rejected by ABRI itself?

Reformasi

No less, the months following the May events had seen an unprecedented upwelling in public protest in Indonesia and, as discussed in a penultimate chapter, also in East Timor. Not only did Habibie mandate the free formation of political parties leading to a promised election in mid-1999, he also recognized several independent unions, freed up the press, and selectively released political prisoners in certain categories. In so doing, he went further than certain of his critics expected in pushing a reform agenda, albeit without seriously questioning the parameters of military involvement in Indonesia's public life. Such prudence pacified Western creditors, although not the radicals within the reform movement.

Meanwhile, the probe into Suharto's wealth proceeded inconclusively, just as the internal military probe into the role of Prabowo in disappearances proceeded with a calculated indeterminate conclusion. Indeed, Prabowo fled abroad. Probes into various ABRI killings and abuses were also allowed to run their indeterminate course. But there were clear limits, however. On his part, Army Commander Wiranto set limits on civilian investigation into army excesses and massacres, covered up or protected the chain of command or taint of the same, and further sullied the army's image by using disproportionate force in neutralizing mass demonstrations in November. For his part, Habibie held back from restoring Megawati Sukarnoputri to her rightful place as head of the leading opposition party, PDI, of which she had been stripped two years earlier by pro-Suharto forces. Indeed, by early 1999, it was clear to many observers that not only had Suharto survived investigation, but that his business empire had emerged from the crisis all the healthier, owing to its links with foreign partners. More ominously, Suhartoists from within the military began to flex their muscles, impatient with Habibie's reformist rhetoric, and, as analyzed below, concessions on East Timor.

Dismayed by the dilatory reform agenda which pledged only a reduction of military seats in Indonesia's parliament, people's power once again came onto bloody collision course with the military in Jakarta in November 1998. Atavistic forces were also unleashed as communal violence flared (Aceh, Ambon, West Timor, and Kalimantan), seldom spontaneous in Indonesia, raising questions as to, variously, the long shadow of Suharto, the role of the military in actively organizing agitators, including, as discussed in a final chapter, death squads in East Timor. Especially.after the infamous military-led rape of Timor following the U.N.-conducted ballot of 30 August 1999, questions were also being raised as to disunity within the armed forces, Habibie's expendability, and, once more, darker scenarios of military takeover.

Just as infusion of IMF funds arrested the worst-case scenario of food riots and anarchy, so the promise of elections appeased Jakarta's Western backers, drawing a critical line between the moderate slogan of *reformasi* and the logical conclusion of the reform process, some kind of social and economic *revolusi*, at least meeting populist demands for renewal. While electoral provisions were being drafted, some 120 new political parties emerged under the new mandate: among them, 33 Muslim parties, a Catholic party, and a Chinese party, including Partai Murba, as discussed in a separate chapter, the banned social democrat party formed by Tan Malaka on 7 November 1948. Keeping the army out of politics was but one of many anticipated problems in the runup to the June 1999 national elections. Even the World Bank hedged on a major tranche of funds, fearing its largesse would once again influence the outcome in favor of the incumbent Golkar machine.

East Timor, Aceh, Irian Jaya

Debates and concerns over Indonesia's boundaries, center-periphery relations, ethnic rights, questions of federalism versus the unitary state principle not only concerned outsiders but came to the heart of political debates, unilateral actions, and people's struggles across the archipelago, especially as communal violence flared. While all provinces of Indonesia in some way demand greater autonomy over their resources and livelihoods from Jakarta, the federalism-autonomy-separatism-independence debate or struggle is focused on three regions, each on the extremity of the archipelago.

While, as observed, PIJAR first coined the phrase *reformasi* taken up as a battle cry for students and moderate reformers throughout the nation, by late 1998 PIJAR was calling for "reformasi total," a demand that would see the end of *asas tunggal* (the Panca Sila or state ideology and the 1945 Constitution). It also sought the abolition of *dwi fungsi*, a view shared by many other sections of society. While the campaign to bring Suharto and his family to trial for economic and other crimes had support across a wide spectrum, including leading moderate Muslim opposition figure Amien Rais, PIJAR targeted not the Suharto family alone but the wider oligarchy. According to George Aditjondro,[3] their vision is a federalist Indonesia and for people's self-determination even within the old colonial boundaries of the Dutch East Indies. But their socialist vision is emphatically not shared by those Aditjondro has called "proportionalists" or Muslim Indonesians who champion rights proportional to their demographic supremacy. Even so, he interprets, the two share concerns over Suharto family nepotism and collusion and military-linked crimes affecting Muslims, namely Aceh and Tanjong Priok.

To better understand the federalist position, we should

observe the problem. One case is Aceh, the historically Islamic region of northern Sumatra that resists Jakarta's rule as vehemently as it resisted Dutch pacification in the nineteenth and early twentieth centuries. Declared a Special Military Region (DOM) by Suharto, as discussed in a separate chapter, Aceh waged a righteous separatist struggle through the 1980s and 1990s only to suffer some of the worst excesses and human rights abuses in Indonesia at the hands of ABRI. Conscious of his large Islamic constituency, these wrongs were recognized by the Habibie government and some forms of redress and healing have been undertaken, including the withdrawal of DOM status.

The second region where separatist sentiments runs high is that of Irian, the western half of the island of New Guinea, incorporated into the Republic of Indonesia only in 1963, after a campaign of subversion by the Sukarno regime and a sham vote of self-determination conducted in 1969 by the U.N. Prodigiously rich in resources and home to an ethnographic mosaic of broadly Melanesian peoples unrelated by history or kin to the mostly Javanese-encadred ABRI, the OPM or Free Papua Organization has waged a 30-year armed struggle in defense of independence. In June 1998 ABRI brutally crushed an OPM flag-raising event inside Irian, signalling its determination to prevent independence at any cost. While Habibie/Wiranto also withdrew DOM status from Irian, for the Irianese this concession hardly compensates for three decades of plunder, cultural assimilation, and loss of resources and land to immigrants. While some voices in Jakarta favor more autonomy for such provinces as Irian, there is little sentiment in favor of a "separatist" outcome, and attitudes in Jakarta remain firmly colonial vis-a-vis the indigenous cultures of this outpost.

Such patronizing attitudes in Jakarta have also governed its military overlordship of East Timor, the Portuguese colony and stillborn independent state invaded in flagrant breach of international law by ABRI in December 1975. Given East Timor's even more unfavorable ecological situation, the attrition wrought by ABRI in the half-island has far exceeded that of even Irian and Aceh, leading, in the words of the 1996 Nobel

Peace Prize Committee, to the loss of one third of the population. If news of such genocidal actions was often ignored or disbelieved in the West, then it is not hard to imagine that for ordinary Indonesians, to the extent that they had even heard of the place, ABRI's work inside East Timor turned Indonesia's 27th province was simply a righteous struggle against variously, as the regime —and even the Western media—made out, communist rebels, separatists, or bandits. While Jakarta long considered East Timorese as ingrates for snubbing Indonesian-style development, unlike the Aceh and Irian cases, in January 1999 the establishment, bowing to international pressure, announced that it would entertain cutting East Timor free, thus reversing its rigid 23-year-old position on annexation. Nevertheless, as discussed in a final chapter, the historic New York agreements on East Timor, the culmination of many years of negotiation between Portugal, Indonesia, and the U.N., offered both hope for change but equally pessimism, as it dawned upon the world community that senior elements within the Indonesian armed forces sought to subvert the outcome of the agreements by diverting arms and money to militia-style death squads.[4] Still defying international pressure, Habibie disallowed the release from custody of the Nelson Mandela-stature political prisoner, labelled criminal, and acclaimed East Timorese leader, José Xanana Gusmão. Eventually, Gusmão was released into the protection of the British Embassy in Jakarta, but only after the U.N.-conducted ballot of 30 August 1999, and the brutal army-led assault on his people and country that followed in its wake.

The crisis and response

It is clear that the 1997-98 collapse of the Asian "miracle economies" not only caught government officials and captains of business in Thailand, Indonesia, Malaysia (also known as the Southeast Asian or SEA-3 countries), and South Korea off guard, but also was not predicted by most development economists. Even after the crisis broke in mid-1997, the Asian Development Bank was predicting growth. But, by 14 August 1997, Indonesia abandoned exchange controls as the rupiah shredded value. The following month the IMF announced its first rescue package. Yet, in the first week of the new year, the rupiah continued to plummet after Indonesia announced what was viewed as an unrealistic budget. But even as a second IMF accord was signed on 15 January the rupiah continued its decline, reaching a record low of 17,000 to the U.S. currency after Suharto further frightened international confidence by suggesting B.J. Habibie become Vice President.

By March 1988, the Thai baht had lost 32 percent of its value over the previous year, Malaysian ringgit 31 percent, Philippine peso 29 percent, Korean won 35 percent, and the Indonesian rupiah 71 percent. Regional stockmarkets began precipitous declines. Growth assessments were scaled back radically, although few were even bold enough to predict negative growth. Private-sector debt that had driven the Asian boom blew out as asset values in the property sector began to collapse across the region. As a proportion of GDP non-performing loans in Malaysia reached 22.9 percent and in Indonesia 10.8 percent. Hyperinflation threatened as the cost of imports soared and production contracted. All this led one political economist, Richard Robison, to declare "a defining moment in the evolution of global capitalism in the post-cold war period," even raising the question of the end of "Asian capitalism." No less, debates as to the origins or causes of the crisis, as to whether they stemmed from "institutions that incubate corrupt systems of nepotism and cronyism" or were broadly external, along with the question of reform strategies as mediated by the IMF, raged on both within and without government circles.[5]

By early 1999, press reports on Asia were no longer debunking the "economic miracle" and the supposed Pacific Century but were comparing the effects of the economic collapse, which had seen not only the decimation of the region's *nouveau riche* middle classes, but had seen millions sinking into poverty, to the level of the Great Depression of the 1930s in Europe and North America. While, to be sure, the effects of the crisis are felt differentially across the region, by far the worst case in terms of disillusionment, loss of jobs and hunger was Indonesia.

There is a sense that prior to the crisis two mainstream

perspectives dominated the debate on East Asian development. Burkett and Hart-Landsberg have outlined these positions as the dominant neo-liberal position championed by the IMF, the World Bank, the U.S. government and most mainstream economists, a view which praised the SEA-3 for their openness to foreign direct investment, their labor market stability, and their fiscal monetary discipline. The minority view held by some Japanese and other regional government officials, also known as the structuralist-institutionalist position, emphasized the positive role played by activist state policies in promoting new industries and exploiting comparative advantages. Nevertheless, as the authors argue, the shared presumptions of the two positions must be seen as having failed and having left no room for ecologically and community-grounded alternatives. In short, "they ignore the self-limiting character of capitalist 'success' nationally and globally."[6]

Particularly shocking to many Indonesians must have been the images of the signing ceremony of 15 January 1998 by IMF President Michael Candassus, portrayed as standing over a visibly dissembling Suharto, reluctantly agreeing to imposed economic reform conditions. In the event, neither Candassus nor Suharto came out of this tryst looking well. Suharto's threats on 9 February to create a "currency board" mechanism may well have been a last-ditch attempt to salvage national face and to quarantine the New Order political-economic system from the kind of medicine prescribed by the IMF that would have seen even more bank closures and dissolution of Suharto-crony-linked monopolies. On the other hand, to the liberal Western media *(Economist* magazine, etc.) Suharto was now identified as the single political obstacle to economic reform, although for practically 32 years the Western media could be counted on to put the best gloss on the dictatorship.[7] In the event, the IMF-brokered US$40-billion bailout of Indonesia survived U.S. Congressional opposition, and continues at this writing to be virtually unconditional as to political reform, demilitarization, the international status of East Timor, and many other scandalous and reprehensible legacies of the Suharto regime.

Replete with irony, former Japanese Prime Minister Ryutaro

Hashimoto saluted Suharto in Jakarta at a banquet hosted by the aging dictator/kleptocrat on 9 January 1997 with the words, "In Japan, we say that a friend in need is a friend indeed. This is truly the kind of relationship that we have with Indonesia, and that I hope to keep growing." [8] Japan never disappointed. The friendship theme for services rendered by the Indonesian New Order, namely oil deliveries during the "oil shock" years, recurred in Hashimoto's statement on Suharto's resignation. Where *even* U.S. President Clinton called for progress towards democracy, the Japanese Prime Minister came down firmly for "stability," economic recovery, and some vague notion of reform.

Even in the depths of its deepest postwar recession, Japan led the international current for Indonesia's recovery, looking for a profitable future, and kicking off a veritable "Marshal Plan," for Asia, even when that prospect appeared as it does at this writing, like throwing good money after bad, especially when transparency is not even a condition at home or abroad. Even the best-intended donations of Japanese rice to poverty-stricken regions of Indonesia fell afoul of that country's notorious profiteers, as protested by City Forum at a rare demonstration outside the Japanese Embassy in Jakarta in January 1999. But by May 1999, as the World Bank began to impose conditions upon its disbursements, Japan moved to circumvent the World Bank by working directly with Jakarta.

Ripples in the Malay world

But the footdragging, the dissembling, the evasions, the favoritism that had come to characterize almost all the ASEAN or Association of Southeast Asian Nations' economies without exception, in their allocation of licences and rewards, came home to roost in the calls for greater transparency, greater accountability, and the end of nepotism, not only on the part of the pro-democracy movement in Indonesia, but, by mid-1998, on the part of a burgeoning anti-government opposition in Malaysia as well.

Prime Minister Mohamad Mahathir of Malaysia attracted both secret admiration for his position in keeping the IMF at bay and, more dubiously, in September 1998, for introducing currency controls. But he also attracted international ridicule for certain of his off-key comments on the causes of the crisis, namely, blaming individuals and even religious groups (Jews). But, just as relations between the core ASEAN countries began to unravel over national animosities—somewhat putting the ASEAN dogma of non-interference in the internal affairs of fellow member-states, in the shadow, the tide against Mahathir's "soft authoritarianism" began to turn. This was not especially because marginal NGOs or Non Governmental Organizations began to draw parallels between his and his ruling party's authoritarian style and that of Suharto, but because the darling of the Japanese political and business establishment, at least, shot himself in the foot by sacking (and publicly damning) his pro-reformist deputy, Anwar Ibrahim, on "immorality" charges, stripping him of his official and party position and throwing him in prison under the Internal Security Act (ISA), pending trial for alleged misdeeds. Unprecedented in postcolonial Malaysian history, massed demonstrations in Kuala Lumpur in October-November 1998 found in Anwar's treatment a pretext to mobilize for change, albeit not necessarily pro-Anwar, just as certain of Malaysia's ASEAN and Western backers sought to distance themselves from the person of Mahathir at the then upcoming Asia Pacific Economic Cooperation (APEC) summit meeting in Kuala Lumpur in November. When U.S. Vice president Al Gore addressed this meeting offering consoling words for the opposition movement in Malaysia, Mahathir's ruling party answered back by kicking off an anti-U.S. campaign, playing upon crude nationalism, citing the old doctrine of "non-interference." Street demonstrations in Kuala Lumpur rekindled in April 1999, following the sentencing of Anwar to six years' imprisonment for "corruption," leading many inside and outside the country to question the integrity of the Malaysian judicial system. In these new bold public responses it can be said that, as with oppositionist forces in Indonesia, access to uncensored news from Internet sources played its part in eroding the government's near-monopoly on news.

Nevertheless, no such political space even exists in the

staunchly pro-Western Sultanate of Brunei Darussalam, still ruled
under emergency measures as a family enterprise following the
crushing of a rebellion in 1962. Scarcely making headlines outside
of London's society pages, and sometimes scandal sheets, the
removal in 1998 by the Sultan of his high-living brother, Prince
Jefry, as Minister of Finance, only began to make sense in
September that year when the government revealed that "large
sums of money" had been misappropriated by the Prince from
the Brunei Investment Agency, the principal business vehicle of
the Sultanate's accumulated oil riches, believed to have been
worth between US$40 and 60 billion before the crisis, albeit
vastly reduced in its wake.[9]

The Book

Chapter 1, "Ideology and the Concept of Government in the
Indonesian New Order," sets down the broad parameters of the
Suharto-military dominated New Order in full flight, an
ideological and institutional system that survived with little
modification down to May 1998 and, indeed, outlives Suharto.

Chapter 2, "Tan Malaka in Indonesian History," profiles the
life and times of the Indonesian revolutionary against Dutch
power, in exile, in Java at the critical moment of independence,
and, as a legend, not only in the heart of Indonesia's first
president Sukarno, but in memory today.

Chapter 3, "The Garuda and the Dragon: Indonesian-Chinese
Relations," steps back from the ideology-and-culture theme and
addresses the way that two regimes, poles apart, would seek
political and economic reconciliation by the late 1980s. One of
the ironies of this relationship was the recriminations entered
into between the two regimes after Beijing—reluctantly —broke
its silence on the alleged outrages committed against ethnic
Chinese, especially women, by military-linked gangs in Jakarta
in May 1998.

Chapter 4, "Radical Islam in Southeast Asia: Rhetoric and
Reality in the Middle East Connection," sets down the facts,
strikes at certain of the myths surrounding "fanatical" Islamic
influence stemming from, variously, Libya and Iran, and the

direct and indirect influence of these countries on the Islamic communities of Southeast Asia.

Chapter 5, "Death and the State in Malaysia," not only profiles the largely forgotten execution of two Western drug addicts, but offers a rare critique in print of Malaysian-style authoritarianism, including the political use of the infamous ISA, the critique of which lately entered mainstream Western media, due to the demands of the much harassed Malaysian political opposition to the arrest in November 1998 of Deputy Prime Minister Anwar Ibrahim.

Chapter 6, "The Image of Brunei in Western Literature," replays Edward Said's concept of Orientalism with reference to the former British protectorate and oil-rich state of Brunei, finding a wealth of literary riches, warts and all.

Chapter 7, "Rentier Capitalism in Negara Brunei Darussalam," identifies the political-economic system that sustains Sultanism in this micro-state with reference to the Middle Eastern literature on "rentier economies."

Chapter 8, "Wartime Portuguese Timor: The Azores Connection," places within context the complex interactions between Australians, British and Americans, and Portuguese, on the one hand, and Japanese (and Nazis) and Portuguese, on the other, in the horse trading over the wartime and even postwar status of Timor with the Lajes airforce base on the mid-Atlantic island of Azores as the Portuguese bargaining chip.

Chapter 9, "Language, Literacy and Political Hegemony in East Timor," describes the complex ways in which language use and cultural defenses have irremediably changed in East Timor since the Indonesian invasion and occupation of 1975.

Chapter 10, "From Salazar to Suharto: Toponymy, Public Architecture and Memory in the Making of Timorese Identity," explores the political uses of toponyms and public architecture in East Timor under two colonialisms, that of Salazar and that of Suharto, and with what effect for posterity and memory.

Chapter 11, "East Timor: Autonomy versus Independence: Rise of the Student Solidarity Movement," addresses the responses of East Timorese to the rise of the *reformasi* movement in Indonesia, and responses of the East Timorese to

Habibie's "autonomy" plan.

A concluding chapter, "East Timor and the U.N. Ballot of 1999" analyzes the UN-mediated ballot arrangements for East Timor—its virtues and flaws—against the background of the nefarious activities of Indonesian military-supported death squads and militias.[10]

Notes

1. Allan Nairn, "Indonesia's Disappeared," *The Nation,* 8 June 1998.

2. Max Lane, "Mass Politics and Political Change in Indonesia," paper delivered at conference "Democracy in Indonesia—The Crisis and Beyond," University of Melbourne and Monash, 11-12 December 1998.

3. George Aditjondro, in paper delivered to conference, "East Timor History and Conflict Resolution," Osaka University of Foreign Languages, 4 October 1998.

4. Jose Ramos-Horta, *Funu: The Unfinished Saga of East Timor,* (Trenton, N.J.: Red Sea Press, 1987); Gunn, *East Timor and the United Nations: The Case for Intervention,* (Trenton, N.J./Asmara, Eritrea: Red Sea Press, 1997).

5. Richard Robison, "Currency Meltdown: The End of Asian Capitalism?," Homepage NIAS nytt, 2, 1998.

6. The ASEAN-Western media-academic-business and governmental nexus in support of the Suharto dictatorship is analyzed in Gunn (with Lee), *A Critical View of Western Journalism and Scholarship on East Timor,* (Manila: Journal of Contemporary Asia Press, 1974). Even so, this field remains wide open for research. Singular in this respect have been the writings of Indonesian academic George Aditjondro, with respect to both the Jakarta oligarchy and the East Timor military-business connection.

7. Paul Burkett and Martin Hart-Landsberg, "East Asia and the Crisis of Development Theory," *Journal of Contemporary Asia,* 28, 4 (1998): 435-56.

8. Japan MOFA (Gaimusho) Homepage.

9. "Large Sums of Money 'Misappropriated'," *The Straits Times Interactive,* 22 September 1998; John Sweeny, *Guardian,* 24 April 1999.

10. See author's *East Timor and the United Nations: The Case for Intervention,* (Trenton, N.J./Asmara, Eritrea: Red Sea Press, 1997).

1. Ideology and the Concept of Government in the Indonesian New Order

During the 1950s a number of scholars proclaimed the "end of ideology." While this assertion may have some validity in the West, it seems to be less relevant to the politics of the new states in the developing world. With the eclipse of the Old Order in Indonesia and the demise of its main ideological expositor—the charismatic Sukarno—observers of the New Order might be excused from noting a decline in ideology. Few observers of contemporary Indonesia have noted the sense of continuity with the Old Order, at least at the level of symbols and institutions.[1] The conscious creation of a national ideology by both Sukarno and Suharto can be viewed as a task of nation-building or the welding together of a national consensus. That this creation is not just an epiphenomenon is illustrated by the attempts of other new states to attain national consensus; the formulation of the *Rukun Negara* (state ideology) in Malaysia is an example in hand.[2]

This article, then, is addressed to the question of determining the saliency of ideology in the New Order and to explain how ideology makes the concept of government in Indonesia meaningful. It is apparent that the literature reflects conceptual problems of Westerners coming to terms with an Indonesian notion of government. In attempting to overcome this ethnocentric bias, here credence will be given to indigenous expositions on this concept of government.

It is significant that since the birth of the nationalist movement in Indonesia, ideological formulations have been informed by a tradition that reflects the specificity of the Javanese cultural heritage. Indeed it is apparent that Suharto and ideologists of the New Order have at once invoked the rule of law in the formal constitution of 1945 and traditional Javanese notions of power. Through their interpretation of Pancasila Democracy (Pancasila incorporates the five principles of monotheism, nationalism, humanism, social justice, and democracy), the leadership has asserted the primacy of traditional values over a strict adherence to Western-derived law. The leadership inculcates supportive values through the educational systems and mass media. However, the various loci of opposition to the regime challenge the leadership's monopoly over the determination of truth.

A number of scholars of political development in modern Indonesia have noted that precolonial patterns of Javanese values have been revived. Anderson argues that in times of stress an older residual idea of power may emerge, in which institutions explained and legitimized in terms of the hegemonic cultural mode appear to be breaking down or in decay. [3] Wilner has addressed the question of how indigenous values affect the exercise of authority. Referring to the Guided Democracy period of Sukarno, she has noted a process of "political traditionalization" that began with or even before political independence. [4] Pertaining specifically to the New Order, Budiman has provided an analysis of the cultural legacy of the Indonesian power holders. Although Budiman concedes that to a certain extent Suharto is playing the role of the old Javanese king, he is skeptical of this "cultural game." He argues that when Suharto's power base is threatened, his cultural sense is overridden by practical material interests. [5]

Equally important is the theoretical question raised by Budiman. He has noted the debate over methodology contained in the two regnant paradigms in contemporary sociology, ie, between cultural determinists as represented by Parsonian functionalists, and Marxist structuralists. The cultural argument, then, holds that it is culture that should be taken into account in the last instance to explain human behavior and social change and that society is integrated through a common value system. The orthodox Marxist holds that determination in the last instance is by the economic mode of production on the one hand, and by the relative autonomy of the superstructure on the other. Budiman favors the Althusserian interpretation, whereby the elements of the superstructure (eg., religion, ideology, the legal system, the state) have their specific effectivity, which means that these elements are determining as well as being determined.[6] The question at issue here, as raised by Mortimer, is what weight is to be attached to cultural analysis in comparison with other factors, especially those located in the social and politico-economic structures.[7]

In summary, the theoretical postulates guiding the following analysis are the essentially Parsonian questions—(a) what is the relationship between values, authority, and power within the Indonesian social system, and (b) how effective, if at all, are the institutions of the New Order in the management and resolution of political conflicts versus the essentially Hegelian-Marxian questions—(a) to what extent is the Pancasila democracy of the New Order an independent variable and an epiphenomenon in the superstructure of ideas, and (b) to what extent are culture and ideology dependent variables (structure in dominance in Althusserian terms) rooted in the dominant structure reflecting practical political interests.

Role of the military in the formulation of a national ideology

Following Jackson's formulation, the Indonesian political system is here understood as a bureaucratic polity with political power and participation monopolized by the highest levels of the civil and military bureaucracies. The main arena for political competition is not the country at large but the bureaucratic, technocratic, and military elite circle in close physical proximity to the president of the republic.[8] However, a longitudinal view of the New Order necessarily must account for the progressive elimination of centers of power outside the government.

The New Order of General Suharto emerged in the aftermath of the 1965 Untung "Coup," which brought down the triangular system of politics of President Sukarno, the PKI, and the armed forces. Symptomatic and illustrative of the new political orientation was an army seminar convened in Bandung in August 1966 (SESKOAD) that can be regarded as a new watershed in the army's political thinking. This seminar presented the main principles, programs, and intentions of the armed forces in the New Order. Not only were senior army officers present, but, as MacDougall has noted, the team of Western-trained academic economists from the University of Indonesia joined the SESKOAD seminar.[9]

The important guiding doctrine emerging from the SESKOAD seminar was a reformulation of the 1965 *Tri Ubaya Cakti* (doctrine of struggle of the army).[10] This Sanskrit formula is not without significance since its symbolism invokes in the mind of its Javanese beholder traditional notions of power (Sanskrit was the language of the Hindu-Buddhist priest scholars of the *kraton* [royal court]). Tri means three, containing (1) the Doctrine of Basic National Security, (2) the Doctrine of *Kekaryaan* (civil action), and (3) the Doctrine of Development. Ubaya means promise. *Cakti* means *sakti* in bahasa Indonesia, and Anderson has rightly noted the conceptual and linguistic problems in the translation of this latter term.[11] Suffice it to say that the nuance is that of spiritually reinforced power or the notion of power in Javanese culture. Indeed, the continuity with tradition has been reflected in the linguistic Sanskritization undertaken generally in the post-colonial period but more particularly in the early years of the New Order. This is inextricably connected with the resurrection of Javanese *kepercayaan* (literally belief but more accurately Javanese mystic belief) and is given the imprimatur of President Suharto himself.

So much for the symbolic level; at the programmatic level the *Tri Ubaya Cakti,* reveals much about the leadership perception of government. The following analysis reflects the seemingly paradoxical commitment to the *ubaya* (promise) of *pembangunan* (development), and the *cakti* (the sacred devolution of power to a moral and righteous force—ie, to President and General Suharto and his guarantor TNI-AD (Tentara Nasional Indonesia-Angkatan Darat) army.

As referred to in the *Tri Ubaya Cakti* and as constantly reiterated in the media pronouncements, the Pancasila represents not just a philosophy but a programmatic guide to action or state ideology. The Pancasila was formalized in Sukarno's address before the members of the Investigating Committee to the Constitution (BPKI) on June 1, 1945. Dahm has elaborated on Sukarno's original contention that the Pancasila is no product of recent years but is drawn from the essentially religious, cultural tradition of Java.[12] It is no accident that despite a professed goal of modernization and development, a countercurrent of continuity and neo-traditionalism can be perceived to coexist in the Indonesian bureaucratic polity. Whatever the locus of opposition to the regime and the dominant ideology of Pancasila, whether from liberal intellectuals, students, regionalists, or Muslims, it is not the Pancasila per se that is criticized (its sacral quality has taken its place in the national consciousness) what is challenged is the regime's monopoly over the interpretation of the Pancasila and its actualization. To be sure there are institutional guidelines that theoretically allow mass participation; the question is to what extent participation is actually practised.

But first it is imperative to analyze the military-bureaucratic elites' interpretations of Pancasila. As the self-styled ideologist of the New Order, Ali Moertopo provides an illuminating interpretation of Pancasila democracy. In an essay entitled the "New Order, Pancasila, and National Strategy," Ali Moertopo has built upon preceding interpretations of the Pancasila to impress the viewpoint of the present bureaucratic polity.[13] The sense of continuity in Moertopo's interpretation of the Pancasila is best illustrated by comparison with the formulation of Sukarno's policy during the Guided Democracy Period, which declared that "the basic ingredient of any national ideology must be the national inheritance of that nation itself, its heritage—from the past, the traditions which bind its peoples together and set the pattern of their life."[14]

For Ali Moertopo and other ideologists of the New Order, traditional as opposed to foreign elements are invoked in the redefinition of a national ideology. The function of ABRI (armed forces) is that of "defender of the Pancasila both as a philosophy or state ideology and as a philosophy of people's livelihood." ABRI, then, takes upon itself to guarantee the purity of Pancasila and "to raise the ideological consciousness of the masses to defend the Indonesian revolution."[15]

Traditional concept of government

In the following sections the actualization of Pancasila democracy will be examined by analyzing the system of meaning embodied in the regime's ideological symbols and by analyzing how this system of meaning is comprehended and acted upon by the various political-socio-religious *aliran* (literally, streams) —ie, the essentially Javanese village *abangan* peasant subtradition, the Islamic *santri* trader subvariant, and the *priai* aristocratic or bureaucratic style of life.[16] Necessarily the process of depoliticization of the political arena will be addressed by giving attention to what Huntington calls the "institutionalization of politics, the creation of a system in which political processes are effected according to established norms." It will be shown that the ongoing process of creating a Pancasila democracy is at once a legitimizing rationalization of the status quo and a particularization of political life to an essentially Javanese power and cultural elite. It is argued here that the deliberate consolidation of formal institutions that strongly stress the executive power, and the particular pattern of the delegation of authority, is a neo-traditional manifestation of: the Javanese concept of power.

The New Order's power elite have formalized institutions that acknowledge the symbiotic dependence of ruled upon ruler, the essentially *abangan* world view upon the symbolic universe of the *priai*. Geertz has posited this dominant *priai* cultural elite as one whose ultimate basis of power is their control over the central symbolic resources of the society (religion, philosophy, art, science, and writing). The mirror image of this cultural elite is a subordinated food-producing peasantry. Traditionally, the Javanese aristocracy extracted rice and manpower from this peasantry by recourse to military terror and by inculcating religious enthusiasm. What is at issue, then, is to determine whether the New Order elite has appropriated religious-cultural symbolism (the hegemonic mode) in the service of self-seeking military-class interest, or whether the New Order is pandering to the *abangan* world view by fulfilling their millennial expectations—the older Javanese idea of a returning savior-monarch (*ratu adil*) and that of the Islamic conqueror (Madhi) who will sweep away the heathen (anti-God PKI) and restore macrocosmic/microcosmic symbiosis or national harmony.

Conflict management

The mode of conflict resolution at the institutional level requires further analysis. The New Order literature constantly reiterates the regime's legality and legitimacy from the dual standpoint of condemning the Old Order and stressing continuity with an essentially precolonial past. At the level of institution-building, the New Order can point to some achievements over and above Sukarno's arrogation of executive power during "Guided Democracy." Suharto's own estimation of these institutions bears analysis. He can claim that:

> both the supreme state institutions, the People's Consulta-
> tive Assembly (MPR) and the higher state institutions
> such as the Supreme Advisory Council (DPA), the par-
> liament (DPR), the state Audit Board and Supreme Court
> ... are constituted on the basis of laws especially designed
> for their establishment. The formation of these institu-
> tions according to these laws signifies that these institu-
> tions have been established in accordance with the 1945
> Constitution. Whether it is recognized, or not, this alone
> is a very significant achievement of the New Order era.[17]

Suharto has pointed to the constitutionality of the Supreme Court as the highest judicial power. He claims that by carrying out their duties on the basis of these laws, the position of these judicial institutions and their performance are assured of free-dom and noninterference from outside, including the government. In the judicial system, judges and lawyers have acquired a more important status, but courts have not become independent of the government although they are less dependent than before.[18]

Prior to the New Order, the state budget was submitted to parliament after the fiscal year had passed. Suharto points to the achievement of the New Order under which the state budget is now approved first by the parliament, and its use is then strictly supervised and examined by the State Audit Board, which reports its findings to parliament every year. It is generally agreed that fiscal management in the New Order is a substantial improvement over the ruinous economic policies of the Guided Democracy period.

But clearly, the principle of separation of powers is not adhered to in the Western liberal sense, and the notion of individual rights in Indonesia must be qualified by the primacy of integration and unity over divided loyalties. Elaborations on the Pancasila have stressed the responsibility of individuals to order and peace in society. Necessarily, the relative degree of autonomy of the legislature from the executive must be examined with reference to Indonesian notions of government.

In discussing the March 22, 1973 re-election of Suharto as President by the Majlis Perwakilan Rakyat (MPR), the largely appointed upper house of the parliament, Rosihan Anwar maintained that the fact that no counter candidate was fielded against Suharto was a manifestation of consensus politics. The political parties therefore decided to give their support to the single candidate, thus perhaps avoiding "loss of face" in a straight contest through voting. Moreover, this act of unanimous support for the single candidate was also thought to be in harmony with the political culture and value system. Whether this was democracy or not, Anwar affirms that it was consistent with Pancasila democracy.[19] Opponents of the regime aver that Suharto's re-election was a manifestation of steamroller politics. Thus, the function and structure of the MPR must be analyzed to gain an insight into the operational aspect of Pancasila democracy.

The basic political functions of the MPR are to determine the Constitution and the Broad Outlines of State Policy (GBHN); to elect the President and Vice President; and to accept or reject the President's account of his performance under the mandate given to him. Theoretically, the President is responsible to the people, since sovereignty is invested in the people. But the MPR, as the people's supreme council, theoretically exercises that sovereignty. On its part, if the Dewan Perwakilan Rakyat

(DPR), or legislature, considers that the President has acted against the Constitution or any other MPR decree, it can in special session call the President to account. In theory, the ultimate sanction of the people through the MPR is to withhold the mandate of office from the President, a right exercised in the 1967 and 1968 MPR sessions. This in itself can be viewed as a check against abusive dictatorship. Sadjidiman Surjohadiprodjo has described the process whereby a hasty vote may not be in accord with common interest; in such a situation the question is resubmitted for deliberation and a new consensus reached.[20] For each of his major decisions Suharto has sought ratification from the MPR, and the legality of all actions is traced back to the fount of legitimacy, the 1945 Constitution.

Apart from the emasculated Communist Party (PKI), the main opposition to Suharto's mandate came from the Muslim fraction within the MPR. Their spokesmen declared that they would oppose Suharto if there was no government compromise on the issue of the status of *kepercayaan* (Javanese mystical beliefs). The government plan to promote *kepercayaan* to a status equal to Islam was taken by the Muslim fraction as a deliberate campaign to erode the power of political Islam. Despite their minority position in the MPR, the Muslims voiced strong disapproval of the government's stand. Rather than risk a polarization of the *alirans*, pitting Muslim *santri* against the *abangan-priai* (traditional Javanese world view), the government reached a new consensus. The President emphasized that the government's support for recognition of the existence of *kepercayaan* in no way meant that mysticism was to be accorded the status of a separate religion. This example serves to support the thesis that the conflict resolution between *alirans* indeed has become institutionalized and potential conflict thus contained. In this sense, the operation of the institutions is supportive of the philosophical tenets of Pancasila democracy.

Rosihan Anwar takes the view that the Armed Forces often act as an "honest broker" in the inter-cameral sessions of the MPR, and that concessions are made in order to avoid open conflict that would affect society at large.[21] Mashuri notes that harmony and balance are the operative principles of these groups; in contrast, under liberal democracy the basic attitude is one of confrontation and opposition, which plants the seeds of destruction by opening up the possibility for social conflagration. Such a polity therefore cannot be afforded by a developing country such as Indonesia.[22] This sentiment has been reiterated by the government media. Suharto notes that "Pancasila Democracy does not recognize opposition groups as known in the liberal democratic system, it only recognizes *musyawarah* leading to *mufakat* [discussion leading to consensus] through representation in both the DPR and MPR."[23] This view is shared by all groups represented, none of which would want to regard itself as in opposition to Pancasila democracy.

As it happened, Suharto's resumption of a new five-year mandate was carried in the March 1978 plenary session of the MPR by the support of three generals representing Golkar (an acronym from Golongan Karya, meaning functional groups), the military fraction, and the regional representative fraction. Together, the three generals spoke for 86.1% of the 920 members of the MPR. The Muslim-backed PPP (Development Unity Party), with 99 seats, and the PDI (Indonesia Democracy Party), with 29 seats, followed the endorsement in the interests of consensus and national harmony. The Muslim walkout, however, forced government recognition over the single issue of their interpretation of the first *sila* of the Pancasila, ie, belief in the ultimate God.

In the legislature (DPR), the facade of legality and formality has been upheld. In the pre-1971 legislature the parties were able to obstruct, delay, and alter parts of the government's programs on such subjects as education, marriage law reform, and electoral legislation. By the time of the 1977 elections, the excesses in the delivery of the Golkar vote did not prevent the Muslims from marginally increasing their percentage of the vote. Indeed, the formation of the new parliament (DPR) and the MPR after the May 1977 elections gave rise to heated debates involving the PDI and PPP over institutional forms and procedures, including the issue of the accountability of the President and the leadership of parliament and the MPR.[24] Debates over the Broad

Outlines of State Policy (GBHN) and the relationship between *agama* (established religion) and *kepercayaan* in the legislature are supportive of the Indonesia notion of *musyawarah* and *mufakat*.

Consolidation of the political system

The move to an anti-party proportional representation system was originally made at the SESKOAD seminar mentioned above. Sajidiman Surjohadiprodjo has argued that the best system for an archipelagic nation is a direct representation form of government that simplifies the political system away from representation by self-interested parties and groups. His views reflect the thinking of the New Order regime. "How can the *gotong-royong* [mutual assistance] environment be shaped and how can *musyawarah* be based on wise guidance if the representatives of the *dewan* [parliament] are not representatives of the people but representatives of organizations? How can simplification of political life be attained if political organizations are not forced to create qualitative improvements?[25]

On February 2, 1970 Suharto insisted that socioeconomic forces in Indonesia divide themselves into three main groups that were spiritual, material, and functional in structure. On March 13, 1970 the Nahdatul Ulama (NU), Partai Muslimin Indonesia (Parmusi), the Masjumi splinter group, PSII, and Muslim Perti parties "reached agreement" to form a spiritual unity group while the Catholic and other Christian parties, the Partai Nationalis Indonesia (PNI), Ikatan Pendukung Kemerdekaan Indonesia (IPKI), and Murba parties reached accord to uphold the materialist group. However, a regulation to formalize the so-called functional groups, issued by the Home Affairs Department, was criticized by political parties as working against their interests.

Suharto's own estimation of the new party configuration as spiritual and material groupings is indicated in his statement that "all political parties and other social-political forces must possess spirit and new orientation which *cocok* with the development of the nation." [26] *Cocok,* a Javanese word and concept, in this context means to be fitting or suitable, but it also contains the nuance that life takes on its true import when human actions are attuned to cosmic conditions. In the Javanese concept of power it is not unreasonable for the *ratu adil* to decide which parties possess this new spiritual orientation. The appeal to congruence or appropriateness is concordant with appeals for the maintenance of harmony. In the jargon of political science, this then is a manifestation of conflict control.

In actuality the parties were not ready to dissolve themselves. Yet, to create a loyal grassroots structure, Suharto revamped Sukarno's original Golkar organization. Liddle has noted that the creation of Golkar was eased by the employing of old-guard leaders in new positions, but that real power in the making of campaign decisions and the solicitation of votes was divided (and competed for) among the Ministry of Foreign Affairs, the Ministry of Defence and Security, and the central Golkar campaign headquarters. [27] Golkar dominance of the political input process was facilitated by the appeal to *monoloyalitas* (single loyalty), which had the effect of co-opting all the *Pamonpraja* (civil service) and, equally important, of creating new political structure of dependence in the villages by a co-optation of village heads, landlords, and the middle-level peasantry.

As part of this Golkarization process, workers, farmers, fishermen, youth, teachers, etc, were grouped under the Golongan Karya symbol. The professed purpose of these organizations is to "aggregate professional interests and to pursue those interests, to provide a vehicle for communications with the authorities and to encourage their members to take an active role in development." Ali Moertopo's opinion is that all of these new political and social institutions are still in the consolidation stage. His optimistic view is that it will take about 10 years before they can begin to perform their designated roles. [28] If politics was *panglima* (in command) during Guided Democracy, what can be said of the New Order is that the military is *panglima* and demonstrates no inclination to return to the barracks while it remains committed to its *kekaryaan* (civil mission) and while the military leadership believes that it is the only social force capable of realizing the objectives of *pembangunan*.

The first parliamentary election of the New Order, however, while creating a simplified political structure, had the effect of institutionalizing and legitimizing the *dwi-fungsi* (dual function) role of the military: as both defense and as a social-political organization. The overwhelming supportive vote for Golkar thus was interpreted as providing evidence of a mandate of approval for the regime—in line with the notion that representative parties did not *cocok* (harmonize) with a Pancasila society. The simplification of the party system in the interests of conflict management was to erode further the participation aspect of government without entirely overwhelming the representation aspect. Fissiparous tendencies run deep in Indonesian society and cannot be removed by decree. The NU emerged from the election with 18.717 percent of the vote and religious faith was transformed into political support through the efforts of rural *kiai* (Muslim religious teachers) who legitimized the NU's political activities in terms of religious imperatives. Anderson denotes this phenomenon as an example of religious groups using politics for essentially religious ends.[29] It should be noted that the main loser of this 1971 election was the PNI, whose former support from the *pamonpraja* was reoriented towards Golkar.

Referring to the 1977 elections, which again endorsed Golkar (although some intellectuals, students and others had withdrawn their support), Suharto could again point to the mandate provided for the New Order, and the *dwi-fungsi* role of ABRI. Suharto could note that the principle that ABRI should have a presence in the representative institutions was fully endorsed by all social and political forces, the latter combining the political parties and functional groups."[30] The endorsement was not unanimous, however, but conflict was managed by the continued consolidation of the political forces in the three groups: the PPP (Development Unity Party) containing NU and three smaller Islamic parties; the Functional Groups (Golongan Karya); and, the PDI (Indonesian Democracy Party) containing the old PNI, the two smaller nationalist parties, and the Christian parties. This realization of "our common determination to refine and simplify our political life and structure" was for the regime a manifestation of the management of civilian conflicts through formalized institutions. The doctrines of *kekaryaan* and development have been noted as constituting two of the pillars of *Tri Ubaya Cakti.* This *dwi fungsi* or *dwi dharma* (dual laws [Sanskrit]) concept— the doctrine of the military's twin functions—serves as the principal ideological justification for military involvement in politics. Implicit in the doctrine is the notion of *modernisasi* (modernization), to which the military as a group are committed. Liddle conceptualizes an administrative model of development in Indonesia, containing a triadic formula of economists as policy makers, armed forces as stabilizers, and the bureaucracy as implementers. Crouch postulates that the complexity of the society demands that the military must share more power with the technocrats. He is less optimistic about the depth of the military's commitment to *modernisasi* given their propensity to enhance corporate interests.

Neither of these analyses has been expressive of the value orientations of the military-technocratic-bureaucratic elite. Clearly a legal rational approach to power configurations is not going to explain elite goals and motivations fully. Indeed, it is argued here that the New Order has been characterized by the phenomena of both increasing military intervention into the civilian sphere and increasing military interpenetration of the business, diplomatic, and political elites. The common shared denominator of this elite, despite their secular pursuits, is an enduring commitment to the *priai* world view, which, as Geertz has made clear, remains the model not only for the elite but ideally for the entire society.

Sundhaussen, in analyzing the position of the president and the way decisions are made within the military, observes that the New Order has come to resemble a personal regime whereby Suharto makes the decisions while the military inner circle is used for policy implementation but is denied a role in policy formulation. The regime, then, is not a junta, although the military is the main pillar of power, nor are there alternative poles of power.[31] This centralization of power accords in a high degree to the personification of unity of society in traditional notions of powers and kingship. Accumulation of power in the traditional mode, thus recognized by the officer cadre, is a reflection of the cadre's value system and social obligations to the center or to *Bapak* (Father) Suharto.[32]

Religion, culture, and hegemony

It has been widely observed that both Sukarno and Suharto have been partial adherents to *kejawen* (traditional Javanese religion). Each has his own guru or *dukun* (spiritual counsellor), heir to the syncretic Javanese animistic/Islamic *abangan* tradition. It has also been observed that both these presidents, after assuming power, took on the trappings of the traditional Javanese monarch. Of course, the sacred regalia of tradition and the panoply of power that surrounds the Presidential *istana* (palace) has taken on a modern guise; so much so, in fact, that observers might be excused to believe that this concentration of wealth and power is an extension of the international metropolitan superculture of a nationalist bourgeois elite. It has also been noted that Suharto's predilection for traditional forms of nepotism and corruption has enriched an inner circle of beneficiaries.

Anderson has observed of the Sukarno and Suharto regimes that they have captured the traditional notions of power and kingship. He views their behavior as a re-emergence of the patrimonial model temporarily distorted by the colonial interregnum. Anderson's formulation is that power is seen to flow out of the concentrated center and not from the diffuse perimeter; moreover, that ministerial behavior should reflect the wishes of the former rather than the latter. This argument, he continues, helps to explain the ease with which many Javanese accepted the emergence, under the authoritarian regimes of both Sukarno and Suharto, of formal power groups outside the "rational-legal" structure of the bureaucracy, eg, Suharto's *Staff Pribadi* (personal agents and confidants).[33] But how consonant is this traditional concept of power with corporate-interest analysis whereby the power elite has self-serving interests at heart? How Suharto maintains his position of power thus becomes as compelling a question as the consideration of how power devolved to him in the first place.

Suharto, as heir to the hegemonic mode of the Javanese *ratu adil*, had, as it were, the divine right to extract tribute, rice or manpower, and religious enthusiasm (the king being the divine incarnate) through resort to randon terror, as practised in the Hindu-Buddhistic inland Kingdom of Java and by the coastal Muslim trading principalities. To carry on this patrimonial analogy to contemporary Indonesia one can view a parallel trilogy. Now it is *Bulognas*, the National Logistics Board, that is responsible for the purchase and distribution of rice. Religious enthusiasm of those *abangan* with a *priai* world view is being appropriated into a semi-formalized world view called *kepercayaan*, subscribed to and given the imprimatur of Suharto and other leading military-bureaucratic elite figures.[34] And third, the *satrya* (warrior role) of the ABRI/TNI general, Suharto, is not inconsistent with precolonial notions of *sakti* (spiritually reinforced power).

To answer the question posed at the introduction of this article—what precisely is the degree of relative autonomy of cultural superstructural factors?—it will be necessary to preview the relationship between the socio-politico-religious *alirans* and hegemonic power in Java. In the New Order, it has come to pass that the basically abangan Generals have given their endorsement to *ilmu* (science of) *kejawen,* otherwise known as *kebatinan* (spirituality) or, more generically, *kepercayaan* (beliefs). What must be determined is whether secularists are promoting tradition and religion for narrow secular interests or whether religionists are using secular politicians to promote religious interests.

Kebatinan has been characterized as "the attitude of always looking for a supernatural explanation of natural phenomena."[35] Although in abeyance during the colonial period, *kebatinan* is experiencing a revival in the New Order period. When Suharto expounds on *pembangunan*, not only is he referring to material development but also to spiritual and moral rearmament. *Kebudayaan nenek moyang* (the culture of the ancestors) provided an appropriate panacea in the spiritual catharsis unleashed by the massacre of the anti-god PKI. In those dark days, the instinct to return to the fold of religiosity was reinforced by the atheistic stigma attached to the PKI by the Suharto government.

Djipojono elaborates how the Javanese ideal of the so-called *ratu adil* greatly facilitates the creation of spiritual groups, especially in periods of social turmoil. Moreover, the impressive performance of a spiritual leader and the devotion of his pupils appears to be modeled on the ideal of a *ratu adil*. [36] So much the better for Suharto as *ratu adil* if he is widely believed to have received the cosmic beneficence. The *abangan* adepts of *kejawen* thus merge harmoniously into the fold of "little tradition"—"great tradition" symbiosis of the *zaman adil makmur* (the age of justice and prosperity).

Slamet has noted the dialogue between reformist Islam and *kebatinan*, which in broader terms is a kind of Indonesianization of the religious faith. For the PNI, which has been on the wane politically, its other manifestation as a religious *aliran-ilmu kejawen* has received official approval. In the previous section it has been noted how religious aliran conflicts have been subsumed under the interests of national harmony in the highest representative institution, the MPR. But clearly for Suharto and the *abangan* generals whose strength and power base is Java, this de facto Javanization works to enhance the hegemonic mode. It can also be shown that regional representation in the MPR is a throwback to the cosmogonic hegemony of Majapahit in which outer appanage groups and outer islands paid tribute to the king in Java.

Of the Golkarization process already discussed, Slamet points out that the pauperization of the masses (otherwise known as agricultural involution) is interpreted as *nasib* (fate) and an acceptance of subordination to particularistic patrons. It has already been described how the institutionalization of politics and the simplification of the party system has worked towards this end. Diverse groups and obstructionist parties were discredited for opening up communalist wounds and have been subsumed by the politics of consensus. Indeed, the purification and cleansing of political life after the 1965 coup can be regarded as a macrocosmic manifestation of the purification of the *kebatinan* adept occasioned in a time of psychic stress.   If unity and harmony is the ultimate goal of the *kebatinan* adept, then tolerance, consensus, and national unity, *Bhineka Tunggal Ika* (Unity in Diversity), is the national goal.   Suharto's political longevity is testimony of his skills at playing this "cultural game"; indeed, it seems improbable that a totally secular Westernized politician could rise above second-echelon positions in the contemporary *kraton* in Jakarta (nor for that matter, a non-Javanese).

What can be said of the *satrya* (warrior) feudal and patriachal view of society assumed by the generals is that it perpetuates a polarization of society between the few rich and the impoverished many.   That this order of affairs is accepted generally by a passive peasantry is testimony to the skills of Suharto and his cohorts in channeling and making routine religious enthusiasm.   The resilience of patrimonial social relations serves well the new *pangerans* (new princes) as it did the sultans of old.

Up until this point elite *priai* representations of *Pancasila* democracy and *priai* world views have been presented.   In terms of the Hegelian-Marxian categories raised in the introduction, the views as expressed by Suharto, Moertopo, Sajidiman Surjohadiprodjo, and others belong to the realm of superstructuralist ideas and reflect the hegemonist view of power.

Scott has raised the very valid question of to what extent the process of hegemony with its attendant mystification applies to the peasantry.   One way of addressing the question is by asking to what extent the institutions of ruling elites penetrate the rural sector and organize the experience of the peasantry.   He says that hegemony depends upon the pervasiveness of institutions, the courts and civil bureaucracy, schools, the media, and churches (in Indonesia, the Muslim *pesantren* schools).   However, the symbolic reach of the state, he argues, is likely to be more tenuous in the countryside than at the center.   In an archipelagic nation such as Indonesia, these generalizations are valid.   In a culturally pluralist society, there exist alternative value orientations distant from the ideological influence of the ruling class, eg, the more orthodox Islamic viewpoint. But Scott advances his thesis to argue that the radical potential of the peasantry is frequently antithetical to the values of hegemonic institutions.[37] In light of this argument, it is worth looking at the tradition of millennial peasant revolts. In recent historical times the quietistic Saminist revolt best illustrates an *abangan* challenge to the *priai* worldview. Saminists tried by the Dutch courts responded to the *priai* with *ngoko* (low Javanese), a language level that says that "the people I am speaking to are no better than myself."[38] While the ideal social relationship of *abangan* and *priai* is the mirror-image view of social harmony already mentioned, the Saminists, or the *wong cilik* (the peasants), to use Scott's vocabulary, "contain almost inevitably the seeds of an alternative symbolic universe." Indeed, the phoenix-like rise of the PKI out of the ashes of the suppressed Madiun Revolt can be partly explained by the same thesis. It cannot be dismissed entirely as a secular phenomenon, since redemptive promise plays its part as well.

What becomes imperative for Suharto and the *priai* is that symbolic opposition does not become socially organized, which would disrupt social harmony. Rather, the symbolic abangan opposition is channeled by skillfully countering rumor with rumor, by getting the influential *dalang* (puppeteer) of the popular *wayang* (shadow play) alongside, by allowing a safety valve of dissent, and by reinforcing social-cultural-religious orderings by the promotion of traditional values. The cultivation of *kepercayaan* among the bureaucratic polity and *golongan karya* fractions in Java through devotion to what might be called a spiritual *monoloyalitas* can be viewed as a manifestation of the ruling-class hegemonic mode that works to withdraw social approbation from those who "digress" by promoting divisive *aliran* interests.

However, the loose, voluntaristic, and spontaneous aspects of these *kebatinan* sects posit a potential challenge to the New Order president, not from their organizational proclivities, but in their role as *resi*. Budiman has described these *resi* as hermits or sages whose typical role is to diagnose decay within the kingdom and to give warning of the impending downfall of the dynasty; moreover, the Javanese *resi* derive prestige from the mystical world of power itself. Suharto, as heir to this tradition, knows well that to suppress the *resi*, who have no personal interests, is taken as a sign of the center's impending disintegration. Moreover, when a Javanese ruler senses impending disorder, there is a strong tendency to become an authoritarian ruler.[39] That characterization befits Suharto's New Order, particularly since the January 1974 riots occasioned by the visit of Japanese Prime Minister Tanaka. For Suharto it is vital to have the *resi* alongside.

Dipojono has noted that the government will always be suspicious when new movements by *kebatinan* adepts are created. This is especially true when the movements internalize the *ratu adil* attitude, which greatly enhances devotion to the spiritual leader and promotes the fighting spirit of the group. Moreover, it is not easy to determine readily whether new movements may have political aspirations as well as their spiritual qualities.[40] The claim of the mystic Sawito abundantly illustrates Suharto's dilemma and for the sceptics exposes his hypocrisy. Sawito, as *resi*, charges that Suharto's *pamrih* (use of power for personal indulgence) has undermined the Head of State's right to rule. His claim to have the *wahyu* (cosmic revelation) has thus landed him a charge of subversion. Suharto's embarrassment over this incident and the attention that Sawito has elicited points to the propriety of "moral force" that transcends exclusive Western-derived notions of power and legitimacy. Similarly, the resignation of the Sultan of Jogjakarta as Vice President could be viewed as a diminution of power at the center. The Sultan's proximity to Suharto was regarded as a consolidation of his legitimacy.

Conclusion

Although credence has been given to the cultural and traditional aspects of power as manifested in the New Order Pancasila democracy, one cannot minimize the fact that the purification and simplification of the political party system has had the effect of progressively neutralizing potential sources of opposition.

Conflict between socio-religio-political *aliran* as formulated by
Geertz, while the most sophisticated conceptualization yet
formulated to explain Indonesian society, does not afford an
explanation of the interest group ties to particular patrons that
have emerged in clear configuration in the New Order. The
military interpenetration with the business elite has distorted its
declared *dwi-fungsi* role of serving Pancasila democracy and
guaranteeing the security of the nation, to that of *"tri-fungsi"*
(three functions), with an additional self-serving profiteering
mission. Empire-building is symptomatic of excesses displayed
by certain generals in alliance with the *cukongs* (Chinese
middlemen) and foreign multinationals. While these enterprises
and foundations make individuals within ABRI/TNI the most
prominent beneficiaries of the New Order (and not excluding
the president), they are important engines of economic growth
and foci of modernization, visibly changing the face of the
economic base in Indonesia.

The display of wealth compounded by power at the center,
however, has brought forth an opposition whose political and
cultural enthusiasm is less than total. Dissatisfaction is
expressed in the symbolic ridicule of *abangan* folk humor, the
cryptic jokes of the *wayang* puppeteer (the *dalang)*, rumor, the
ridicule of Madame Suharto by the students, the *santri* outrage
at immorality at the center, and more tellingly by those
millenarian *abangan* who would dare speak *ngoko* to the *priai*.
If it transpires that those *abangan* (whose world view assumes
an alternative symbolic universe in their pursuit of millenarian
goals) translate their frustrations into a consciousness that
transcends the syncretic *abangan/priai* mirror-image view of
social stasis, then Suharto is in deep trouble. That is to say, if
the burden becomes too onerous for the *abangan* peasantry,
the *ABRI/Golkar/Bulog* patronage networks would be perceived
as straining the interests of village and national harmony.
Suharto, if indeed equated with the *ratu adil,* would be further
perceived as unable to realize the *zaman mas* (the golden age)
and the *wahyu* withdrawn. Of the first Parsonian question,
concerning the relationship between values, authority, and power,
the preceding analysis has not provided fully worked out answers

or predictions but rather has afforded a probabilistic explanation. The second Parsonian question, which was addressed to the efficacy of institutions in resolving conflict, has been positively answered. A longitudinal view of the implementation of Pancasila democracy through two elections and 12 years of relative social and political stability illustrated that the New Order was devoid of the worst features of divisive and parochial politics. In this highly pluralistic society, it is to the credit of the New Order that their concept of Pancasila democracy offers the way out of the impasse borne of the ruinous Guided Democracy years and the traumatic after-effects of the post-1965 coup, the PKI massacres. Politics as the allocation of resources demands the just distribution of religious, cultural, ethnic, and economic opportunities. If it is perceived that any of these tangible or intangible resources become identified with any single group, then the system is perceived to be out of harmony. Contained in the concept of Pancasila democracy is the potential to attain harmony. If tradition provides the national resilience to overcome the divisiveness inherent in the Old Order, then that is an achievement of the New Order regime. Whether the Magelang Generation of ABRI (those officers trained at Magelang since 1960) can bring off their succession to the ABRI generation of 1945 by continuing to address social welfare with the same political commitment to *dwi-fungsi* remains to be seen.

The final two questions posed in the introduction of this article raise the dilemma of Suharto. If Pancasila ideology functionally remains as a superstructural epiphenomenon, then, as with the kings and sultans of the past, sacral religious symbols contain the danger of being perceived as nostrums. Enthusiasm then becomes "an opiate of the people." If the ideology is affirmed as a socially/structurally dependent variable, then the New Order through economic actualization can affirm its legitimacy, just as the legendary *ratu adil*, through attention to the irrigation system and good public works, pandered to the needs of his subjects.

It has been shown that for the *abangan* peasantry of Java, it is still consciousness that determines existence; the millenarians, the students, the mystics, the *kiai*, and even the officer cadre are in accord with pervasive traditional value systems, although reflecting different degrees of cultural-religious diffusion, hence the enduring *aliran* conflict. It cannot be said that the shift from a traditional patrimonial model to a totally rational-legal pattern of authority has been effected. Neither can it be said that the idealized *priai* value system has been superseded by a pervasive secularism. Although, as has been shown, the relationship between *abangan* and *priai* contains contradictory elements of allegiance and alienation, it cannot be said of the *abangan* and even the PKI that existence determines consciousness as in the Marxist schema.[41] The symbolic universe of the individual is thus prefigured by the society he lives in. One can conclude that the relative autonomy of culture in society thus defies quantification by either the functionalist school or by the Neo-Hegelians. Neither can one agree with the religious fatalists who exclaim *"Insya Allah"* (It is the Will of God).

Notes

This paper arose out of a series of postgraduate seminars in Indonesian Government at the University of Queensland. It has profited from the critical attention given by Ulf Sundhaussen and Michael Tioeng.

1. For an appreciation of the ideological antecedents to the New Order in its formative stages, see Donald E. Weatherbee, *Ideology in Indonesia: Sukarno's Indonesian Revolution* (Yale University, South-East Asian Studies, 1966), passim.

2. See R. S. Milne, "'National Ideology' and Nation-Building in Malaysia," *Asian Survey*, X, 7 (July 1970), passim.

3. Benedict R. O'G. Anderson, "The Idea of Power in Javanese Culture," in Claire Holt (ed.) *Culture and Politics in Indonesia* (Ithaca: Cornell University Press, 1972): 1-69.

4. A. R. Wilner, "The Neotraditional Accommodation to Political Independence: The Case of Indonesia," in L. W. Pye (ed.), *Cases in Comparative Politics*: Asia (Boston: Little Brown, 1970).

5. Arief Budiman, "The Student Movement in Indonesia: A Study of the Relationship Between Culture and Structure," *Asian Survey*, XVIII: 6 (June 1978): 624-625.

6. Ibid., 610-611.

7. Rex Mortimer, "Culture and Politics in Indonesia," *Australian Outlook*, 26, 3 (December 1972), passim.

8. Karl D. Jackson, "The Prospects for Bureaucratic Polity in Indonesia," in K. D. Jackson & L. W. Pye (eds.), *Political Power and Communications in Indonesia* (Berkeley: University of California Press, 1978).

9. John James MacDougall, "The Technocratic Model of Modernization: The Case of Indonesia's New Order," *Asian Survey*, XVI, 12, (December 1976): 1166.

10. "Doctrin Perdjuangan TNI-Tri-UBAYA CAKTI, Second Army Seminar from 25 to 31 August 1966, Staff of the Army Command and General Staff School (SESKOAD), Bandung.

11. Anderson, "The Idea of Power,": 4.

12. Bernard Dahm, *Sukarno and the Struggle for Indonesian Independence* (Ithaca: Cornell University Press, 1969): 336-350.

13. See, Ali Moertopo, *Strategi Politik National* (Malang: Paragon Press, 1974).

14. From an address by President Sukarno before the Belgrade Summit of Non-Aligned Countries in 1st September 1961 (Department of Information, Republic of Indonesia): 9.

15. *Kompas* (Jakarta), February 17, 1975 (American Embassy Translations of Indonesian Newspaper Editorials).

16. Clifford Geertz, *The Religion of Java* (New York: Free Press, 1960), contains the most developed exposition on the *abangan, santri,* and *priai (priyayi) "aliran."*

17. U.S. Foreign Broadcast Information Service (FBIS) monitored report on Suharto's March 11, 1978 speech before the MPR.

18. See Ulf Sundhaussen, "The New Order of General Soeharto," *Internationales Asienforum*, 4 (1973): 60. It should be further noted that "crimes" regarded as endangering national security may well be handled by a military tribunal rather than a civilian court.

19. Rosihan Anwar, "Social Political Aspects of the MPR," *The Indonesian Quarterly*, 1, 3 (1978): 11.

20. See Sajidiman Surjohadiprodjo, *Langkah-Langkah Perdjuangan Kita,* Departemen Pertahanan Keamanan Pusat Sedjarah ABRI, 1971, p. 81. The author at the time of writing was a Brigadier-General of the Army (TNI).

21. Anwar, "Social Political Aspects of the MPR."

22. Mashuri, "Pancasila Democracy," *The Indonesian Quarterly*, V, 4 (October 1977).

23. *Pandangan Presiden Soeharto Tentang Pancasila,* Center for Strategic and International Studies, Jakarta, 1976: 61.

24. C. van Dijk, "Prelude to the 1978 General Session of the Indonesian People's Congress," *Review of Indonesian and Malayan*

Affairs, 12, 1 (1978): 105-111.

25. Sajidiman Surjohadiprodjo, *Langkah-Langkah*.

26. *Pandangan Presiden Soeharto Tentang Pancasila*: 67.

27. R. W. Liddle, "Evolution from Above: National Leadership and Local Development in Indonesia," *The Journal of Asian Studies*, XXXIII: 2 (February 1970): 290.

28. Ali Moertopo, "Political and Economic Development in Indonesia in the Context of Regionalism in South-East Asia," *The Indonesian Quarterly*, VI, 2 (April 1978): 34.

29. B.R.O.'G. Anderson, "Religion and Politics in Indonesia Since Independence," in *Religion, and Social Ethos in Indonesia*, (Clayton, Victoria, Australia: Monash University, 1973).

30. From FBIS monitored broadcast of Suharto's March 11 speech before the MPR.

31. Ulf Sundhaussen, "The Military: Structure, Procedures and Effects on Indonesian Society," in K. D. Jackson and L. W. Pye, *Political Power*.

32. Ulf Sundhaussen, "Social Policy Aspects in Defence and Security Planning in Indonesia, 1947-1977," (Uppsala, August 1978). This is an unpublished paper submitted to the IXth World Congress of Sociology, Research Committee on Armed Forces and Society. Sundhausen notes that in the case of Indonesia the officers' behavior must be explained in terms of their value system, just as the behavior of other groups involved in public life is usually not only analysed in terms of narrow egotistic interests but also in regard to their ideals and spiritual orientations (Ibid: 53).

33. See B.R.O'G, Anderson, "The Idea of Power."

34. In the 1977 Congress debates over agama (religion) it is significant that bureaucratic-military elite figures supported *kepercayaan*. For example, Adam Malik at various meetings with Islamic organizations stated that because *kepercayaan* did exist in society its existence should be recognized. The minister of Home Affairs voiced the same support. See van Dijk, "Prelude,": 117.

35. See Bonokamsi Dipojono, "Kebatinan and Kebatinan Movements for the Javanese," *The Indonesian Quarterly*, 11, 1 (October 1973).

36. Ibid.

37. James Scott, "Hegemony and Peasantry," *Politics and Society*, 7, 3 (1977): 273-275.

38. See B.R.O'G. Anderson, "Millenarianism and the Saminist Movement," in *Religion and Social Ethos in Indonesia*. Anderson asserts that what millenarianism means basically is that people in the

millenarian movements and the authorities that represent them in some real sense share a common cosmology.

39. Budiman, "The Student Movement,": 616.
40. Bonokamsi Dipojono, "Kebatinan and Kebatinan Movements."
41. See Sartono Kartodirdjo, "Agrarian Radicalism in Java, Its Setting and Development," in Holt (ed.), *Culture and Politics in Indonesia*: 113. With reference to the political dimension of millenarianism in Java, Sartono notes that its ideology is suffused with religious symbolism because the world view of the rural people to whom millenarianism appeals is still dominated by religion.

2. Tan Malaka and the Indonesian Revolution

The role of Tan Malaka (1897-1949) in Indonesian nationalist history has always been provocative, just as the Sumatran-born former chairman of the Indonesian Communist Party (1921), subsequent Comintern representative for Southeast Asia (1923), and erstwhile "father" of the Indonesian nationalist revolution, has attracted the attention of a wide range of both Indonesian and non-Indonesian historians.[1] In turn, Tan Malaka was a prolific author, penning, besides his three-volume autobiography, some scores of booklets and tracts often written under great adversity.

It is vitally important, thirty more years after the consolidation and institutionalization of the Indonesian New Order regime of General Suharto, and fifty years after the proclamation of Indonesian independence by Sukarno/Hatta in August 1945, that Indonesian history, including "nationalist" history, be written from the outside. All the better that it be written on the inside, were it not for the powerful sway of state agencies—the censorship apparatus, official institutes of history and think-tanks—that have made a small industry out of rewriting modern Indonesian history in line with the ascendancy of Suharto and the army. For obvious reasons such key events as those surrounding the coup of September 1965 and its bloody aftermath, are subject to major obfuscation inside Indonesia today. Similarly, the full panoply of propaganda services have been brought into play to parlay the armed invasion and annexation of East Timor in 1975 into a "liberation." No less, as this work engages, the events of 1945-46 leading to the proclamation of the Republic and its defense against armed colonial restoration (1945-49) are equally subject to official revisionism.

Conversion to bolshevism

The case of Tan Malaka stands out, for he was thrice imprisoned and banished by three colonial powers in Asia. First, he was arrested and briefly imprisoned by the Dutch authorities prior to banishment from his native Indonesia in mid-1922 for alleged various revolutionary activities. Second, he was arrested in August 1927 by the American authorities in the Philippines and subsequently banished. Third, in 1932, he was arrested by the British authorities in Hong Kong, imprisoned and likewise banished. As Tan Malaka has himself written, in the last two cases the countries concerned had broken with their political traditions by denying him the right of asylum.[2]

Born in 1896, Tan Malaka was the son of a high official in the Minangkabau region of Sumatra. The year of the Bolshevik revolution, 1917, found him in Holland, where for six years, he continued his schooling. Attracted by the tumultuous events unfolding in Russia, and having broken with his patrician Dutch sponsor, he traveled to Moscow, where for several months he absorbed at first hand the lessons of the revolution. Thus armed, he returned to the Indies (November 1919), found employment as a supervisor of schools for the children of plantation coolies in the Deli region of Sumatra, but also helped form the Indonesian Communist Party (PKI), the Sarekat Islam (SI), and communist schools. Moving on to Java, where he set about organizing a school in Semarang, Tan Malaka was elevated, at the age of 25, to the chairmanship of the PKI at its eighth congress in December 1921. But expelled from the East Indies in March 1922, after two months in prison, he proceeded to the Netherlands where he stood successfully for the Dutch Communist Party in the parliamentary elections of that year. Prevented by age from holding a parliamentary seat, he then proceeded to Moscow via Germany to attend the Fourth Comintern Congress, arriving in October 1922 to become an active Comintern organizer.[3]

As representative of the Communist Party of the Dutch East Indies (PKI) at the Moscow Congress, Tan Malaka came to attention for his critique of the blanket condemnation of Pan-Islamism as contained in the theses approved by the Second

Congress of the Communist International, reflecting, inter alia, the Eurocentrist viewpoint among European Marxists, Lenin included. Tan Malaka argued with great force that this attitude had been taken up by bourgeois nationalists in the Dutch East Indies in order to isolate the Communists from the peasant masses.[4] Writing of the collaboration of the Party with the Sarekat Islam, 1 to 4 million strong, Tan Malaka lamented a split occurring in 1921, owing to the "tactless criticism of the leaders of Sarekat Islam."

> The government through its agents, made use of this split, and also of the decisions of the Second Congress of the Communist International, to fight against Pan-Islamism. The government agents said to the simple peasants that the Communists did not only want to create a spit among them, but also that they wanted to destroy their religion. This was too much for a simple Moslem peasant. The peasant thought to himself that he had already lost everything in this world and that he was not willing to lose heaven as well. Such was the mood of these simple-minded people, and the government propagandists and agents made use of it. Thus we have a split." (Chair [Marchlewski]: "Your time is up") "I have come from India, it took me forty days to come here." (Applause.) "The Sarekat Islamists believe in our propaganda. They are with us "with their stomachs" (to use a popular expression), but with their hearts they remain with the Sarekat Islam—with their heaven, which we cannot give them. Therefore they boycotted our meetings and we could not carry on propaganda any longer. [5]

As B. O'G. Anderson has commented upon this intervention, throughout his life and often at odds with the Comintern, the Indonesian stressed the revolutionary potential of Islam in the colonized territories and the need for communist parties to cooperate with radical Islamic groups.[6] Yet, as mentioned below, Tan Malaka was also prepared to change his mind on that question, especially as he came to know better the concrete situation in colonial Malaya and Singapore. In any case, whatever the mixed reception in Moscow, the Indonesian revolutionary was

appointed Comintern Agent for Southeast Asia at the Executive
Committee of the Comintern International (ECCI) plenum of June
1923.

Tan Malaka in Guangzhou (late 1923-June 1925)

Following his new appointment, Tan Malaka set up headquarters
in Guangzhou (Canton), arriving in the southern Chinese city in
mid-to late 1923. Here he plunged into the demi-monde of
underground Comintern work, especially on labor issues, which
brought him into contact with the leadership of the Kuomintang,
including Dr. Sun Yizian (Sun Yat Sen), whom he met in
December 1923, and also with a network of agents who linked
the bustling river port city with the revolutionary anti-colonial
stream in the British and French colonies. In his biography, Tan
Malaka writes that discouragement, a sense of alienation in the
Chinese city, and deteriorating health obliged him to move on to
Manila in June 1925.[7] It was in Guangzhou in April 1925 that
Tan Malaka first published his *Naar de Republiek Indonesia*.
    What was the situation in Guangzhou that helped shape Tan
Malaka's thoughts? Under the control of Sun Ko, Sun Yizian's
Western-trained son, Guangzhou in 1923 was a quintessentially
Chinese city in a modernizing phase. At least up until the boycott
or general strike of 1925, Guangzhou under the Kuomintang-
Chinese Communist Party alliance experienced, in the words of
one student of the city, a "remarkable expansion of commerce,
industry and public services." Under the protection of Sun Yizian,
the city became a magnet for such future giants of the Chinese
Communist party as Mao Zedong, who taught in the Peasant
Training Institute in Guangzhou; Zhou Enlai, who was political
commissar in the Whampoa Military Academy where Lin Piao
was a student, and Jiang Jieshi (Chiang Kai-shek) was
superintendent. From 1923, until the "White Terror" of 1927,
Guangzhou was the site of joint action in mass movements by
peasants and labour groups.[8] The impression gained from a
reading of Tan Malaka's autobiography confirms that these events
deeply impressed themselves upon the young revolutionary, just
as one can safely draw the inference that they influenced his

intellectual and political development.

Tan Malaka's return to Southeast Asia (July 1925)

Arriving in the Philippines in July 1925 in the guise of a returnee Philippine student, Tan Malaka immediately threw himself into revolutionary activity. There he made contact with a number of prominent Filipino nationalist leaders, including Jose Abad Santos and Manuel Quezon and labor leader Francisco Varona. Although not mentioned in Tan Malaka's autobiography it is also possible that he made contact with future Filipino communist leaders. Helen Jarvis, a Tan Malaka biographer, believes that it was Varona who helped him bring out the Manila edition of *Naar de Republiek Indonesia* while Tan Malaka made himself useful as a correspondent for the nationalist newspaper *El Debate*.[9]

Anderson describes how in Manila, still as chairman of the party, Tan Malaka came into increasing conflict with his party comrades. In particular, he sought to heal the widening breach between the PKI and the old Sarekat Islam groups around Tjokroaminoto and Haji Augus Salim. He also warned of the dangers of sectarianism in a situation in which the masses were national-socialist rather than proletarian socialist in orientation.[10]

For the Indonesian revolutionaries-in-exile, Tan Malaka included, the colonial port city of Singapore provided perfect cover, especially in the Arabo-Malay quarters of the city. As a British colony, Singapore—like Hong Kong—also allowed certain legal cover for banishees from other European colonialisms in Southeast Asia. Although the matter is not clear, Tan Malaka probably first visited or passed through Singapore in late 1925. In any case, at the age of 29 he arrived back in Singapore in June 1926 and, following another short absence from the colony, found employment as an office clerk in a German trading company.[11]

Among the first group of Indonesian communists drawn to the attention of the British police in the Straits Settlements, since the foundation of the PKI in 1920, were probably Raden Semaun, who passed through in 1922, and Alimin, who stopped over

briefly in 1924 en route to the Pan-Pacific Labour Conference
held in June of that year in Guangzhou.[12] Other known Javanese
revolutionaries then sojourning in the bustling multiracial port
city included Musso, Winata, Boedisoejitro, Subakat,
Djamaluddin Tamin, Sutan Djenain, Sardjono, Mohamed
Sanoesi, Soegono, Sutan Said Ali, Abdul Ghaffar, and Sutan
Perpatih. All became refugees in the British colony following
the failure of the communist-inspired strikes in Semarang and
Surabaya of 1925, or, in some cases, earlier. All made Singapore
their base.[13] Some of this group, like Alimin, survived into the
1960s, or 1970s, in the case of Semaun. Others, like Musso,
went down fighting in the Madiun rebellion in 1948. Yet others,
like Tan Malaka, were victims along the way. As revealed by a
British report, the activities of this band of refugees and banishees
from Java were not restricted to the Straits Settlements and the
Netherlands East Indies, but also to Sarawak, and the Philippines
as well.[14]

It is possible that Tan Malaka made more than one
furtive visit to Singapore during this period. British police
records contain a letter written by Tan Malaka in Singapore
on 6 November 1925, ie, seven months after the publication in
Guangzhou of *Naar de Republiek*. This was a letter addressed
to Boedisoejitro, then in Java. Contrary to his earlier optimism
as to Islam, this letter baldly states his conviction that the Malays
of Malaya did not hold out too much revolutionary promise: "In
brief, if one looks for a movement in the FMS, it is not sought
from the side of the Malays. It will certainly come from the
Chinese and Klings, whatever sort of movement it may be." [15]
Perhaps, in this, Tan Malaka foresaw the problem of ethnic
competition in the revolutionary struggle in Malaya, competition
that was bound to be unequal and weighted on the side of the
Chinese and the Indians, as he implied in his letter. Nevertheless,
membership of the first mass Indonesian nationalist organization,
Sarikat Islam, and its adjunct *merah* or "red" inclined sections,
also proliferated on the other side of the Malacca Straits.

As Yuji Suzuki has pointed out in an essay on the evolution
of Tan Malaka's political thinking in the 1930s, the Indonesian
became convinced that nothing but a mental transformation of

the Indonesian people could break through the tautology of feudalism and imperialist oppression. As Tan Malaka wrote in *Massa Actie,* also penned and published in Singapore in 1926:

> You, 55,000,000 people of Indonesia, you will never become free and independent, as long as you do not throw all the dirt of magic out of your head, as long as you still hold to the ancient culture which is full of fallacies, resignation, and fossilized notions, and as long as you still have a slave mentality...Only when your society produces men who are better than a Darwin, a Newton, Marx or Lenin, can you be proud.

Suzuki comments that, from individual liberation through the absorption of Western science, Tan Malaka inferred a progression to national liberation from Western domination, or from *ketimuran* to materialism, as he later expressed the matter. It is also important in this context to take note of Tan Malaka's lifelong avocation as teacher, a role to which he would return in the 1945-46 period when *pemuda* or youth became his favored force in the struggles ahead.[16] In this text, Tan Malaka also set down his ideas on the nature of the Indonesian revolution and the course by which it should be advanced, as well as his concept of Aslia, a socialist federation of Southeast Asian countries and north Australia, an idea to which he would return in 1946.

Tan Malaka's scarlet pimpernel role was now well established, at least if colonial police records are to be believed. British colonial sources reveal that following one of his trips to Singapore (via Penang?), he travelled to Thailand, bypassing Bangkok for Chiang Mai, where he arrived on 24 September 1925. As the concerned Dutch intelligence operative noted at the time, "If Tan Malaka is established there, he can be up to no good..." Indeed, British reports hint that he established the "elements" of a communist organization in Chiang Mai, dangerously close to British Burma.[17]

In April 1926, Singapore emerged as the forum for a key conference of the exiled Javanese leaders of the PKI. In attendance were Alimin, Budisutjitro, Subakat, Winata and Musso.

The idea of bringing together delegates from the Netherlands East Indies and various groups at Singapore was Tan Malaka's. He sought to temporarily transfer the PKI executive to Singapore and to reorganize the *Sarekat Rakyat* along the lines suggested in his writings and as endorsed by the Comintern Executive. Tan Malaka's concerns stemmed from his foreknowledge of the decisions brought down at the PKI Congress in Solo in central Java (the Solo resolution actually convoked at Prambangan in December 1925 under the leadership of Alimin) to initiate strike actions the following May, to be succeeded by a call to revolution in Sumatra and then Java. In response, Tan Malaka drew up a set of theses arguing the futility of such an adventurist course of action. He argued that the situation in 1926 did not meet the minimal conditions of, first, iron discipline of the party; second, the broad acceptance by the Indonesian masses of the leadership of the PKI; and third, division among enemies at home and abroad. In this sense, Tan Malaka took a strong position against the adventurism of the call to putsch, small-scale rebellion, and individual anarchism, as opposed to broad program of education of the masses, strikes, boycotts and mass rebellion. The *Thesis* was passed on to Alimin with a view to having the matter discussed by PKI leaders in Java.[18]

Other members of the PKI remained in exile in Singapore where, as mentioned, the decision was made—in Tan Malaka's absence—to launch the rebellion.

Tan Malaka, who vigorously opposed this foolish line of action, and, angered that the PKI leadership had tried to prevent the dissemination of his arguments, met with Alimin in Manila in February 1926, sought the latter to return to Singapore, report his views, and influence the Party to reverse its stand. In the event, Alimin did not read Tan Malaka's thesis at the Singapore conference, as agreed, and did not defend Tan Malaka's position that revolution under the present circumstances was not appropriate. Another member of the circle, Subakat, who concurred with Tan Malaka's point of view, was only informed about the thesis when he arrived in Singapore in June 1926. While Tan Malaka's strong reservations were registered by the PKI Central Committee, it had the effect of postponing, rather than countermanding, Musso's call for action. But 6 May 1926 saw the Indonesian back again in Singapore. On this occasion, according to British police intelligence, Tan Malaka narrowly missed a rendezvous in Geylang Serai, the still characteristically Malay suburb of Singapore, with Alimin and his comrade, Musso, who departed for Moscow (via Guangzhou) in search of arms. Only Subakat, the sole remaining PKI leader in Singapore, sided with Tan Malaka's view and together they worked to reverse the decision to promote the rebellion through the publication of pamphlets and the writing of letters.

After the news of the temporary postponement of the uprising had been received, the Padang Panjang (Sumatra) Sectional Committee directed an appeal to Tan Malaka in Singapore, seeking his approval for insurrection without further delay. The letter was hand-delivered to Singapore on 10 September by a group including Zainun gelar Radja Marah from the Padang sub-section. Two days later, Tan Malaka called together his comrades in Singapore and repudiated Musso's call to action, thus effectively countermanding the Solo resolution. It was resolved to establish a new Central Committee at Penang, headed by Tan Malaka.[19]

Tan Malaka and the 1926-27 rebellions

The much-discussed rebellions broke out in West Java in late 1926 and, in early 1927, on the west coast of Sumatra. In these actions, metal workers and dock workers struck in Surabaya and were supported by tram and railway workers. In Jakarta, pro-communist groups briefly seized the telegraph office. In West Java and Bandung, the Dutch pressed military units into action against communist forces. To some extent, vacillation among the party leadership helped the colonial authorities to crush the rebellions, facts not forgotten by Tan Malaka's adversaries.[20] In all, about 13,000 persons were arrested, about half of whom suffered imprisonment, many interned in the notorious Bogen Digul prison camp in West Irian, from which they were not released until June 1943 ahead of a planned Allied attack against the Japanese.

Certain sections of colonial Dutch opinion tended to place the blame for the rebellion onto the British for not deporting those Javanese revolutionaries who had through the years resided or passed through Singapore. This is a reference to two of the inner circle of Javanese revolutionaries, Musso and Alimin, who were arrested in Singapore on 18 December 1926, having arrived on the SS *Deli* the same day from Bangkok. For instance, as an article in the Dutch newspaper *Nieue Rotterdamsche Courant* of 28 December 1926 pointed out, the leaders of the revolt remained in close contact with the communist centers of Guangzhou and Singapore. Further, the PKI leadership in residence in Singapore, and the central committee of the party in Java, were practically indistinguishable. More damningly, it was alleged, the arms used by the rebels came from Singapore, and the banks which financed this traffic were also located in Singapore.[21]

As it happened, an official Dutch enquiry into the communist rebellion of 1926 in West Sumatra and West Java traced the "propaganda and criminal agitation" experienced in the Dutch colony to a "secret center" in Singapore. This was described as a link between the PKI and the Comintern, between ECCI and the Profitern, between Indochina and the East Indies, between India and the Far East, and the meeting point between Chinese, Japanese, Australian, Indochinese, and Javanese communists. At the heart of this center was alleged to be a eighty-man secretariat divided into two sections, one concerned with propaganda, and the other, "direct action." [22]

The truth probably lay somewhere in-between. In the event the British authorities in Singapore saw to a more active cooperation with their Dutch counterparts. As the British Consul in Batavia, Crosby, remarked, the Dutch were permitted to send special detectives, including a European police officer to Singapore. Together, the colonial police forces identified leaders of the movement, and intercepted and deciphered encoded correspondence between the leaders. Notwithstanding what Crosby described as "close and effective" cooperation, the British were not about to waive the law by surrendering up Alimin and Musso as strongly requested by the Netherlands' authorities. [23]

Tan Malaka in Bangkok (May-August 1927)

The years following the failed rebellion of 1926-27 in Java and
Sumatra are described by Helen Jarvis as the most shadowy of
the revolutionary's career.[24]

As the west coast rebellion in Sumatra ran its course, Tan
Malaka and Subakat departed Singapore for Bangkok, and, from
this relatively safe base, tried to reassess the situation.
Djamaluddin Tamin, however, remained in Singapore helping
those communists who managed to escape from Indonesia and
gathering information on the extent of the damage suffered by
the party. In May 1927 he joined Tan Malaka and Subakat in
Bangkok and, on the first day of the following month, the three
established the Partai Republik Indonesia (PARI), a broad
nationalist party. Djamaluddin Tanin subsequently returned to
Singapore where he acted as PARI agent and kept up contact
with PKI members until his arrest in 1932. Jarvis notes that
several vain attempts to hold PARI congresses were aborted.[25]
While, as Tan Malaka wrote in his autobiography, the creation
of PARI was not "an attempt to liquidate communism,"[26] his
plan was nevertheless rejected by Moscow as unorthodox and
Trotskyite and he was obliged to resign his membership of the
executive committee of the communist international (ECCI).
According to Jarvis, it is clear that Tan Malaka broke with the
PKI and the Comintern in an endeavor to create "his own leftist
tradition" (arguably Trotskyist).[27]

Meanwhile, offices of PARI were established in such Asian
cities as Shanghai, Singapore, and Tokyo. While PARI continued
to exist for the next ten years, at least as a tenuous connecting
link between the pre-1926 PKI and the Indonesian nationalist
revolution of 1945, Tan Malaka appears to have distanced himself
from the party following its foundation.[28] Two of Tan Malaka's
underground PARI organizers in pre-war Java, Adam Malik and
Sukarni, however, would later emerge as staunch allies, after
the 17 August 1945 proclamation of the Republic.

Tan Malaka in the Philippines (August 1927)

Shortly after founding PARI, Tan Malaka departed for the
Philippines. Betrayed to the American authorities in the
Philippines—many fingers point at the Dutch—Tan Malaka was
summarily arrested on 12 August 1927; but the case backfired
and Tan Malaka became a cause celébré for local nationalists.[29]
Tan Malaka describes in his own words how he was soon bailed
out of prison by Ramon Fernandez, an ex-senator and ex-mayor
of the City of Manila and a "non-cooperator against American
imperialism." Even though, as Tan Malaka explains, the full
weight of the American merchants backed by the American Army
and Navy and, ultimately the acting Governor General, was
arrayed against this opinion, eventually, by August 1931, he won
his freedom in the form of a deportation order to China.[30]

Tan Malaka in Hong Kong (September 1932-October 1932)

Having eluded the Dutch police who were awaiting his arrival in
Amoy, where he disembarked, Tan Malaka moved to Shanghai.
Apparently he met Alimin in the international port city in August
1931. But driven out of Shanghai by the Japanese attack of
September 1932, Tan Malaka proceeded to Hong Kong where he
arrived early the next month. Together with a PARI comrade,
Djaos, Tan Malaka was arrested on 10 October and interrogated
by British officials from Singapore.[31] Although the only charges
against him were illegal entry, he did not fight the issue, as Ho
Chi Minh had done before him, but agreed to deportation to China
in order to protect his local allies.

The arrest of Tan Malaka in Hong Kong was foreshadowed
by the arrest in Singapore the preceding month by his comrade
Jamaluddin Tamin and his circle of confidants. According to Tan
Malaka's own admission, his earlier visit to Bangkok was to
meet with the leaders of PARI to decide whether or not the time
was ripe for direct action in the Netherlands East Indies. But
PARI, he insisted, was a purely nationalist body concerned with
rallying the Javanese and Sumatran proletariat to drive the Dutch
from the Indies. He also denied the incriminating evidence

contained in the papers of the arrested Comintern agent, Noulens, that he was charged by Moscow to proceed, along with Alimin, to Burma and foment revolution. While the British had no proof, they found it hard to believe that an internationalist of Tan Malaka's caliber could not be implicated in subversive actions against the British empire.[32]

As Tan Malaka wrote in his biography, such was British ambivalence towards this cosmopolitan native, that he was moved backwards and forwards between a European cell and a native cell. When granted permission to write a letter, he took the opportunity to cable Lansbury, leader of the British Socialist Party. Secretly, he also sent a letter to independent Labour MP, James Maxton, and member of the British parliament. A second secret letter was sent to Manila and attracted a statement of support.[33] Finally, on 27 October, Tan Malaka was informed by the British that an official Dutch case for extradition was not legally supportable and that he was to be allowed to leave Hong Kong. The choice of country was one that the revolutionary agonized over. [34]

Even though his case was taken up in the British parliament by Maxton, Tan Malaka was deported to Shanghai. Clearly a skilled linguist after three years in China, he traveled slowly back to Singapore, via Burma, where he settled in September 1937 masquerading as a Chinese and teaching school. [35] A witness to the Japanese invasion of Singapore, he continued in this employment until the middle of May 1942, when he was spirited across the Straits of Malacca to Medan in northern Sumatra with the help of his former Chinese students.

Tan Malaka and the republican ideal

Returning to the East Indies from Singapore in early 1942 Tan Malaka entered the final phase of his life, arguably also coinciding with the pinnacle of his revolutionary career. In the period up until independence was declared on 17 August 1945, Tan Malaka had already joined with nationalist and revolutionary youth in Jakarta, including certain influential members of the nationalist leadership. Just whom he met among this circle, and in what circumstances, remains obscure and the subject of much speculation. It is also clear that, while the left wing, including communist party organizations, remained dormant during the period of the Japanese occupation, old networks were easily stirred by propaganda in the underground. The question of Tan Malaka's contacts with the Japanese is also at issue.

It is of more than passing interest that during Tan Malaka's years in Singapore, up until his return to Indonesia still under Japanese rule, a series of novels appeared in Medan entitled *Patjar Merah Indonesia* ("The Scarlet Pimpernel of Indonesia"). The characters of these stories, set in the 1930s, are Indonesian nationalists, expatriated by Dutch colonial authorities, who fought against the oppressive power of imperialism and Stalinism. The superhuman hero was widely believed to have been Tan Malaka. Such stories did much to add to the legendary aura of Tan Malaka and his shadowy life and prepared the way for his reception as a "superhuman" figure when he later returned to the public stage in the newly independent Republic.[36] While Tan Malaka learned at first hand of the Tan Malaka myth—he writes of finding one such book in a Medan bookshop he acknowledged that he returned as a "Rip Van Winkle," unrecognized and badly out of touch with local realities.

This reality Tan Malaka discovered at first hand, following a hazardous journey across the island of Sumatra from Medan via Padang, Palembang, and Lampang to Jakarta, where he arrived in May 1942, renting a room in the mixed rural-urban Rawa Djati quarter. Here, he eked out a bohemian existence writing what he considered his classic work *Madalog* and half of the manuscript of another work called *Aslia*. In his autobiography Tan Malaka describes a rhythm of writing in the mornings, conversing with his working class *kampong* dwellers in the afternoons, and studying in the Gambir public library in the evenings.[37] Now going by the name of Ilyas Hussein and masquerading as an ex-clerk from Singapore, Tan Malaka got himself hired in late 1943 as a clerk in the Bajah Kozan, a coal mining enterprise in south Banten on the remote coast of West Java controlled by Sumitomo interests. This was no ordinary coal mine, however, but an example of what he described in his

1945 publication *Rentjana Ekonomi* as an example of "economic plunder" through the use of slave labour. In this position until mid-1945, when news of a Japanese capitulation gained increasing currency, Tan Malaka mediated between his Japanese military bosses, whom he evidently impressed with his energy and administrative skills, and the needs of the 10,000 or more *romusha* or indentured laborers, literally worked to death in the mine, and whose respect he also gained. As an example, he describes how he gained the confidence of other colleagues, as much the *romusho*, by scripting *sandiwara* or plays with historical themes, albeit loaded with appropriate and subtle anti-imperialist messages.[38]

There is no question, however, that Tan Malaka owed his position to the Japanese authorities, although that is not the same as saying that he collaborated with the Japanese, as was definitely the case of Sukarno and Hatta. As Tan Malaka explains, such Japanese-fostered mass organizations as the Hokokai, the "Three A" movement, and Putera, touched all youth in Bajah Kozan. Tan Malaka explains, however, that in the local *pemuda* movement, two streams emerged. The former, the Angkatan Muda, with its focal point in Bandung, rejected Japanese promises of independence as improbable, and, the Jakarta-based Angkatan Baru, to which he sided, recognized that to actually win independence it was necessary to work with the Japanese and obtain it from within. To this end, Tan Malaka was chosen as a local (Bantem) delegate to represent the Aliran Baru at an upcoming conference in Jakarta aimed at forging a consensus between the two tendencies or at least finding sufficient middle ground for cooperation. In accepting the position, Tan Malaka is emphatic that he rejected any connection with the Hokokai (in which Sukarno and other members of the elite had been involved). But upon arrival in Jakarta, Tan Malaka was somewhat shattered to learn that the Japanese forbade the meeting. Still going by the name of Hussein from Bantem, he nevertheless used the occasion to forge key links with certain (unnamed) *pemuda*.[39] These contacts included Chairul Salch, future Vice President of Indonesia under Sukarno, and Adam Malik, the enigmatic future Vice President of Indonesia under Suharto.

Meanwhile, on 14 August 1945, two days before the dropping of the atomic bomb on Hiroshima, Sukarno and Hatta returned from Saigon, where they had extracted promises of independence from the Japanese Commander of the Southern Area. But, in the way of obtaining independence outside of Japanese auspices, the two senior nationalist leaders were kidnapped by a group of *pemuda* whose loyalties lay with Tan Malaka and whose number included Adam Malik and Chairul Saleh. It is tempting to see the hand of Tan Malaka in this putsch but, equally, he saw advantage in working with his Japanese contacts, namely in the person of Dr. Achman Subardjo, the Dutch-educated Indonesian advisor to the Japanese navy, and head of the Asrama Merdeka Indonesia under the sponsorship of Rear Admiral Maeda Tadashi, the "leftist" head of Japanese Naval Intelligence. It was Maeda who dispatched Subardjo to rescue Sukarno and Hatta from the *pemuda*. Thus, when the proclamation of independence was made by Sukarno and Hatta two days after the official Japanese surrender on 17 August 1945 in Maeda's Menteng residence, Tan Malaka, the *pemuda* groups, and, indeed, an outraged Japanese High Command, were presented with a fait accompli.[40]

While the matter is controversial, contemporary American sources reveal that "according to documents that had come to light," Tan Malaka, "Father of the Repuolic," had a hand in this proclamation of independence, or, more accurately, a unilateral declaration of independence, and that he had urged Sukarno and Hatta to proclaim it without delay before the return of the Netherlands or the Allies.

> This could explain the political will, signed by Soekarno and Hatta, and dated October 1st 1945, in which they stipulated that their power could be transferred to "Comrade Tan Malaka," should they themselves became incapacitated to continue the struggle for the independence of Indonesia. [41]

These basic facts are acknowledged in Tan Malaka's biography, where he describes a meeting with Sukarno on this date at which the latter, now first President of the Indonesian Republic, assured him that, "if I am incapacitated *[tidak berdaja]*, I would transfer the leadership of the Revolution to you."[42] Anderson confirms that, not only were the Maeda group informed as to Tan Malaka's whereabouts through Subardjo, later appointed Minister of Foreign Affairs in the first Sukarno cabinet, but that, after 25 August, he moved in with the Subardjo family and was soon introduced to such prominent members of the Indonesian elite as Sukarno, Hatta, Sutan Sjahrir and others.[43]

As Tan Malaka wrote in his autobiography on the republican ideal:

> Forced by the people of Jakarta under the leadership of the *pemuda* headquartered at Menteng 31, on 17 August 1945 Sukarno and Hatta proclaimed the independence of Indonesia, and chose a republican form of government. To me this momentous event for the people of Indonesia meant stepping from the world of ideas to the world of reality in a period of little over twenty years (I had written *Naar de Republik* in January 1924 in Singapore).[44]

Tan Malaka's alienation from Sukarno's nationalist government became open, however, in November 1945 with the replacement of Subardjo by the moderate socialist, Soetan Sjahrlr, who, as prime minister, reserved to himself the position of foreign minister. In was on Sjahrir that the main task of negotiating the controversial Linggadjati Agreement (as discussed below) fell. For a short period, in June-July 1946, Sjahrir was abducted by Tan Malaka's supporters.

Tan Malaka and *perjuangan*

From September 1945 to November 1946, the British command assumed responsibility for taking the Japanese surrender in Java, although widely believed by Republican forces to be a cover for a planned Dutch restoration. As witness of the conflict between the British forces and the people of Surabaya in November, Tan Malaka took a firm position in favor of the *perjuangan* or struggle line, as opposed to the *diplomasis* line represented by the Sjahrir government. To this end, in early

1946, Tan Malaka set about organizing a "Persatuan Perjuangan" (literally, "struggle front") but also going by the name or "People's Front," appealing to all revolutionary, nationalist, and republican groups. Dutch intelligence saw this move as a typical tactic of using nationalism as a guise for communist aims.[45]

As many as 133 parties, associations, and groups joined the "People's Front," including Pesindo or "Pemuda Sosialis Indonesia," a party of extreme left-wing socialist youth, and certain who formed into guerrilla bands, who owed allegiance to Amir Sjarifuddin, then Minister of Information and later Defense Minister and Prime Minister of the Republic, in July 1947. It was also supported by the PKI under Mohammed Yusof, a figure who rose to prominence under Japanese sponsorship, not pre-war communist affiliation.[46] While the Labor Party (PBI) and Masjumi (the Muslim organization) also joined the People's Front, in March 1946, along with Pesindo, they withdrew to take up seats in Sjahrir's cabinet. Youth leaders, such as future New Order Vice President Adam Malik, and the radical nationalist intellectual Mohammad Yamin, were likewise attracted.

At the general meeting of the "People's Front" held on 4-5 January 1946, attended by General Soedirman, the Commander-in-chief of the Republican Army, Tan Malaka developed his "minimum program" around the slogans of *"Merdeka atau mati"* (freedom or death) and application of the policy of the "pointed bamboo." By this he urged rejection of all negotiating proposals tendered by the Netherlands, the withdrawal of Allied troops, and the recognition of Indonesian independence as a precondition for any negotiations. He also invoked the support of the Soviet Union on the principle of its opposition to any form of colonial rule.[47] While Sukarno had addressed one of the People's Front meetings, it is clear that the Republican government began to view the growth of the People's Front movement with suspicion. The matter came to a head in February, when the People's Front demanded the resignation of the Sjahrir cabinet and adopted "an increasingly aggressive attitude." According to Dutch intelligence, the conflict then resolved itself into a struggle for power between Tan Malaka and the government in the person of Amir Sjarifuddin. At first, members of Pesindo were forbidden to attend the People's Front meetings, and then Pesindo resigned as a body from that organization. Thus, by the time of the March 1946 meeting of the People's Front, only forty of the original political organizations were still affiliated with it.[48]

Now emboldened by its newly won support, the Republican government launched a counter-coup, effectively pre-empting the emergence of a dominant socialist current in the nationalist revolution. On 17 March, Tan Malaka and other leaders of the Persatuan Perjuangan, including Subardjo, Sukarni, and Mohammad Yamin, were arrested by Republican troops on the pretext of leading Tan Malaka to a meeting with President Sukarno. They were subsequently interned—albeit not imprisoned—in an isolated village where they languished for a long time. In a recent study the Indonesian writer, Aboe Bakar Loebis, claims to have knowledge which contradicts Tan Malaka's own assertion in *Dari Pendjara ke Pendjara* that he surrendered to Republican forces as he was promised a meeting in Jogjakarta with Sukarno. Rather, he claims, Tan Malaka's arrest order was unconditional and actually ordered by Sukarno, not Sjahrir.[49] In the same month, in shadowy circumstances, the Republican side moved against Mohd. Yusof, chairman of the PKI, and erstwhile ally of Tan Malaka. After his arrest, a special Republican committee was formed to purge the communist party of its revolutionary leftist-Trotskyist drift. While Yusuf's PKI was repudiated as the legal successor of the old PKI of the 1920s, the "official PKI" was re-established under the chairmanship of Sardjono. A former PKI leader back in 1925, Sardjono had recently returned to Java from Australia, where he had presided over the Central Committee for a Free Indonesia in Brisbane. Australia had been host during the war for 800 "Digulists," including veterans of the 1926-27 rebellions spirited out of West Irian in June 1943. With his return, a manifesto was issued proclaiming that the Party would support the (nationalist) revolutionary movement and that it would fight for the maintenance and consolidation of the government of the Republic.[50]

The temporary relief on the part of the Dutch at the coup against Yusof's PKI, and the arrest by the government in the

same month of Tan Malaka and followers, is carried in the following, just as the sense of conspiracy is described in general
Western relief that Tan Malaka was temporarily out of the way:

> The danger of the domination of a Tan Malaka type of com-
> munist government was hereby averted. Soon the regular
> communist party, which had little or nothing to do with Tan
> Malaka's proposed coup d'état, would make its bid for power
> in other and subtler ways.
>
> Whether or not Tan Malaka will again play a role of any
> importance can only be proved by events. As the original
> sponsor of the Republic, as a veteran communist leader, and
> as a former, though renegade, disciple of Moscow he will
> always command and a certain prestige in some communist
> circles.[51]

In captivity, however, Tan Malaka proved as much an embarrassment to the Republic as on the outside. Not only did he
produce a torrent of prison writings but plotted the kidnapping
of Sutan Sjahrir, the Prime Minister, and Foreign Minister of
the Republic. This was effected by Tan Malaka's proteges in the
last week of June 1946, leading to Sukarno being presented with
an ultimatum demanding Sjahrir and Sjarifuddin be dismissed
and that Tan Malaka form the new government.

Increasingly, however, Sukarno came under mounting pressure from Tan Malaka's supporters to modify his position, notably in a démarche presented on 3 July 1946. This 3 July affair,
as it was styled, was used, in turn, by the government as reason
to continue Tan Malaka's imprisonment. On the other hand, Jarvis
observes, the government was interested in developing an alternative left-wing pole to undermine the PKI around Musso, who
had arrived back from Moscow in August 1948, and whose position on diplomacy had become more hard-line than the Gerakan
Revolusi Rakyat or GRR. After two and a half years of forced
captivity, Tan Malaka was released on 16 September 1947, some
time prior to the outbreak of the Madiun revolt.[52]

Tan Malaka and *diplomasi*

In his aptly entitled autobiography, *Dari Pendjara ke Pendjara (From Prison to Prison)*, actually penned during this period of captivity, Tan Malaka reminds us that the Indonesian *"hari pahlawan"* (literally, heroes' day), which commemorates the people's defence against the bloody British attack against Surabava on 10 November 1945, was actually mounted at the head of the Bengawan-Solo valley, the location he targeted for the defense of the revolution in 1924. Notably, Tan Malaka deplored the attitude of Sukarno and Hatta, supported by Amir Sjarifuddin, in resisting the actions of British forces in Surabaya and Magelang in September-October 1945. As vindication he cites *Naar de Republiek Indonesia,*[53] There is no question that, from a reading of the text, Tan Malaka argues again and again the futility of making an armed stand in the large cities of Java and that some form of worker-peasant alliance based in the albeit densely populated East Javanese countryside would be the ideal site.

In fact, by time that British troops departed Java at the end of November 1946, some 55,000 Dutch troops had already landed, and, in the following months, by a combination of military and other methods, including the deployment of economic blockades, the Dutch re-established civil administration in Jakarta and other coastal cities of Java. Elsewhere in Indonesia, Dutch forces mounted a bloody "pacification." Against this background, a series of compromises were worked out known as the Linggadjati Agreement (drawn up before the departure of the British but not ratified until 25 March 1947). In essence, the Dutch recognized de facto republican control in Java, Madura, and Sumatra, while at the same time creating puppet states in the rest of the East Indies with a view to subordinating the Republic within a greater Netherlands-Indonesian Union. On 20 July 1947—in the face of world opinion—Dutch forces launched an attack on Republican territory, the so-called first police action, in an attempt to restore the prior colonial status quo.

Tan Malaka also made his views on Sukarno clear in print.

Described variously as "embodiment of all the bad qualities of Hindu-Javanese culture," non-revolutionary, opportunist, elitist, Sukarno clearly stood in opposition to the values Tan Malaka upheld, namely his *"kerakyatan"* or people-based, progressive and non-compromising anti-imperialist position. This criticism, not surprisingly, extended to the question of Sukarno's collaboration with the Japanese administration. As Mrazek observes, Tan Malaka's own non-collaboration became one of the most important values of his second return (even if it is true, as we have seen, that he had contacts with the Japanese Naval Liaison Office in Jakarta prior to the transfer of power). [54]

As the Dutch account points out, even after Tan Malaka's release from prison, remnants of his following carried on in the "Akoma" or "Angkatan Kommunis Muda," a communist youth organization, whose members were still faithful to the aging leader and who had never joined the official Communist Party.[55]

Meanwhile, in January 1948, an agreement called the Renville Agreement was brokered between the two sides on board a U.S. warship of the same name. Under U.S. pressure, the Republic accepted the terms of the agreement, which left the Republic virtually encircled by the Dutch. In part, PNI and Masjumi protest over the terms of Renville led to the resignation of the signatory of the Agreement, Amir Sjarrifudin. Meanwhile, on 1 February 1948, Tan Malaka's supporters from the Persatuan Perjuangan established the GRR as a front opposed to Renville, with Tan Malaka as the spiritual head. Jarvis writes that one of the precipitating factors in the establishment of this front was the PKI's shift in line in 1948 from all-out support of Renville, and in the Amir Siarifuddin government, to opposition to the Hatta government that was implementing it.[56]

The GRR, in turn, was a merger of the following parties: Partai Rakyat (People's Party of Maroeto Mitimihardjo); Partai Rakyat Djelata (Common People's Party of St. Dawanis); Permai, Persatuan Marhaen Indonesia (Indonesian Union of Proletariats); Laskar Rakjat Djawa Barat (semi-military organization); Persatuan Invaliden Indonesia (Indonesian Union of Disabled Soldiers); Partai Buruh Merdeka (Independent Labor Party of Sjamsoe Harva Oedaja); Partai Wanita Rakyat

(Womens' Organization); Barisan Bantang Republik Indonesia (semi-military organization of Dr. Moewardi); Angkatan Komunis Muda (Akoma, youth movement of Ibnu Parma); and Angkatan Komunis Muda, Youth-movement of Ibnu Parna). The chairman of GRR was Dr. Moewardi (kidnapped on 13 September 1948 at Solo); Samsoe Harya Oedaja was Deputy Chairman and Chairul Saleh, Secretary-General. According to American sources, the objectives of the GRR became clear at its first meeting on 1 February 1948 where an overwhelming majority urged, first, the seizure of power within a week's time, second, annulment of the Renville Agreement, third, formation of a revolutionary Cabinet with adequate representation of Tan Malaka's following and, fourth, implementation of the minimum program of Persatuan Perdjuangan (Tan Malaka's People's Front, which was dissolved in May 1946).[57]

The *raison d'etre* and aims of the GRR were further clarified by B. Sirogar, who chaired a GRR meeting in Jogjakarta. He clarified that as the GRR was a merger of anti-colonial parties based on the declaration of independence of 17 August 1945, it opposed negotiating with the Dutch [Linggajati (November 1946) and Renville (January 1948) agreements]. Consequently, it opposed the Hatta cabinet policy of compromise with the Dutch (as with the former Sayap Kiri or left-wing cabinet) and, sought to create a revolutionary government of the Indonesian Republic extending to the whole of the former Netherlands East Indies.[58] In fact, while general meetings of the GRR were held in Jogjakarta, Solo, Madiun, Kediri, and other places, the planned coup did not transpire and the GRR remained relatively inactive until August 1948.[59]

The Madiun revolt and aftermath

Meanwhile the communist leader, Musso, who had spent the war years in the Soviet Union, returned to Java in August 1948 under the guise of Soeparto. At a party meeting later that month he revealed his true identity, was elected party chairman, and joined the revolt, which broke out in Madiun in early September. Musso, who refused to work with radical nationalists otherwise accused of Trotskyism, evinced both an uncompromising, albeit Stalinist, anti-bourgeois, and anti-imperialist position. Musso's authority in a new PKI Politburo, nevertheless, was quickly accepted by Amir Sjariffudin and other Central and East Java members of the People's Democratic Front. Newer and younger figures rallying to Musso included the future PKI leadership group of D.N. Aidit (1923-65), M.H. Lukman (1920-65), Njoto (1925-65), and Sudisman (1920-68).[60]

The rift between the PKI around Musso and the American-backed (or at least pro-Western) Hatta government, reached crisis level on 11 September 1948 following a wave of disappearances of PKI officers in the Solo area. Lower-echelon communist leaders in Madiun responded to this and moves by the Republican High Command to demobilize their forces by storming the local Silawangi Division barracks. By 18 September, following an outbreak in fighting, pro-communist officers were in control of Madiun and surrounding towns. Musso and Sjariffudin, who had gone over to the PKI, were thus presented with a fait accompli when they arrived in Madiun on that day. In the event, the Silawangi Division under General Abdul Haris Nasution crushed the so-called Madiun "soviet" within a month, leading to the death of Musso, bloody repression of the PKI, and flight of remaining leadership.[61] Tan Malaka could have wryly noted that it was the second time in thirty years that Musso erred on the side of adventurism, exposing the party to destruction. Needless to say, the crushing of the PKI was met with relief on the part of the West, including the U.S., even if the communist setback did not translate into immediate military advantage for the Dutch.

But this time, with the destruction of the PKI at Madiun in August 1948, Tan Malaka remained the foremost proponent of the *perjuangan* line. On 7 November 1948 various pro-Tan Malaka groups and parties established the Murba or Proletarian Party. Within a month Murba had attracted a membership of 80,000. The Party's minimum program announced late that month was based on the old Struggle Front and included expropriation of Dutch property and armed opposition to the enemy. A maximum program charted a course towards a socialist Indonesia. Tan Malaka, for self-preservation among other reasons, departed in November for the Solo River Valley accompanied by thirty-five guerrilla fighters.[62]

On 21 December 1948, in the face of the long-expected Dutch attack on the beleaguered Republican government seated in Jogjakarta—the so called Second Dutch police action—Tan Malaka went on the East Java service of Radio Republik Indonesia, broadcasting a statement rejecting negotiation, such as pursued by Sjahrir and Hatta and compromise, such as reflected in the Linggajati Agreement and the Renville Agreement. As monitored and summarized by the local Republican delegation, Tan Malaka required his supporters and potential allies to annul all "inventions" as Linggajati, Renville and Hatta's *aide memoire*; to root out all puppet states created by the Dutch with the help of their henchmen; to recapture every patch of ground occupied by the enemy's troops; to seize all foreign property; to restore self-confidence and annihilate all fifth columnists; to ignore all truce regulations; to reject any negotiations if not based on complete independence as proclaimed on August 17 1945; and to unify all parties and fighting organizations and maintain the people's army.

U.S. sources claim not to have been aware of Tan Malaka's whereabouts at this time except that he was known to be moving about the countryside "somewhere to the north and east of Solo." Earlier that month, the U.S. Consul General in Batavia, Livengood, reported that Republican forces were closing in on "Tan Malaka Trotskyists" in the wake of arrest of Sjarifuddin and the leading communists. As evidence, he cites the closing of a Murba newspaper and a GRR radio license.[63] As Livengood wrote prophetically on 6 December 1948:

> That the Communists have failed in their first postwar attempt most certainly does not mean that the Communist movement have been permanently broken. The Communist group may have new leaders, Musso is reported to be dead; Alimin has surrendered or been captured; Sjarifuddin, Suripno, Daroesman, Djokosujono and, according to republican reports, even Sarjono have all been captured. Tan Malaka, who had been released from jail in September to split Musso, following, appeared to be the logical successor

to leadership. It was thought that he could use the Gerakan Rakyat Revolusi (People's Revolutionary Movement) to rally the Left. The GRR published the daily newspaper. Murba, and operated the radio station GRR. The former leader of the movement, Rustam Effendi, had been killed in the early stages of the revolt at Solo, so that Tan Malaka should have had little opposition in gaining control of the Left.

But Tan Malaka has run into difficulty. Sjarifuddin and the last rebel leaders were captured on November 29th. Within 48 hours the Republic announced that it was banning indefinitely the publication of Murba, suspending indefinitely the license of Radio GRR.

If Tan Malaka is in fact to rebuild the Communist structure, he will have to construct, first, new propaganda organs. What the strategy will be can be learned only by careful investigation in the Republic. But if the new Communist movement is to be truly a part of Stalin's international communism, it seems that the strategy will have to follow the International's Thesis on the national and Colonial Questions.[64]

In fact, such pessimism or apprehension by the U.S. as to a communist revival in Indonesia based upon opposition to a colonial restoration tipped Washington in support of the Republic against the Dutch, who launched their second "police action" in December 1948. In this military action, in the face of UN Good Offices Committee, the Dutch forces bombed the airport of Jogjakarta and captured Sukarno, Hatta, and several other Republican leaders. While the situation looked hopeless for the Republic, the Dutch troops soon found themselves facing armed guerrilla resistance and civilian non-cooperation. It would not be until May 1949 that the two sides entered into negotiations leading to the Round Table Conference at The Hague and the official transfer on 27 December 1949 of sovereignty of the former Netherlands East Indies to the new Republic of the United States of Indonesia.

Tan Malaka, however, would not live to celebrate this event. According to Republican sources, relayed by Livengood to Washington in March 1949, Tan Malaka was believed to have moved from East Java back to Surakarta (Solo), his home base. "Republicans interpret this to mean that Tan Malaka has been unsuccessful in attempts to organize Trotskyist cells in East Java Republican Army units and may have returned to Surakarta to reorganize his activities." The same report confirmed that the Front Demokrasi Rakyat (FDR) was still active in Jogjakarta.[65]

On 1 April, as Livengood reported, Musso was killed in October by Republican armed forces (TNI) while Sjarifuddin was executed, by Republican forces in Solo on 19 December. The same report signalled the presence of 2000 of Tan Malaka's troops in the Kediri area "not necessarily communist."[66] In circumstances which are still fairly obscure, Tan Malaka was seized and summarily executed "most probably" on 19 February 1949 on the orders of the military governor of East Java. His corpse was never found.[67] Aboe Bakar Loebis, who concedes not to know who shot Tan Malaka, claims he was killed near Dewa Mojo beside the Sungai Brantas in East Java.[68]

Tan Malaka in Indonesian history

Although Tan Malaka was out of the picture, his ideals survived him in two forms: first, in the form of armed struggle, and second, in the form of parliamentarianism. With respect to the first, Tan Malaka's followers, organized as the Laskar Rakyat Jawa Barat (West Java People's Brigade), constituted the last sizable band of armed guerrillas to resist the Republican leadership prior to their defeat in October 1949 in south Banten, and the capture of their leader, Chairul Saleh, in March of the following year. In mid-November 1949, this group denounced the Republic's leadership and proclaimed itself as the Tentara Rakyat or People's Army to fight for independence [69] outside of the U.N. framework. With respect to the parliamentary or at least organizational struggle, the formation of Partai Murba (on 7 November 1948) just after the Madiun uprising was significant, according to Feith, in the way it expressed "oppositionism" to participate in any cabinet, and, after the Round Table Conference Agreement, which it opposed, refused to recognize the "practical difficulty of governments." Nevertheless, according to Feith, Murba was able to broach a "radical nationalist appeal and a radical socialist one." Needless to say, Murba's "inchoate" Trotskyism and broad links with other parties, such as the PNI, brought it into conflict with the PKI orthodoxy. True to Tan Malaka's concept of armed struggle, it also forged links with the People's Army and "Bamboo Spear" organizations in West Java.[70]

How is Tan Malaka's role in modern Indonesian history perceived? As seen in official PKI historiography, the first four phases of growth of the Party since its founding on 23 May 1920 were (1) the foundation of the Party and the Struggle against the First White Terror (1920-1926); (2) twenty years underground and the anti-fascist front (1926-1945); (3) the August Revolution and the Struggle against the Second White Terror (1945-1951); and (4) the broadening of the united front and the building of the Party (1951-). Until killed in Java in February 1949 by a Republican soldier, Tan Malaka played a central and sometimes determining role in the first three of these phases, whether *in situ* in Indonesia or whether in exile, the PKI line is less charitable. In a 1958 publication, then Chairman of the PKI, D. N. Aidit, dismisses Tan Malaka's role in the November 1926-February 1927 revolts in Java and Sumatra. Looking back, he blamed the failure of the revolts on a vacillating party leadership, poor coordination, the lack of resolute action once the revolt had broken out, and Tan Malaka's "Trotskyist" practices, especially in setting up PARI at a time when the PKI faced the full brunt of colonial "white terror." All of this, he continues, made the work of the PKI more difficult and eased the divide-and-rule policies of the Dutch in mounting their repression.[71]

Curiously, perhaps, it was the first President of the Republic of Indonesia, Sukarno, who went out of his way to defend Tan Malaka and Partai Murba. By 1956, as Sukarno began to elaborate upon a form of "Guided Democracy," he increasingly looked to the 1945 generation of youth leaders, including Chaerul Saleh. Murba reciprocated. For example, in the course of an address to the Fifth Congress of Partai Murba in Bandung in December 1960, Sukarno described Parti Murba as "a revolutionary nationalist party of consequence," but also a party which concerned itself with social questions. On this occasion,

Sukarno revealed that he had been acquainted with Tan Malaka, that he had read his writings, and had discussed them with him for hours.[72] In 1963 Tan Malaka was awarded the title of "National Hero" by Sukarno. For Sukarno, Tan Malaka was both a nationalist and a socialist.

It is of interest that Tan Malaka's role in Indonesian nationalist history has, paradoxically, been permitted some backhanded rehabilitation in the fading days of the New Order regime, albeit in the world of private letters outside of the state-controlled history institutes. For example, Aboe Bakar Loebis, writing in his 1992 book, *Revolusi: Kenangan, Pelaku dan Saksi*, observed of Tan Malaka that, whatever his shortcomings, he was a "brilliant nationalist fighter, thinker and theoretician. Even among our modern revolutionary leaders, Tan Malaka was a giant."[73]

While Tan Malaka's "national communism," outside of the Stalinist tradition, came to be acknowledged inside Indonesia in the revolutionary period (indeed, we have shown him to be in the forefront of the revolutionary struggle), at the same time, his leftist tradition hostile to the capitalist underpinnings of the beneficiaries of the republican governments makes him anathema to the heirs of that tradition, today in power in Jakarta.

Notes

1. Rudolph Mrazek, "Tan Malaka: A Political Personality's Structure of Experience," *Indonesia*, 14 (October 1972): 1-48; Harry A. Poeze, *Tan Malaka: Srijder Voor Indonesies Vrijheid Levenstoop Van 1897 Tot 1945* ('S-Gravenhage: Martinus Nijhoff, 1976); Yuji Suzuki, "Tan Malaka: Perantauan and the Power of ideas," L.Y. Andaya, C. Coppel, Y. Suzuki, *People and Society in Indonesia: A Bibliographical Approach* (Monash University, 1977): 31-50; Helen Jarvis (trans., ed., intro.) *From Jail to Jail* by Tan Malaka, (3 vols.) (Athens, Ohio: Ohio University for International Studies, Monographs in International Studies, Southeast Asia Series, No.83, 1991).

2. Tan Malaka, "Letter to China league for Civil Rights," South America, February 1933 cited in Poeze, *Tan Malaka: Strijder Voor Indonesies...*: 573.

3. Benedict R.O'G.Anderson, *Java in a Time of Revolution*, (Ithaca and London: Cornell University Press, 1972): 271-272, and see Helen Jarvis,"Tan Malaka: Revolutionary or Renegade?," *Bulletin of Concerned Asian Scholars*, 19, 1 (January-March, 1987): 44-45.

4. Fernand Claudin, *The Communist Movement: From Comitern to Cominform*. (Part 1), (New York and London: Monthly Review Press, 1975): 258.

5. *Bulletin of the Fourth Congress of the Communist International*, 7: 6-8, Ibid, 258n.

6. Anderson, *Java in a Time of Revolution:* 272.

7. *Dari Pendjara ke Pendjara* (Vol. I): 104-105.

8. Ezra Vogel, *Canton under Communism: Programs and Politics in a Provincial Capital, 1949-1968* (Havard University Press, 1969): 33-34.

9. Jarvis, "Tan Malaka: Revolutionary or Renegade?": 46.

10. Anderson, *Java in a Time of Revolution*.

11. *Dari Pendjara ke Pendjara*, Vol.II: 106.

12. cf. Yong Mun Cheong, "Indonesian Influence in the Development of Malay Nationalism, 1922-38," *Journal of the Historical Society*, (July 1970): 5

13. Various PRO C0273 sources drawing upon colonial police record.

14. PRO CO 273 534, J. Crosby, "Notes on the Native Movement and the Political Situation in the Netherlands East Indies generally," Batavia, 26 March 1926.

15. PRO CO 273535, MBPI, 6 November 1925.

16. Yuji Suzuki, "Tan Malaka's Mental Revolution: Development of Political Thinking in Indonesia in the 1930," Jabatan Sejarah, Universti Malaya, Kertas Seminar, No.7. The English translation of the passage fom *Massa Actie*," taken from this paper.

17. PRO CO 273 533, J. Crosby, 28 November 1925.

18. Harry J. Benda and Ruth J. McVey, *The Communist Uprisings of 1926-1927* in *Indonesia: Key Documents* (Ithaca, N.Y.: Modern Indonesia Project, Southeast Asia Program, Cornell University, 1960) 136; 153-157.

19. Ibid: 153-157.

20. On the uprisings see Ibid; and Ruth T. McVey, *The Rise of Indonesian Communism* (Ithaca: Cornell University Press, 1965), chapter II, and George McT. Kahin, *Nationalism and Revolution*, (Ithaca: Cornell University Press, 1952): 80-85.

21. PRO CO 273 535, "Granville," British Legation, The Hague, 4 January 1927.

22. Blumberger, *Le Communisme aux Indes Neerlandaises...* p.72.

23. PRO CO 273 535, Crosby, Batavia, 7 and 16 February 1927.

24. Jarvis, "Tan Malaka: Revolutionary or Renegade?": 46-47 and cf. McVey, *The Rise of Indonesian Communism:* 322.

25. Jarvis, Ibid: 48-49.

26. *Dari Penjara ke Pendjara,* (Vol. II: 114).

27. Jarvis, "Tan Malaka: Revolutionary of Renegade?": 49.

28. Ibid.

29. Ibid.

30. See Poeze, *Tan Malaka: Strijder Voor Indonesies:* 362-380 for very detailed analysis of official and press accounts relating to the Manila trial and its aftermath.

31. Ibid., and see Jarvis, "Tan Malaka: Revolutionary or renegade?": 49.

32. PRO CO 273 589 13040 1933, "Raj Bhadur Prithvi Chand."

33. *Dari Pendjara ke Pendjara:* 43-45.

34. Tan Malaka, letter, in Poeze, *Tan Malaka-Srijder Voor Indonesies...*

35. *Dari Pendjara ke Pendjara,* (Vol.II), and Jarvis, "Tan Malaka: Revolutionary or Renegade?": 51.

36. Noriaki Oshikawa, "Pantjar Merah Indonesia and Tan Malaka: A Popular Novel and a Revolutionary Legend," *Journal of Sophia Asian Studies, No.4.* 1986: 1.

37. *Dari Pendjara ke Pendjara* (Vol. II): 137-177.

38. Ibid.

39. Ibid.

40. See, eg. Nugroho Notosusanto, *Tentara Peta pada Jaman Pendudukan Jepang di Indonesia* (Jakarta: Penerbit PT Grameda, 1979).

Adam Malik stated that his first contact with Tan Malaka was on the night of 14 August 1945 but with a man going by the name of Husin from Banten (see Kahin, *Nationalism and Revolution in Indonesia:* 119.)

41. "Communism In Indonesia," compiled by the office of the Netherlands Representative to the Combined Chiefs of Staff, Washington DC, February 1946.

42. Tan Malaka, *From Jail to Jail* (Vol III: 63).

43. Anderson, *Java in a Time of Revolution:* 276-277.

44. *From Jail to Jail,* (Vol. III)...:55. See Anderson, *Java in a Time of revolution...* : 280, for discussion on the so-called Testament conspiracy.

45. "Communism in Indonesia."
46. Ibid.
47. Ibid.
48. "Political Developments of the Communist Revolt in Indonesia," based on information compiled by Netherlands Intelligence sources.
49. Aboe Bakar Loebis, *Revolusi: Kenangan, Pelaku dan Saksi* (Jakarta: Universitas Indonesia Press, 1992).
50. U.S. document dated 24 November 1948.
51. "Communism in Indonesia..."
52. Jarvis, "Tan Malaka: Revolutionary or Renegade?": 53 and see footnote on Jarvis on Tan Malaka's publications in this period.
53. *Dari Pendjara ke Pendjara...*: 133.
54. Rudolf Mrazek, "Tan Malaka: A Political Personality's Structure of Experience," 14 (October 1972): 1-48.
55. "Communism in Indonesia..." and, see Jarvis, "Tan Malaka: Revolutionary or Renegade?": 54, writes that AKOMA retained a revolutionary approach up until 1965 when it was banned. In 1956 it was represented at the World Congress of the Fourth International by Ibnu Parna.
56. Jarvis, Ibid.: 52.
57. U.S. source: "Political Developments after the Communist revolution in Indonesia," based on information compiled by Netherlands Intelligence Sources, Annex: Gerakan Revolutie Rakjat.
58. Ibid.
59. "Political Developments after the Communist Revolt in Indonesia."
60. M.C. Ricklefs, *A History of Indonesia*, (London: Macmillan, 1981).
61. See the judicious analysis of the Madiun revolt in Julie Southood and Patrick Flanigan, *Indonesia, Law, Propaganda and Terror* (London: Zed Press, 1983): 26-30.
Sjarifuddin, who had conducted the negotiations with the Dutch leading to the Renville agreement, had signed the premiership on 23 January 1948 and launched a leftist campaign against the Dutch. He emerged as one the leaders, of the Madiun rebellion, prior to his arrest by Republican forces and subsequent execution.
62. Jarvis, "Tan Malaka: Revolutionary or Renegade?": 53.
63. Livengood to Secretary of State, 2 December 1948.
64. Charles A. Livengood, American Consul General, Batavia, 6 December 1948. Subject: Indonesian Communist Party claims. No. 471.

65. Livengood to State, Batavia, 15 March 1949. Subject: Communist propaganda Opposition to republican negotiation with the Dutch.

66. Livengood to State, 1 April 1949 (incoming telegram).

67. Jarvis, "Tan Malaka: Revolutionary or Renegade?": 54 and cf. V. Thompson and A. Adloff, *The Left Wing in Southeast Asia,* (New York: William Sloane, 1950): 285.

68. Aboe Bakar Loebis, *Revolusi...*: 159.

69. cf.Ulf Sudhaussen, *The Road to Power Indonesian Military Politics, 1945-1967* (Kuala lumpur: Oxford University Press, 1982):. 53.

70. Herbert Feith, *The Decline of Constutional Democracy in Indonesia,* (Cornell: Cornell University Press, 1962): 55, 131-132.

71. D.N. Aidit, "The Birth and Growth of the Communist Party of Indnesia," in *The Selected Works of D.N. Aidit,* Vol. I, (Djakarta: Jajaan Pembaruan, 1959), JPRS, 6551, CSO 3477-D: 283.

72. *Bung Karno tentang Partai Murba, Tan Malaka dan Perjuangannja: Pidato Amanat Presiden Sukarno kepada Resepsi Pembukaan kongres ke V,* 1960.

73. Aboe Bakar Loebis, *Revolusi...*: 159. Notable also, in this sense is, *Memperingati empat puluh empat tahun wafatnya pahlawan kemerdekaan national Tan Malaka* (Jakarta: Yayasan Massa, 1993). While I have not had a chance to consult this book, the "national hero" status accorded Tan Malaka by this *festschrift* condition, suggests that not all scholars inside Indonesia are bound to accept all the standardized official histories and historical verities on this epoch.

3. The Garuda and the Dragon: Indonesian-Chinese Relations

While it is clear that the 1955 Bandung Conference commemoration hosted by the Indonesian President, Sukarno, in May 1985 lacked the symbolism, the purpose, and the unity of that inspired by the original, it did signal, as widely observed, the re-emergence of Indonesia on the international stage after some twenty years of semi-seclusion.[1] More important—at least from the perspective of this article—is that the conference provided the first forum for official Indonesian contacts with the People's Republic of China (PRC), since diplomatic ties were broken off after the failed communist coup in Indonesia in 1965.

But if the expectations of outsiders as to a Sino-Indonesian rapprochement were not met at Bandung, unlike other initiatives in the recent past, the log jam in relations was breached, as demonstrated by the subsequent agreement of both sides on 5 May 1985 to resume direct trade. Some regional effects of this development should also not be ignored. The visits by the Prime Ministers of Singapore and Malaysia to the PRC in, respectively, September and November 1985 were no doubt timed to give minimal offense to the Indonesian side. While Malaysia along with Thailand and the Philippines established relations with Beijing in the mid-1970s, Singapore defers to Indonesia on the China recognition question, although Singapore has gone further than Indonesia by setting up a trade office in Beijing.

Thus while Indonesia has moved into line with its ASEAN partners in seeking to take advantage of Deng Xiaoping's "Open Door" policy, at the same time it has gone further in extending an opening to the Council for Mutual Economic Assistance (CMEA) or communist trading bloc of countries including Vietnam. Indonesia's new assertiveness on the diplomatic front also has been indicated by the pretensions of the Indonesian President in seeking a leadership role within the Non-Aligned Movement (NAM). Similarly China's motivations in seeking to restore links with Indonesia have to be assessed in light of its own fluid domestic and regional political environment and in line with its avowed status as a Third World nation equidistant between the two superpowers.

In this article, then, we will seek to interpret both Indonesian and Chinese motives for the opening with reference to official statements and journalistic interpretation. Namely, on the Indonesia side, whether the new emphasis is just in line with Indonesia's traditional "independent and active foreign policy," as sources close to official thinking have put the matter,[2] or whether economic pragmatism in an era of dramatically falling state revenues reveals (or compels) a loosening in the ideological rigidity of the regime. And, on the Chinese side, whether sincerity to put the past aside and mend relations with the non-communist countries of Southeast Asia overrides or dovetails with considerations closer to heart, namely an interest in determining the future reordering of political alignments in the Indochinese peninsula. As Wong has phrased the matter, in a detailed study of China's changing relations with the region, the failure to restore more positive links with Jakarta and with the ASEAN group constrains China's strategy of checking the hegemonic ambitions of the Soviet Union and by extension the regional ambitions of Vietnam, and acts, moreover, as "a constant reminder to the Chinese of their past diplomatic failure."[3]

Twisting the tail of the dragon

The central validating myth which sustains the Indonesian New Order is the "understanding" that the nation was rescued from a Communist Party of Indonesia (PKI) takeover in September-October 1965. Although the Chinese side has denied, since the outset, any involvement in these events, Chinese residents in Indonesia were among the victims of the Army-led communal massacres which ensued in the aftermath. With the destruction of the Chinese Embassy budding in Jakarta and the subsequent expulsion of the Chinese Ambassador in 1967, relations between the two countries were suspended. Indeed, as one authority has written of post-coup events, Beijing's verbal opposition to army brutality against Chinese residents and suspected communists was termed, by the anti-communist press in Indonesia, "evidence of China's complicity in the coup."[4] The fact that individual Chinese entrepreneurs/financiers (*cukong*) have risen to positions of economic and social pre-eminence in the Indonesian New Order over the past two decades, through their comprador or collusive activities with the military and not excluding the Palace, has not disguised deep-rooted mistrust of the Chinese community in Indonesia. Neither has the passage by the Chinese National People's Congress of a new citizenship law in September 1980, to the effect that no dual nationality would be recognized for any Chinese national, had the effect of laying to rest the Indonesian fear of the "overseas Chinese bogey."[5]

Yet since 1977 relations between Indonesia and China have thawed, encouraged by the pronouncements of both former Foreign Minister Adam Malik and his successor, Mochtar Kusumatmadja. The stumbling block, then and now, has been China's alleged links with the Indonesian Communist Party (PKI). But the ten years since the death of Mao have seen China open up to the rest of the world, with only a few states clinging to relations with Taiwan. Seen in this light, the failure of Indonesia and China to re-establish relations appears all the more anachronistic.

Clearly, then, the thirtieth anniversary of the Bandung Conference attended by Chinese Foreign Minister, Wu Xueqian, afforded the most propitious occasion for the re-establishment of diplomatic ties. As editorialized in the pro-Government Indonesian daily, *Berita Buana*, in the leadup to the Bandung Commemoration, among other benefits foreseen for Indonesia were a "possible consensus by Indonesia and the PRC to normalize diplomatic relations." The "peaceful political climate" surrounding the meeting was seen as conducive to fruitful talks between the foreign ministers of the two countries. Wu, the paper noted, served as vice-Foreign Minister inder a foreign minister who was PRC ambassador in Jakarta until 1965. Citing the broader coincidence of ASEAN-PRC strategy vis-à-vis Vietnam, the paper editorialized in favor of normalization of bilateral relations.[6]

Expectations were even higher on the Chinese side that a meeting between Wu and Indonesian President Suharto would break the ice. As reported by Chinese sources, Wu's visit was definitely seen as signaling an improvement in relations. As Wu told reporters on arrival in Jakarta, "China is positive in the restoration of relations." Indeed, following talks between Wu and his Indonesian counterpart, Mochtar Kusumaatmadja, on 24 April, both indicated that they had agreed to improve bilateral relations.[7] While briefly meeting Suharto in a line-up reception, the time arranged by the Indonesian side for discussions between the pair was—astonishingly—arranged for an hour or so before the Chinese Foreign Minister's scheduled departure.

As Wu recalled the events in an interview given to *Shi jie Zhishi* magazine and broadcast over Beijing International network in Indonesian, his arrival in Jakarta attracted much attention from the local press. Having been *tersekap* (locked up) for years, he indicated, Indonesian journalists expressed interest in domestic changes and developments in the PRC. Wu disclosed that the talks (with Mochtar) and the brief introduction with Suharto took place in a "friendly, frank and sincere atmosphere." Wu further revealed that the two sides had agreed to establish direct trade links and to ask the non-governmental trade boards empowered by the respective governments to hold consultation leading to the signing of a document on direct trade. Explaining the seeming diplomatic slight of not being able to arrange a personal discussion with Suharto as sought, Wu stated that, owing to the short notice of the projected meeting (26 April at 0800), he could not rearrange his scheduled departure (26 April 0930). He pleaded the urgency of a planned (27 April) meeting in Beijing with the Danish Foreign Minister. Instead, Mochtar delivered a five-minute briefing to the President.[8]

How, then, can one explain this seeming instance of breakdown of *tepo seliro*, or mutual understanding as the term might be rendered from the Javanese? According to some analysts, Wu walked into a trap that had been set in Jakarta by elements within the Indonesian bureaucracy, most probably the Defense Ministry, who, as a minimum, expected the Chinese Foreign Minister to bear an apology for his country's alleged involvement in the coup. While Wu's visit evidently had the imprimatur of the Armed Forces commander, Benny Murdani,[9] the Foreign Ministry and the Palace, as articulated by the mouthpiece of the armed forces, *Harian Umum AB*, the army expressly demanded a Chinese apology as a condition for normalization. Indeed, as Nations has written, the fact that Wu had the temerity to arrive in Jakarta without bearing an apology was seen as an affront by some Indonesians, namely military hard-liners.[10]

In fact, Mochtar expressly denied the 23 May report that Jakarta had sent feelers to Beijing to request an apology. Mochtar countered that Indonesia would have been satisfied with a declaration from Beijing that it would no longer support underground movements against Southeast Asian governments.[11] This comment was made to newsmen following Mochtar's meeting with Suharto.[12] Asked to comment on such a condition, Wu replied to a pro-China source in Hong Kong that "China handles its relations with all countries in the world on the basis of the five principles of peaceful coexistence. That is, we do not interfere with the internal affairs of any country."[13]

In response to statements by Indonesian leaders that the PRC must denounce its links with the PKI before normalization could proceed, Wu answered in two parts. First, he pointed out that it is an internationally established practice for political parties to maintain relations with parties of similar ideology elsewhere in the world. It is not only a communist practice but is upheld by other nationalist and socialist parties around the world, he stated. Second, the Communist Party of China (CCP), ever since its 12th National Conference in 1984, has set down four principles that must be upheld by the CCP in its relations with communist parties and other political parties around the world, namely independence, equality, mutual respect, and noninterference in each other's internal affairs. Accordingly, Wu avowed, the CCP will never interfere in the internal affairs of another country—a fact stated by Secretary General Hu Yaobang during his 1985 visit to Australia. Wu further emphasized that the allegation which links the PRC with the 30 September Movement or the coup attempt in Indonesia in 1965 "contradicts historical facts."[14]

As reiterated by Wu in an interview granted to an Indonesian newspaper on the occasion of his visit for the Bandung commemoration, "China has not supported the PKI for the past 18 years," and in any case most of the former PKI leaders residing in China after the coup attempt had gone there "on their own free will."[15] At least one Western analyst has affirmed that in contrast to the pro-Moscow faction in exile, the Beijing faction, especially since 1981, have been "soft-spoken."[16] As affirmed by the author during a visit, Chinese returnees from Indonesia in the post-coup period and who have found their way onto State farms in Hainan Island in Guangdong province of China—remain if wistfully—reconciled to the political realities, which mean permanent absence from their former country of adoption.

While there would be few official Indonesian political figures convinced by the Chinese disavowal of interference in at least fraternal party affairs, the fact remains that the demonstrated quid pro quo entered into with China by other ASEAN states such as Thailand and Malaysia has been the re-establishment of diplomatic relations in return for pledges from the Chinese side to downplay support for communist insurgencies in Southeast Asia. In the case of the Philippines, a nation that has benefited from diplomatic relations and direct trade with the PRC since 1975, there is no evidence whatsoever of Chinese support to the major self-styled Maoist insurgency in the region, that of the New People's Army.[17]

Any illusions that the Chinese side may still have harbored as to the resumption of diplomatic relations with Indonesia would have been shattered on the occasion of the Malaysian Prime Minister's visit to China in November 1985. According to one source, the Indonesian President requested the Malaysian Prime Minister to convey to the Chinese side Indonesia's position, namely no normalization unless China renounces support for communist insurgent movements in the region.[18] The whole episode of the 1985 opening between Indonesia and China was thus highly reminiscent of the on-off approach adopted by the

Indonesian side in 1980. As described by one observer, a case of the "proud Javanese...twisting the tail of the dragon."[19]

The KADIN visit to Beijing

Clearly economic crisis at home has been a major stimulus to Indonesia in its search to diversify trade outlets and to expand non-commodity exports. Two international aspects of the crisis are of relevance here. First, the raising of barriers to the penetration of Indonesia's traditional markets in Japan, the United States, and Europe, and second, the dramatic fall in 1985-86 in the price of oil, Indonesia's main source of state revenues. Also, Indonesia could not but have noticed the forwardness of its ASEAN partners—Singapore and Malaysia included—in reaching out to China to take advantage of that country's Open Door policy. Thus, the Indonesian decision to resume direct trade with China was not taken without a great deal of soul-searching. This was reflected in the pages of the semi-official Indonesian journal *Indonesian Quarterly*. While noting that the reforms taking place within China might well be of relevance to Indonesia's future trade, the journal also pointed out that China's own developmental successes would provide Indonesia with competition in certain areas. In fact, the journal noted, Indonesian oil is already being ousted from the Japanese market by Chinese oil. The arguments against direct trade the journal saw as being equally persuasive. It had to be conceded that traditional intermediaries in the Sino-Indonesian trade, namely Hong Kong, Singapore, and Japanese business houses, held clearly demonstrated skills in managing international trade that could not be easily replicated by Indonesia and China if the trade was on a direct basis. More tellingly, the journal continued, the traditional indirect trade conveniently circumvented the potential problems of (political) "contamination" implied by the direct trade.[20]

In the absence of accurate figures for the overall indirect Sino-Indonesian trade (estimates vary from US$200-900 million) per annum, figures for the re-export trade between the two countries through Hong Kong (1978-1983) are illustrative. In line with other estimates of the overall Sino-Indonesian trade, these statistics reveal that trade is overwhelmingly in China's favor by a factor of 7 to 10. And while China has been able to increase dramatically the volume of its exports to Indonesia over the 1978-83 period, Indonesian exports to China peaked in 1982. The same source reveals that Indonesia's trade via Hong Kong is made up overwhelmingly of natural products—in rank order of value; plywood, rattan, duck feathers, marine products, etc.[21]

Having several times failed in earlier initiatives to open up direct trade with China, Indonesian Foreign Minister Mochtar braved criticism from military hardliners in November 1984 by again lending public voice to the venture. Preliminary talks between Indonesian and Chinese representatives on the trade issue spanned six months and eventually notched up a further ten months in Jakarta, Beijing, New York, and Singapore. Unwilling to give the talks an official imprimatur, the Indonesian side was represented by KADIN, the Indonesian Chamber of Commerce and Industry, while the Chinese body concerned was CCPIT, or the Chinese Council for the Promotion of Trade. One important intermediary between the two parties was apparently a Singaporean shipping magnate, Tong Djoe.[22]

Thus, even prior to the Bandung commemorative meeting, China had already played host to the vice-chairman of KADIN, the Indonesian President's millionaire half-brother Probosutedjo. During a four-day tour of China in April 1985 along with a group of Chinese businessmen, the Indonesian met the Chinese Deputy Premier of Economic Affairs, Zhangqing Fu. However, as one observer has written, Probosutedjo travelled in a private capacity. Indeed, such was the sensitive nature of his mission that he waited until early May to comment publicly on the trip.[23] As it happened, the Indonesian Armed Forces Chief, Benny Murdani, branded the visit to Beijing by the delegation as "having no loyalty to government policies and national interests."[24]

The next step in the establishment of direct trade links, following the exploratory talks in Singapore of 30 January 1985, was the endorsement on 5 July of a Memorandum of understanding between the two sides. While the Memorandum stopped short of providing for the establishment of trade offices, it did nominate KADIN and CCPIT as the sole organizations allowed to participate in the direct Indonesia-China trade. The Memorandum also provided for the entry of ships of the two countries flying their national flags as well as for transactions to be carried out in convertible currencies facilitated by the national banks of both countries.[25]

KADIN President Sukamdani Gitosardjono, who headed the Indonesian side, said that the agreement was made possible by "mutual understanding," "mutual friendship" and the "will to cooperate."[26] Wang Yaoting, who signed for CCPIT, declared at the meeting "With constant enhancing of direct trade and exchange of visits, mutual understanding will increase and relations can be improved."[27] Despite these expressions of goodwill, Jakarta evidently requested that references to the names of the two countries be absent from the accords, thus imparting only a quasi-official stamp of approval.[28] On 24 April, Suharto was reported to have approved the opening of direct trade with China. He told the cabinet that general trading rules would be applied and almost any goods exported or imported. He further announced that the ports of Jakarta, Medan, Surabaya, and Tanjung Priok would be open to Chinese vessels.[29]

The first Indonesian trade mission to the Chinese capital since 1976 arrived on 29 July 1985 with the directive from Mochtar not to discuss politics with their Chinese counterparts.[30] The Indonesian mission to Beijing, which included nine official KADIN representatives and more than 100 businessmen with support staff, agreed to buy Chinese capital goods and raw materials, including cotton, asphalt and coal, while the Chinese trading firms agreed to buy more than US$200 million worth of Indonesian goods. These included rubber, textiles, plywoods, timber, aluminum ingots, sheet glass, cement, coffee, and cocoa.[31] This visit was followed up in early September with the establishment of a special committee chaired by KADIN with the promotion and coordination of direct trade with China.[32]

As an Indonesian trade official made it known to the author, Indonesia not only seeks to expand its trade with China in traditional agricultural products, but also seeks an outlet for its manufactured goods, such as paper, cement, etc.[33] Accordingly, the direct Sino-Indonesian trade was expected to eventually replace most of the indirect trade carried on through third parties in Singapore and Hong Kong. Singaporean businessmen, however, were reportedly confident in their long-established trading connections and in the city-state's superior banking and shipping service.[34] Indeed, as the Indonesian source acknowledged, only a "theoretical" expansion of trade could realistically be envisioned as stemming from the direct-trade opening.[35]

The Chinese trade mission to Indonesia

On 10th August 1985, a Chinese trade mission arrived in Jakarta. The 43-strong delegation was led by the chairman of CCPIT, Wang Yaoting. At stake in the visit were some $300 million worth of agreements. Included in the delegation were representatives of state import and export corporations as well as bankers and insurance and transport executives. Although this visit was the first by high-ranking Chinese officials since the 1967 rift, Indonesian officials again played down the political significance of the visit.[36] On this occasion, Wang indicated that through its visit, the group sought first, to develop trade with Indonesia, and second, to strengthen the friendship between the peoples of the two countries.[37] But as Wang told *Sinar Harapan*, further negotiations on direct-trade transactions would have to be taken before these initial commitments could be translated into contracts. Accordingly a joint press statement issued by KADIN and CCPIT noted that the two sides "are aware that more time is needed to bring into realisation trade commitments made..."[38]

In September, three separate and smaller delegations from China arrived to examine prospects for possible textiles, and plywood and light industrial goods sales. A month later, the first Chinese freighter to dock at an Indonesian port since the late sixties loaded plywood in North Sumatra.[39] As Wang put it, aside from the enhanced trade prospects, the opening would go far in helping to "promote the friendship between the Chinese and Indonesian people."[40]

By the end of the year, after six months of direct trade, much of the initial euphoria surrounding the development had disappeared. More sober heads prevailed. The US$35 million in contracts had been signed. By this point the Indonesians were strongly denying the possibility of unfreezing diplomatic ties.[41]

In evaluation of the trade opening, it appears that one year after the resumption of direct-trade ties, Indonesia was ahead by $150 million in a two-way trade of $250 million. Indonesia also gained in a counter-trade deal, worked out in August 1986, that would permit Indonesian ships to carry Indonesian cement and Chinese coal.[42] According to Indonesian sources, then, difficulties in managing the bilateral trade stem from conflicting views on the role played by the Geneva-based Société Générale de Surveillance (SGS), a private body charged by the Indonesian government to streamline the management of the nation's notoriously ill-managed ports. While Indonesia demands SGS surveillance of goods entering or leaving the PRC, the Chinese side reserves this function exclusively to the Chinese Commodities Inspection Corps.[43]

Neither has Indonesia revealed itself willing to resist Taiwanese blandishments, political or economic. Amounting to $694 million, Taiwan's trade with Indonesia was reported to be $133 million in deficit in 1985, mainly owing to oil and gas imports. But lower oil prices have permitted Taiwan to post a surplus on two-way trade with Indonesia in 1986. As part of its trade offensive with Indonesia, Taiwan plans to extend loans to Indonesia to finance that country's imports of capital equipment[44]—all things considered, a positively seductive gesture.

The other side of the coin to the China opening, however, is the steady rise since 1981 of Indonesian trade with the So-viet Union, albeit weighted in Indonesia's favor. Thus, while Indonesian imports of Soviet goods amounted to only $5 million in 1985, the Soviet Union imported Indonesian products to the value of $106 million.[45] Certainly the fact that Indonesia has diplomatic relations in place with the Soviet Union and other CMEA countries is a factor to be considered. Accordingly, Indonesia has been successful over the last two years in cementing barter trade deals with the Eastern European nations, indicative of official Indonesian flexibility in its "look east bloc" offensive. As one Indonesian trade official reminded the author, China stands out in Indonesian eyes as merely the last of the communist bloc countries to re-establish direct-trading ties with Indonesia.[46]

Problems in Sino-Indonesian relations

Basic problems in Sino-Indonesian relations might be described as stemming from two fundamental obstacles, first, the nature of deep rooted anti-communism held by the Suharto regime, and second, the nature of regional Southeast Asian political alignments.

Notwithstanding the openings of Indonesia to the communist bloc countries over the last few years, a number of events in the course of 1985 highlighted domestic political realities vis-à-vis communism at home. Notable was the execution of four long-term PKI detainees, some 17 years after the coup attempt, despite the vigorous protests of Moscow and a number of Western countries. Whether or not the condemned men were pawns in Jakarta-Beijing diplomacy remains a moot point,[47] but it definitely demonstrates the ideological inflexibility of the regime to adapt to change. A second event concerned the firing of around 2,000 senior blue-collar workers, mostly in the oil industry, because of their alleged former affiliation with communist unions. While certainly another exercise in redbaiting, as Kaye termed it, the act is likewise difficult to link with China diplomacy,[48] indeed, pro-Soviet sympathizers could have been the more likely target.

Not only communists have been the victims of control exercises as described above; so have the ethnic Chinese residents of Indonesia. Even at the height of the Sino-Indonesian trade negotiations, certain authorities in Jakarta warned against the threat posed by communist infiltrators and the communist underground in the country. Yoga Sugama, chief of the Indonesian Intelligence Agency, BAKIN, warned a parliamentary hearing in Jakarta that the passage of ships, goods, and people between

Indonesia and China could create an untoward opening for communist activists. To match rhetoric with deeds, twenty-five illegal Chinese immigrants, otherwise family members of those Chinese who fled the country after the abortive coup of 1965, were expelled.[49] As is common knowledge among Chinese businessmen or other visitors to Indonesia, the regime exercises certain discriminatory control measures. For instance, holders of Hong Kong Certificates of Identity can visit Indonesia in groups only, not as individuals, and at discriminatory prices.[50]

With respect to regional alignments, as is well understood in ASEAN circles, Indonesia has sought to balance its anti-communist regional policing role (*tahanan daerah*) with its interlocutor role in negotiations over Kampuchea with Vietnam. While at first glance the two make for curious international bedfellows, their interests have converged to the extent of keeping the PRC at arms length. Some parallels in the treatment accorded their respective Chinese communities might also be observed. As has sometimes been platitudinously asserted by the Indonesian side, the two countries stand out in the region as having won their independence in armed struggles against colonial restorations following the capitulation of the Japanese. That being so, the Indonesian "revolution" departs from the Vietnamese insofar as it has yet to be consummated as a social revolution.

Thus, as pointed out in an editorial in the *South China Morning Post* of Hong Kong, the possible emergence of an *entente cordiale* between Vietnam and Indonesia would be a nightmare for China. These anxieties were raised by the little publicized six-day official visit to Jakarta in mid-April by Vietnamese Defense Minister, Van Tien Dung.[51] On this occasion, a memorandum of understanding on the resumption of trade was signed.[52] The Indonesian side subsequently announced that they would open a trade representative office in Ho Chi Minh City in 1986, thus resuming links cut off during World War II. Meanwhile an Indonesian trade delegation visited Vietnam in October 1985,[53] followed in late March 1986 by an Indonesian military delegation.[54]

A number of signals point to the centrality of the Kampuchea question linked with Vietnam as governing Indonesian thinking towards China. The most vivid articulation of this linkage, was made by Mochtar in early May 1985, when he informed the press that Indonesia would move ahead with the normalization of its relations with the PRC only after relations between the U.S. and Vietnam had been normalized.[55] It also seems to have been the case that China expected, by its diplomacy with Indonesia, to win dividends on Cambodia.[56] If that was the case, the movement has been glacially slow. In August 1986, following a visit to Jakarta by Norodom Sihanouk, Head of the China-backed Coalition Government of Democratic Kampuchea, Mochtar told the press that he was ready to meet Chinese leaders "anywhere, anytime" to act as interlocutor on the Cambodia question. Clearly, in Sihanouk's visit, Mochtar saw China as adopting a more flexible position on Kampuchea, namely accepting a Cambodian government not necessarily dominated by the Khmer Rouge.[57] China, on the other hand, would have been moderately gratified that Suharto promised Sihanouk that Indonesia would continue giving political and humanitarian aid to the Cambodian resistance group.[58]

Conclusion

I will conclude with a number of interrelated generalizations:

1. As with the previous demarche by Mochtar and his predecessor, the Sino-Indonesian rapprochement of mid-1985 foundered on pathological Sino-phobia linked with dogmatic anti-communism and a shrewd estimation of Realpolitik. Clearly military hard-liners in the Indonesian power elite are not yet to relinquish the Chinese bogey, still very much a foundation myth of the New Order government of General Suharto. Neither is the PRC—even in its current reformist phase—willing to renounce links with fraternal parties, the sine qua non of proletarian internationalism.

2. Further underscoring the asymmetry in political perceptions between Indonesia and China are differences over the advantages of the direct-trade opening. For the Indonesians, the opening was seen as one way to capitalize upon an

opportunity to help correct a large trading imbalance. For China, which in any case enjoyed a massive surplus in its trade with Indonesia, the opening was linked with a broader diplomatic offensive designed to bring Jakarta into line with the other ASEAN countries, not only on the question of recognizing China but on acknowledging with China that the primary sources of regional instability were the Soviet Union and, with respect to Indochina, Vietnam. Chinese disappointment at Bandung II was thus compounded by the quickening pace of Indonesia-CMEA ties. To the undoubted alarm of China, Vietnam has beer accorded by Indonesia a high order of trade concessions while Hanoi-Jakarta ties have been affirmed. For the right-wing generals in Indonesia who largely accommodated America goals during the Vietnam War, this is pure realpolitik.

3. The failure of Indonesia to make the necessary concessions and to restore full diplomatic relations with China further calls into account its nonaligned status. Underscoring the differences of the two countries within the nonaligned movement, China and Indonesia are at odds over the question of Indonesian aggression in East Timor. More specifically, Indonesia has failed to follow China in identifying Vietnamese aggression in Cambodia as the source of instability in Indochina. Thus, as interlocutor for the ASEAN countries with Vietnam, Indonesia has been able to keep China guessing its true motives in Indochina diplomacy. Nevertheless, China continues to see its Indonesia connection as useful and worth pursuing.

4. Thus, at the center of Indonesian concerns remains the doubt that Vietnam presents a greater danger than China. Indonesia's flirtation with the CMEA bloc is one way of indicating to the U.S. that it has gone too far in accommodating China. The Jakarta daily *Merdeka* succinctly presented the Indonesian geostrategic view in an editorial of May 1985 entitled "The U.S. is Pampering the PRC." As a defense against such "opportunist and compromising communist forces" (as China), the leader writer pointed out, "We in Southeast Asia have the Indochina barricade in the north the ASEAN barricade in the south and the South Pacific forum in the southeast."[59]

Notes

1. See, eg., R. Nations, *Far Eastern Economic Review* (*FEER*), 9 May 1985; and D. Weatherbee, "Indonesia in 1984: Pancasila, Politics and Power," *Asian Survey*, XXV, 2 (February 1985): 195. "Relations with Socialist Countries," *The Indonesian Quarterly*, XII, 1, (1985).

2. John Wong, *The Political Economy of China's Relations with Southeast Asia* (London: Macmillan, 1984): 34.

3. D. Mozinga, *Chinese Foreign Policy Towards Indonesia 1949-1967* (Ithaca: Cornell University Press, 1976): 249.

5. Wong, *Political Economy*: 63.

6. *Berita Buana*, 23 April 1985.

7. *Ta Kung Pao*, 25 April 1985.

8. "Report on Interview Granted by Foreign Minister Wu Xueqian to Shijie Zhishi in Beijing on the Prospects of Sino-Indonesian Relations." Beijing International Service in Indonesian, 2 May 1985 in Foreign Broadcast Information Service (FBIS), 3 June 1985.

Also see, *Ta Kung Pao*, 6 June 1985.

9. Agence France Presse, 28 May 1985, in FBIS, 30 May 1985.

10. *FEER*, 6 June 1985 and R. Nations, *FEER*, 23 May 1985.

11. L. Kaye, *FEER*, 6 June 1985.

12. Jakarta Domestic Service, 25 May in FBIS, 28 May 1985.

13. *Ta Kung Pao*, 25-30 April 1985.

14. Ibid.

15. *Ta Kung Pao*, 25-30 April 1985.

16. J.S. Mintz, "Indonesia," *Yearbook of International Communist Affairs*, 1984, (Stanford, Cal.: Hoover Institute Press, 1985): 227.

17. AFP, 8 October in FBIS, 9 October 1985. In fact, this is nothing new. An almost identical statement was made by Suharto in a speech to the People's Consultative Congress in early 1973. See E.W. Martin, *Southeast Asia and China: The End of Containment* (Boulder, Colorado: Westview Press, 1977): 41.

18. See, eg. W.R. Hinton, "China and Southeast Asian Communist Movements: The Decline of Dual Track Diplomacy," *Asian Survey*, 22, 8 (August, 1982).

19. Wong, *Political Economy*, p.60

20. *Indonesia Quarterly*, XIII, 2 (1985).

21. *Indonesia: In Commemoration of the Indonesian National Day 17 August 1984 and the Commencement of the Fourth Five-Year Plan: 1945-85*, Embassy, Republic of Indonesia, Hong Kong.

22. *Asiaweek*, 19 July 1985.

23. L. Kaye, *FEER*, 23 May 1985.

24. *Asiaweek*, 19 July 1985.
25. V.G. Kulkarni, *FEER*, 18 July 1985.
26. Reuter, *South China Morning Post* (SCMP), 6 July 1985.
27. *Asiaweek*, 19 July 1985.
28. L. Kaye, *FEER*, 18 July 1985.
29. Agencies, *SCMP*, 25 July 1985.
30. *The Japan Times*, 23 July 1985.
31. AFP in *SCMP*, 5 August 1985.
32. AFP in *SCMP*, 12 September 1985.
33. Interview with Indonesian Trade Counsellor, Embassy of Republic of Indonesian, Hong Kong, September 1985.
34. *Asiaweek*, 19 July 1985.
35. Interview.
36. AP report in *SCMP*, 11 August 1985.
37. Reuter report, Beijing, 9 August 1985 and Reuter report, Singapore, 9 August 1985, SCMP.
38. AFP in *SCMP*, 21 August 1985.
39. AFP in *SCMP*, 27 December 1985.
40. AFP in *SCMP*, 21 August 1985 and 20 August 1985.
41. *Beijing Review*, 36 (9 September 1985).
42. *Asiaweek*, 24 August 1986.
43. *Indonesia Newsletter*, 20 (June 1986), Embassy of Republic of Indonesia, Canberra.
44. *Asiaweek*, 7 September 1986.
45. *Indonesia Newsletter*, 18 (May 1986).
46. Interview, Indonesian Trade Counsellor, Embassy of Republic of Indonesia, Hong Kong.
47. L. Kaye, *FEER*, 5 December 1985 and see *Inside Indonesia*, 6, (December 1985): 3.
48. L. Kaye, *FEER*, 5 December 1985.
49. Kuala Lumpur International Service, 23 May 1985, FBIS.
50. "Jakarta Travel Policy Rapped," *SCMP*, 9 July 1985.
51. *SCMP*, 8 May 1985 and R. Nations, *FEER*, 23 May 1985.
52. *SCMP*, AP and Reuter, 3 November 1985.
53. Jakarta Domestic Service, FBIS, 4 November 1985.
54. Hanoi Domestic Service, 29 March 1986, FBIS, 1 April 1986.
55. Jakarta Domestic Service, 24, 28 May 1985 in FBIS.
56. R. Nations et. al., *FEER*, 5 September 1985.
57. *SCMP*, 23 August 1986.
58. AP in *The Nation* (Bangkok), 20 August 1986.
59. *Merdeka*, 3 May 1985.

4. Radical Islam in Southeast Asia: Rhetoric and Reality in the Middle Eastern Connection

Linked with Syria and South Yemen in the "steadfastness front" (that bloc of radical Islamic states which oppose otherwise collaborationist Zionist solutions to the Palestinian problem), Libya as well as Iran (and North Korea) have been identified by the U.S. Reagan Administration, and hence popular imagination, as the leading purveyors of state terrorism in the contemporary world. To varying degrees these regimes are seen as cat's paws for Soviet expansionism and/or promoting policies detrimental to U.S. interests globally. It is no doubt not lost upon the U.S. State Department that four of these five states are Islamic. Moreover, two of these regimes, Gadaffi's Libya and Khomeini's Iran, not only represent exemplars of Islamic radicalism but most vigorously proclaim the universality of their respective models. It has been well recorded in the Western media that north and Sub-Saharan Africa, Lebanon, and the Gulf have been exposed in varying degrees to the full militancy of Gadaffi-ism and Khomeini-ism. Less attention, however, has been given by scholarly journals (and especially by the left) to the receptivity of the southeast edge of the Islamic crescent (modern Southeast Asia) to the demonstration effect of the overthrow of the Pahlavi monarchy in Iran and the corresponding resurgence of Islamic fundamentalism that has accompanied the ascendancy to power of Khomeini and his clerics. Nor, on the other hand, has the attraction held out by Gadaffi's secularist version of radical Islam been satisfactorily explained with reference to Southeast Asia. It might be said that while "liberation theology" as a political factor in the Catholic/Hispanic world has received the attention it merits from leftist circles in the West, no such willingness to acknowledge the liberationist potential of radical Islam has been reflected in writings on the Islamic world from this quarter.[1]

At issue, then, is the question of whether religion has been or is being used as a weapon by these states, or whether religion— as internalized and practised by local believers—is an end in itself. Thus, in an attempt to discern myth from reality in official Western and popular images held concerning the international behaviour of two of these regimes, Libya and Iran, we will examine in turn the interfaces/interactions of the key states, liberation fronts and peoples in Islamic Southeast Asia with the two leading poles of radical Islamic utopianism in the contemporary world.

The following analytical foci are suggested by the foregoing: (1) Has the upsurge in fundamentalist attitudes reported in certain Islamic circles in Southeast Asia been actively promoted/ endorsed by Iran or is it an autonomous phenomenon, albeit stimulated by the example of Khomeini's Iran? (2) To what degree, and at what level, has Gadaffi sought to intervene in Islam and/or liberationist/separatist issues in Southeast Asia? As a corollary, what resonance has Gadaffi-ism as a liberationist force struck with the target Muslim peoples, fronts, and State actors in Southeast Asia? (3) What is the mix of internalist over external appeals and drives contributing to the political foment of Islam in contemporary Southeast Asia?

Gadaffi's universalism: the ideological basis

It is certainly the case, as the British Middle East scholar, Edward Mortimer, has written, that Gadaffi's internationalist line is not "Islamic" in the sense of taking the Muslim side in any dispute. Indeed, he observes, no mention is made of Islam or religion, for that matter, in the first and second parts of *The Green Book,* the most explicit statement of Gadaffi-ism, published respectively in 1975 and 1978. While the question of religion, but not specifically Islam, is addressed in part three (1979), it is done so, as Mortimer affirms, in a manner that elevates nationalism over and above religion per se.[2] Indeed, the opening sentence of this volume states, "The social, ie, national factor is the driving force of human history".[3] While this sentiment no doubt is due to Gadaffi's Nasserite leanings, it is hardly a statement that would endear him to religionists, much less fundamentalists. Indeed, this conviction is modified ten pages on: "The sound rule is that every nation should have a religion. The contrary to that is abnormal."[4] Even so, as St. John has pointed out in an article on Gadaffi's ideological posture, Islam is central to his view of religion and the Koran is seen as central to his view of Islam.[5]

While viewed as alternatively an apostate and a madman by his Islamic and non-Islamic detractors, it is argued here that Gadaffi has not so much jettisoned religion as rechanneled it to serve political ends. Stated another way, while the secularist thrust of Gadaffi's Al Fateh revolution at home has been pre-eminent, abroad the "natural" universality of Islam has made it the logical medium for seeking political influence and reach. Thus, the international arm of politicized Islam in Libya is the Islamic Call Society, a *dakwah* (missionary) movement that seeks to touch Islamic youth, not only in the Arab/African world but globally. Accordingly, it preaches not only Koranic injunctions but the broader lessons of the Libyan leaders' so-called "Third International Theory." Thus, according to an official Libyan publication, the flow to other countries (including Southeast Asia) of Libyan *dakwah* delegations "comes amid increasing attentions to the great Al Fateh revolution about spreading out the teachings of Islam in different continents and supporting and backing issues of Islam and standing beside Muslims against all crusaders' attempts carried out by American and Zionist imperialism against Islam and Moslems."[6]

Again (as Mortimer has written) while Gadaffi has adopted a version of Nasser's strategy of three circles in international relations (Arab, African, and Islamic), shifting emphasis according to circumstances, he has revealed himself as more than willing to take up revolutionary causes far from the Middle East heartland.[7] We would submit, however, that if Nasser in his day symbolized the struggle of the Afro-Asian and Arab peoples against the constellation of old colonial powers, then Gadaffi, confronted by the U.S. economic embargo and Franco-U.S. encirclement on the military plane, quintessentially symbolizes for the Third World peoples the cutting edge of the nonaligned movements' opposition to neo-colonialism on a global scale.

Most recent instances of support for non-Arab/non-Islamic causes by Libya include reception of a delegation of members of the Kanak National Liberation Front of the French Pacific territory of New Caledonia and a reiteration of support (including arms) for American Indians and blacks. This should not be surprising, as the doctrinal basis of support for minorities is spelled out explicitly in *The Green Book,* part three. A minority, Gadaffi writes, belongs to a nation which provides it with a special framework. Such a minority has its own social rights and its political and economic problems can only be solved by the masses in whose hands power, wealth and arms are placed. The doctrinal foundation upon which Gadaffi places his support for liberationist fronts is no less "socialistic" and owes as much to Western as to mainstream Islamic thought. "Contemporary national liberation movements are themselves social movements. They will not come to an end before every group is liberated from the domination of another group."[8] Clearly, then, the secular basis of Gadaffi-ism, namely its modernist, reformist, and egalitarian-socialist thrust, should be highlighted separate from the image of irrational, fundamentalist, obscurantist, and above all, rogue terrorist, as purveyed by official U.S. spokesmen. Whatever else, these stereotypes cut across the grain of an impressive round of domestic achievements in the Jamahiriyah, a detail invariably glossed over in much reporting on this country.

Khomeini's universalism: the ideological basis

While lacking a single concise statement of ideological principle analogous to Gadaffi's *The Green Book,* it is nevertheless possible to piece together the Khomeini worldview from his books, published versions of his speeches and official pronouncements of the Islamic Republic of Iran. But arguably, in the case of the Khomeini's Iran, actions have spoken louder than words, unless of course these words are those of the Koran. As one student of the question, Ferdous, has written, Khomeini's political philosophy has evolved dramatically. Thus in a 1978 book entitled *Islamic Government,* Khomeini advocated the overthrow of the monarch in Iran and the establishment of a republic. In theory as in practice, Khomeini demonstrates the idea of separation of politics and religion as contrary to Islam. Khomeini thus views Islam as a government of the *ulama,*[9] to be contrasted with Gadaffi's view of the *ulama* as instruments of social change.

Mortimer has written of the Iranian revolution that like the French revolution in 1789 and the Russian revolution of 1917, it proclaimed itself as based on principles of universal applicability. Thus Iran was viewed by its new leaders as "the vanguard or nucleus" around which the Islamic *umma* (community) could be reconstituted as successive Muslim countries threw off their chains and restored authentic Islamic government.[10] As another student of the Iranian revolution has written, "export of Islamic revolution" is not simply a revolutionary slogan; it is a cardinal principle of the foreign policy of the Islamic Republic of Iran."

The general sense of this assertion was given concrete expression by Khomeini in a speech on the occasion of the fifth anniversary of the revolution. Observing with evident pride that, in the preceding five years, the seed of the Iranian revolution had not only been sown at home but in all Islamic lands, he prophesied:

> Once we have properly nurtured the growth of this revolution when we would witness some time in the not too distant future the rising up of all the nations dedicated to glorifying Islam ... [12]

However, in consideration of the internationalist thrust of the Islamic Revolution in Iran, it should be understood that the Islamic Republic of Iran upholds the value of official ties with foreign governments. In doing so it divides the world into three categories: (1) Islamic countries, (2) other Third World states, (3) superpowers. But, and here lies the rub, it considers such ties as "the gates towards the real audience who are the common people."[13] The foregoing is not to suggest that Khomeini necessarily advocates violence in achieving his goals internationally. According to Ramazani, the contrary is the case; rather, the following peaceful strategies are preferred: (1) promoting correct Islamic ethics; (2) broadcasting revolutionary propaganda; (3) proselytising through foreign religious leaders; (4) forging links with pilgrims in Mecca; (5) promoting revolutionary front organizations.

Whatever local support has been forthcoming for acts of terrorism and counter-terrorism by Iranian-inspired Shiite Muslims in such places as the Gulf and Lebanon, it is no doubt fear of the demonstration effect of the Iranian revolution that most worries the Western world. Equally, those Third World countries hosting large Muslim populations feel themselves particularly vulnerable. Bearing in mind the major questions posed above, we will turn in this paper to an analysis of the three major Islamic movements for autonomy in Southeast Asia: the Patani case, the Moros case and the Aceh case. While situating the narrower aspects of the secessionist issue and the broader ambit of political Islam in Malaysia and Indonesia, we shall take the Libyan and Iranian connection in Southeast Asia as the leitmotif.

The origins of Muslim separatism in Patani (Thailand)

There is consensus among scholars of the Patani region of the modern Kingdom of Thailand that the local people were first converted to Islam at some point in the thirteenth century. During the sixteenth century, however, the historic outward expansion of the Thai rekindled. Tributory status was thus imposed by the centralised Thai state over what are now the Muslim majority provinces of Thailand (constituting some three percent of the total population of Thailand): Satun, Patani, Yala, and Narathiwas, as well as over the Malaysian states of Kelantan, Trengannu, Kedah, and Perlis. Prior to Thai military conquests (which could not be regarded as complete, even in the eighteenth century), Patani by all accounts was a flourishing trade and religious center. Intermittent rebellion continued in Patani until the early part of the nineteenth century when, in order to impose administrative rule over the Muslim south, local power was fragmented. Thus by 1902, all the local Muslim leaders were replaced by centrally appointed officials from the Thai civil service. It was at this point that the present border between Malaysia and Thailand was formalized in an agreement signed between the British and the Thai whereby the latter renounced claims to the Malay-Muslim states of Kelantan, Trengannu, Kedah, and Perlis, while the former recognized the sovereignty of Thailand north of these states.

Thomas, a student of the Muslim separatist issue in Thailand, makes the relevant point that in considering contemporary events, it must be recognized that a long period of political unrest has existed in the south, often simmering beneath the surface but flaring up on such occasions as collective refusals to pay tax, demonstrations, or on the occasion of presenting petitions.[15] Prior to the present crisis in the south of Thailand, there have been two major uprisings by the Muslim peoples during this century. The first, in 1922, was led by Rajir Abdul Kadir and other *ulama* (religious leaders) along with sections of the dispossessed Malay nobility and their followers. He was also able to rally support from his fellow Malays in Kelantan. The period, 1922-45, has been described by Pitsuwan Surin, a Thai student of the problem, as a time of struggle on the part of the Thai Muslims to uphold their cultural and political identities in the face of widespread political changes. This is a reference to the limited parliamentary opportunities afforded by the 1932 rebellion against the Absolute Monarchy and, more dramatically, the endeavor by ethnic and religious minorities in Thailand to withstand the aggressive assimilationist policies of the fascist dictator, Pibul Songramm. The other landmark rebellion of 1947-48 occurred in the context of the rising tide of nationalism in the Malay world during World War II. The leader and "father of the Patani struggle," until his death in the early sixties at the hands of the Thai police, was Haji Sulong. In 1948, at the height of this rebellion, 250,000 Thai Malays unsuccessfully petitioned the UN to preside over the secession of southern Thailand and its subsequent incorporation into the Federation of Malaya. Eventually, in the

face of intransigence on the part of Bangkok and in the context
of sustained pressure locally by the Thai police, a modern
liberation front and army was launched in the late 1960s in the
manner of their co-religionists in the Philippines, thus pushing
the struggle for autonomy into a new stage.[16]

One of the first indicators of outside support for the
movement was signaled in a 1963 CIA field report drawing
attention to a purported link between the Muslim irridentists in
Thailand and the Chinese communists who shared the same
general terrain as a rear base, on the one hand, and the Indonesian
Communist Party, on the other. Allegedly an arms shipment from
Sumatra to the Thai-Malay border region was intercepted by
local authorities.[17] While drawing attention to the link between
communists and Muslims in the south has been a favorite ploy
on the part of Thai intelligence along with the CIA, the charge
remains to be substantiated by independent witnesses.

Muslim liberation fronts in southern Thailand

As Thomas has written, there has never been one single
organization which can speak for all or even most separatists;
indeed, not all the population are behind the separatists. Nor is
there agreement among analysts over the nomenclature of the
various fronts and armies.[18] Three fronts with differing political
tendencies stand out, however: the conservative National
Liberation Front of Patani (NLFP), the broadly based Patani
United National Revolution Front (PULO), and the radical Patani
National Revolution Front (PNRF). McBeth, a Bangkok-based
journalist, notes that the overall strength of the three fronts is
thought to be no more than 500 to 600 but that in late 1979 a
parliamentary commission to southern Thailand identified 84
different armed groups in the Muslim-predominant provinces
"most of them with affiliations as unclear as the line between
banditry and separatism."[19] Writing in October 1976, a
correspondent of the *Mimbar Socialis,* the mouthpiece of the
Malayan Socialist People's Party, pointed out that while pro-
imperialist publications have drawn attention to the splits in the
movement, in fact a unity of purpose existed between the fronts

despite differences in detail, especially in the face of the internal colonialism of Bangkok.[20]

The first-mentioned of these fronts, the NLFP, is the oldest among the separatist organizations. Since 1977 this front has sought the restoration of Patani under a Sultanate, but as an autonomous entity within the Federation of Malaysia. With networks extending across the border into Malaysia, it is not surprising to learn that this front has enjoyed links with the "conservative" Kelantan-based Party Islam (PAS), which until its defeat in 1978 constituted the ruling government in Kelantan. It was this front that first apparently canvassed the Patani independence issued abroad, notably in the conservative Middle Eastern countries such as Saudi Arabia and Egypt. The second front, PULO, evidently functions as an umbrella organization "more practical than the former two groups with a wider appeal to all elements within wider Malay Muslim society." Founded in 1967, PULO draws support from three spheres, from some 8,000 Patani Muslims in Saudi, from a "headquarters" in Kelantan, and from locally based *jabatan tentra* (military formations). In 1975 PULO succeeded in organizing the largest political demonstration in Thailand's history. The level of solidarity combined with support from Middle Eastern sources set the tone and the stage for the prosecution of *jihad* by this organization, although how far religious ideology serves as a cover for socially derived frustration remains an area of investigation. No such ambiguity surrounds the motivation and orientation of the third tendency. This is represented by the PNRF (and other like-named fronts), which seek to establish a republic along the lines of Islamic socialism. The PNRF is led by a former *pondok* (religious institution) teacher, Ustaz Karim Hassan, better known as Ustaz Karim. This front is committed to the liberation of Patani and a variant of socialist revolution. Its following is accordingly derived from the young and radical elements of Malay-Muslim society in the south. From this core was derived a Muslim People's Liberation Army launched on 7 August 1977.[21]

Whatever else can be said of the armed struggle being waged by Muslim separatists in southern Thailand is that they have seldom received good press coverage in the region. Nor has the leadership been particularly adept in promoting their cause to the non-Islamic world. In an interview granted in Libya in early 1984, exiled Patani spokespersons of the "socialist" tendency revealed that organizationally—if not militarily—the movement was alive and well.[22]   Addressed to a Middle Eastern audience with little notion of Thai history or geography, a bulletin issued by the Front in the context of an exhibition staged in a Libyan port city underscored the truism that Patani was one of the oldest Malay kingdoms in the Malay peninsula and a sovereign country prior to annexation by the Kingdom of Thailand in 1786. It thereupon existed as a vassal state paying tribute to Bangkok until 1902, the year of its forced incorporation into the modern Kingdom of Thailand. Moreover, repeated attempts by "freedom" movements in Patani, particularly since 1948 to win their "birthright" from Thai colonial power, have been "brutally suppressed by the Thai authorities by means of genocide and in the name of assimilation." According to the same source, the struggle for the "full liberation and complete independence" of Patani actually commenced the year after the original Thai conquest of 1787.

At the present time, the source makes clear, armed clashes between these "freedom fighters" and the "Thai imperialist enemy troops and its collaborators" ensue unabated on the ground in Patani. Although the Libya-based spokesperson of the movement refused to place an upper ceiling on the number of *askar* (guerrilla fighters) in the field, he indicated that the number was in excess of 1,000. Photographs of guerrilla base camps taken *in situ*, as viewed by the author, reveal well-equipped and uniformed partisans.

According to the spokesperson, a Malay Arabic-speaking teacher of Islamic law and who otherwise might be considered the Libya-based intellectual force behind the movement, the militants not only derived support from the local populace but also from the Malaysian people. Moral support notwithstanding, he continued, this did not imply condoning on the part of the Malaysian government. This he attributed to the ASEAN factor, a reference to the political, and on a decidedly more secondary level, military ties between Bangkok and Kuala Lumpur. Again according to *Mimbar Socialis,* a source otherwise sympathetic to the aspirations of the PNRF, far from being a supporter of the rights of the Patani peoples, the National Front government in Kuala Lumpur takes a "cool" and "opportunist" view of the question. This was thrown into high relief at the session of the Islamic Conference Foreign Ministers in Istanbul in May 1976, whereupon representatives of the ruling Malaysian National Front government sided with the Thai (and Indonesian) regime in ignoring the aspirations of the Patani people and in isolating the representatives of the Patani peoples at the conference table.[23] However, while the Islamic Conference endorses the right of the Patani peoples to autonomy, the Libya-based front remains righteous in its commitment to the struggle of the Patani peoples for *merdeka* (independence). Likewise they claim that the movement is not only gaining support from the people of Patani but as well from the "foreign freedom loving peoples and governments of the world" who have "started" to understand the Patani case on a "stronger and stronger" basis. When pressed on the question as to which governments support the Libya-based front, the spokesperson conceded that the movement faces a recognition problem.

Whether or not Libya has formalised support for the movement was not an issue upon which the spokesperson would speak, but if not actively supporting them on the ground, as has sometimes been claimed in official circles in Bangkok, it was acknowledged that Libya provided "backup" for the movement. For instance, Libya is host to at least thirty Patani militants. This would not be surprising, as up to 13,000 Thai migrant workers at a time have in the past been employed in Libya (some in the most menial positions) alongside Pakistanis, Filipinos (including Muslim Filipinos), South Koreans, and other nationals. While hardly supplying a steady stream of military manpower for the movement, the environment for Muslim Thai expatriate laborers in Libya might be termed supportive in terms of financial inducements and political education and some leakage over to the political front cannot be discounted.

Asked to comment upon alleged links with the Communist

Party of Thailand, the spokesperson for the Libya-based front was vociferous in his denunciation of the false propaganda emanating from Bangkok. According to the front's literature, the Patani case exists, "in spite of all the efforts by the Thai colonialists to block up the real facts of the problem, naming it as communist bandits, etc." Rather, "victory is always with truth." Pressed to elaborate on this point in general the spokesperson retorted (in an utterance that would not fundamentally contradict Gadaffi's Third International Theory), "communists are also imperialists, as in Afghanistan."[24]

According to Thai army intelligence, at least 60 Muslim youths who receive "guerrilla training" in an unnamed Middle Eastern country returned to the south during early 1985, some arriving by air via Bangkok with others arriving overland via Malaysia.[25] A separate Thai intelligence account identified these returnees with PULO. However, these armed groups, including "saboteur units," have reportedly been unable to mount armed operations of late but rather have been concentrating on political activities in various localities in Yala. On the other hand the Barisan National movement (a reference to the radical PNRF) has been active in collecting protection fees from business owners in its sphere of influence while stepping up recruitment.[26] According to Paisal Sricharatcharya, such activities have brought the Muslims into conflict with the Communist Party of Malaya. He speculates, however, that the recent sapping of communist strength could well play into the hands of the Muslims. Otherwise, this independent observer holds with the Thai military assessment that the separatists are a spent force.[27]

To take Thai propaganda at face value, official policies vis-a-vis the south are beginning to bite. According to Squadron Leader Prasong Soonsiri, Secretary General of the National Security Council of Thailand, government policy as of early 1985 can be construed as threefold. This involves, first, a nation-building strategy focusing on the promotion of Thai language among Muslim youth, second, seeking to improve the relationship between Thai Muslims and government officials, and third, by promoting a law-and-order approach.[28]

Whatever the long-term efficacy of this traditionalist

incrementalist approach, it is certain that the broader issue of internal colonialism of the south by Bangkok will remain a festering sore until the fundamental question of poverty, economic development, and redistribution are radically addressed. Further, given the fact that the motives of the major external actors in the Patani secessionist struggle are mixed and given the complex historical evolution of the problem, it would be facile to view the holy-war component of the struggle in the south as pre-eminent, as sometimes held by the mainstream press in Thailand. But whatever the heartfelt interests of the Islamic Conference members on the Patani issue, Libyan interests, as revealed above, are probably more in the way of seeking international Muslim allies at the expense of conservative Middle Eastern competitors, as much as striking a U.S. ally at a vulnerable pressure point. No less important, Gadaffi's credibility among the faithful as a true Muslim internationalist rests upon his ability to project his influence to such far-flung frontiers of the Islamic world as Patani.

Contours of the Islamic challenge in Malaysia

Of the Southeast Asian countries, it is Malaysia which has gone furthermost in the development of official links with Libya. This in part stems from Malaysia's active participation in the Islamic Conference, at least since Tungku Abdul Rahman, the former Malaysian Prime Minister, championed that cause. An early high point in official Malaysian-Libyan ties was established by Datuk Hussein Onn, the then-serving Malaysian Prime Minister, who visited Tripoli in 1977. He was there reported as having stated that Malaysia and Libya shared concern over the unresolved problems of West Asia, namely the plight of the Palestinian peoples. Likewise, he thanked Libya for its support of the ASEAN concept of a zone of peace, freedom, and neutrality in Southeast Asia. More specifically, Hussein Onn thanked Libya for its help in promoting the Islamic cause in Malaysia, namely for contributing a $10 million ringgit aid grant to PERKIM (the Malaysian Islamic voluntary agency). Reportedly, Hussein Onn told Gadaffi that "Malaysia was happy with Libya's role in bringing about unity and solidarity among Muslim countries in the spirit of the Islamic Conference." As the semiofficial Malaysian press viewed the matter, the personal contacts between Hussein Onn, Gadaffi, and Abdel Salem Jallaoud, the Libyan second-in-command, laid the basis of goodwill to facilitate bilateral co-operation.[29] But while Malaysian boycotts of Israel go back to 1977, it has been under Prime Minister Mohammed Mahathir that a strong pro-PLO line has emerged. Though anathema to the rejectionist front members, Yasser Arafat's PLO faction receives full diplomatic status in Kuala Lumpur and Yasser Arafat was received as head of state in the Malaysian capital in mid-1984.

It is clear, then, that the momentum of the Hussein Onn-Gadaffi meeting has been kept up under the Mahathir administration, with cooperation between the two countries not only embracing accord on international Islamic questions but expanded to include economic and religious cooperation. In January 1984, for instance, an agreement for religious cooperation was initialed in the Libyan capital by the Malaysian Minister for Culture and Sports (and UMNO Youth leader), Ibrahim Anwar, and the Libyan Secretary-General of the Islamic Dakwah Association. An UMNO Youth delegation accompanying Anwar called for intensifying contacts between Malaysia's International Islamic University and the Islamic Dakwa Association. As reported in the official Malaysian media, Anwar revealed that Libya had agreed to increase trade and cultural relations with Malaysia, assist the new university, assist the establishment of (official) *dakwah* centres in Sabah, and to upgrade the program for exchanges of students and youth leaders between Malaysia and Libya.[30] On the economic front, the Malaysian Overseas Investment Corporation and the Libyan Foreign Investment Company have agreed to set up a joint holding company in Kuala Lumpur for trade, investment, and commerce.[31]

While various phenomena pertaining to a resurgence of Islam in Malaysia have been evident since the mid-1970s, notably the appearance of unofficial *dakwah* groups preaching a fundamentalist Islamic message, by the early 1980s, the Mahathir

administration had actively embarked upon an official
Islamization program. In a manner of casting a shadow over the
future of the secular status of the state, Mahathir in 1982 led
people to believe that he was not opposed to some kind of Islamic
state. This has been explained by observers as an attempt to
meet the fundamentalists' challenge head on, a case of attempting
to out-Islam Parti Islam (PAS) by forcing the Malay-dominated
National Front government to up the ante with respect to
religion.[32] PAS, as the leading Malay parliamentary opposition
force in the country, has been able to challenge on more than
one occasion certain of the core assumptions held by the
government as to the role of religion in society and the nature of
the state. Indeed, PAS under the control of a fundamentalist
"Young Turk" faction has pursued throughout 1983-84 the issue
of Islamic purity and the demand for an Islamic state with such
vigor that it has threatened to split the Malay vote, thus
weakening the Malay UMNO component of the ruling National
Front. Tasker has affirmed that, by preaching fundamentalist
Islamic values to the Malays, PAS appears as more worrisome
than even the Chinese-based parties. A government White Paper
on "The Threat to Muslim Unity and National Security" has
documented evidence of PAS' divisive influence among the
Malays. Specifically, it holds PAS responsible for the situation
in certain parts of the northern Malaysian states where PAS and
UMNO supporters have separate *imam* or religious leaders in
the same mosque. According to the Paper, certain groups
advocate violence as a means to establish an Islamic state.[33]
While some observers have detected a curtailment of the
government's Islamization program during 1984, they are not at
the same time prepared to argue that Islam will not again become
a persistent thorn in the side of the defenders of the secular state
in Malaysia.[34] Indeed, throughout 1984 PAS kept up the charge
that the Mahathir administration was infidel. The administration
responded by imposing a ban on political assemblies in four states
and by invoking the Internal Security Act to arrest three PAS
members. Further, Mahathir came public with the allegation that
elements of PAS were plotting to overthrow the government and
replace it with an "Iranian-style regime dominated by mullahs."[35]

By 1983, charges of Iranian interference in Islamic politics in Malaysia were widespread, the Islamic Republic of Iran having opened an Embassy in Kuala Lumpur in 1981 with a resident Ambassador arriving the following year. Indeed, as early as mid-1979, the Malaysian Prime Minister had issued a public warning that a group of "Malay religious opportunists" were seeking to overthrow the government by extra-constitutional means.[36] In late 1983 the linkage with Iran was made explicit by the deputy Prime Minister, Datuk Musa Hitam, who, inter alia, claimed that radical Muslim republicans were gaining support and were planning to overthrow the system of government. Specifically, he mentioned a group of Malays arrested in Saudi Arabia apparently promoting the Khomeini line that the monarchy was incompatible with Islam. Whatever Musa's interest in making this disclosure—eg, aligning himself with the Malay Sultans vis-à-vis Mahathir—there is no doubt that even the suggestion of Iranian style republicanism strikes at the heart of the Malay political establishment.[37]

While the situation in multiracial Malaysia in the mid-1980s hardly parallels that of pre-revolutionary Iran, the Mahathir government is taking no chances. The major initiative undertaken to neutralize the activities of Iranian or Iranian-inspired Muslim activists appears to be the attempt to upgrade state-to-state relations in order to bind Iranian interests in Malaysia to official and approved outlets. This took a significant step forward during January 1984 when Tan Sri Ghazali Shafie visited Teheran and there stressed the need for further development of official Malaysian-Iranian relations in the economic, trade, and cultural fields. An ensuing joint statement made by Ghazali and his Iranian counterpart underlined the importance of unity in the Islamic world "to effectively confront international Zionism and superpower designs on Islamic and other Third World countries." Together they affirmed their belief in the value of the Non-Aligned Movement to ensure the interest of Third World countries.[38]

James Clad writes that by most accounts Iran now appears to accept that close ties with radical Muslim elements could jeopardize its diplomatic presence in Malaysia.[39] However, in a separate development, Teheran refused to accept a Malaysian proposal for an intergovernmental agreement to approve visits to Iran by Malaysian Muslims, suggesting that the Iranian side does not want to close the "gates" to the real audience in Malaysia, namely the common people.[40]

Thus while Iranian-style epiphenomena abound in Malaysia, eg, portraits of Khomeini carried at PAS rallies, it should not be forgotten that in the Malaysian context, the gulf between the Malay beneficiaries of the National Front governments' New Economic Policy (NEP) and the non-beneficiaries among the rural masses must appear to the latter as almost unbridgeable, even if absolute indices of poverty among the have-nots are not crushing. Indeed, one of the most damaging critics of the NEP has been the Angkatan Belia Islam Malaysia (Malaysian Islamic Youth Movement) (ABIM), formerly led by Anwar Ibrahim until his cooptation via UMNO into government in 1982. Variously alleged to have links with Libya and Iran, ABIM—while under severe government surveillance—articulates a doctrinaire version of Islam as social justice. It thus appears (although this is not the area of focus or investigation of this essay) that both absolute poverty and perceived relative poverty as much as the psychological distance of the rural Malay or uprooted Malay from his city and/or Western-educated cousin provides a fertile ground for the seeds of fundamentalist responses to economic/social alienation.

The origins of Muslim separatism in Aceh (Indonesia)

According to an official Iranian publication, *Kayhan,* as early as the fifteenth century, the great Arab historian, Ibn Khaldun, remarked upon the presence of a strong Muslim state in Aceh. The attempt by the Dutch to annex Aceh to the Dutch East Indies, however, only "aroused the Islamic fervor of the population." Accordingly the defeat of the Dutch at the battle of Banda Aceh in 1873 is explained by this source as a "devastating blow to European prestige." Neither did a second Dutch invasion achieve its purpose. From that point the Acehnese struggle came under the leadership first of Tengku Tilik di Tiro Muhammed Saman and later his descendants. Thus, in rejecting demands of the

Dutch in 1873 (and foreshadowing contemporary Iranian interest in the Aceh question) leaders of the resistance declared:

> The Islamic state of Aceh had always been an inseparable
> part of the universal Islamic state and always acknowledged
> the suzerainty of the Islamic caliphate. To ask us to renounce
> loyalty to the Islamic caliphate and swear loyalty to the King
> of Holland is tantamount to asking us to renounce our reli-
> gion. For our religion and our flag every Acehnese will shed
> the last drop of his blood.

Approvingly, the *Kayhan* reporter attributed the strength of the
Acehnese resistance to the spirit of *shahadah;* nearly half the
population purportedly sought martyrdom in defense of their Islamic way of life. Thus by 1942, the source continues, the Muslims of Aceh were finally victorious in ousting the Dutch from
their territory. Reflecting the viewpoint of the anti-Suharto government, Acehnese rebels of today, the source noted that while
the sovereignty of Aceh was transferred on 27 December 1950,
this was done "over the heads of the people of Aceh Sumatra
without election or referendum" and in violation of international
law and all the decolonization laws.[41]

As the historical record reveals, after the capitulation of the
Japanese conqueror in 1945, the Muslim Association of Religious
Teachers (PUSA) seized power in Aceh with David Beureh as
their Governor. When Aceh was absorbed into the north
Sumatran province, PUSA conducted a campaign against the
central government culminating in the 1953 uprising. Beureh
declared Aceh as henceforth part of the Indonesian Islamic state,
as proclaimed by Darul Islam in 1949.[42]

Iranian sources acknowledge that the "Islamic State of Aceh
Sumatra" was "re-established" by the National Liberation Front
(of Aceh), declared on 4 December 1976 and taking the Koran
as its constitution. Members of the Darul Islam movement of
Sumatra (Darul Islam had during the 1950s confronted the
government in West Java over the issue of an Islamic State) then
regrouped under the leadership of Tengku Hasan di Tiro (a
proclaimed descendant of the famed resistance fighter) in order

to set up an Islamic state. Having regrouped in the hills as guerrilla bands, di Tiro's forces not only endured local hardships but ran the gamut of repression at the hands of the Javanese (ie, the Suharto government) forces, by means of modern rifles, armoured vehicles, and helicopters. Certainly, as the *Kayhan* report underscores, what distinguishes the resistance against the Indonesian Armed Forces is its Islamic character.[43]

Media attention on the National Liberation Front of Aceh Sumatra has been as sporadic as its activities, yet it has had the ability to attract headlines. For instance, in mid-1977 a grenade attack in north Sumatra was attributed to a Komando Jihad, which otherwise might be seen as the action element of the front. During the same approximate period, six ex-Darul Islam members were arrested for plotting to set up an independent state of Aceh.[44] One year later, the apprehended grenade thrower, identified as a member of Komando Jihad, was arrested and executed. It was alleged at his trial that the movement had "tried" to obtain arms and money from the Libyan Embassy in Kuala Lumpur.[45] On 20 April 1981 the government announced the arrest of Iman Bin Mohammed Zein, leader of the so-called Indonesia Islamic Revolutionary Council, along with 19 other members of the organization that had allegedly sought assistance from Khomeini for an attempt to overthrow the Suharto regime. Later in the same year, the arrest of David Beureh was also reported. The arrest of Mohammed Zein and his entourage, however, transpired in the context of the recapture on 30 March 1981 of an Indonesian airliner hijacked to Thailand by a Muslim group, linked by Indonesian intelligence to the Komando Jihad. This group was also linked with a mob attack upon a Bandung police station during the same month.[46]

It is certain, however, as Sacerdoti contends, that government misinformation surrounding the whole question of radical Islam in Indonesia seeks to convey the impression of fanatic, terrorist, and social misfit, an argument—in the absence of informed dialogue—scarcely tailored to allay Muslim grievances.[47] The following example is apposite. It concerns a young *alim* (theologian) prosecuted in Aceh by central government authorities for allegedly making a speech at a mosque opposing the state ideology of Pancasila. The *alim's* trial, according to an Iranian source, backfired as tens of thousands of people turned up at the courthouse in a display of sympathy and out of fear of becoming social outcasts in a deeply religious society. There is no doubt truth in the assertion made by the *Kayhan* reporter on this case that it flies in the face of the government propaganda that the call for an Islamic State is restricted to a few miscreants.[48]

A 1981 Jajasan Lembaga Bantuan Hukum (Foundation of Legal Aid Institute) report, cited by Justus van Der Kroef in a penetrating study of human rights abuses in Indonesia, notes of Aceh, that after participation in the local anti-government protest demonstrations, teachers and students of secondary schools were "subjected to a campaign of organized terrorism and intimidation" by the Indonesian government. This included the beatings and clubbings of teachers as well as students. In one northern Acehnese school, students were tortured by "mysterious" hooligans described as "soldiers in mufti." As van der Kroef acerbicaly commented, "The Indonesian government has not issued a denial." Drawing the inference from this report, he laments, "one senses a deepening brutalization by the government of the treatment of its opponents."[49]

Contours of the Islamic challenge in Indonesia

There is no doubt that the Indonesian government's brutal putting down of the Tanjong Priok riots of 12 September 1984, including the slaying of the charismatic leader (and now martyr) of the Muslim peoples and downtrodden of the port city, Amir Biki, represents a turning point for political Islam in Indonesia; moreover, with the voice of popular Islam in the Indonesian context synonymous with the have-nots is increasingly finding itself drowned out by the modulated incantations of official Islam.[50] This much became apparent in the course of 1983 with the government's insistence that political organizations of all complexions adopt the State ideology, Pancasila. Bowing to the inevitable, the United Development Party (PPP), a forced alliance of four Muslim political parties, fell into line in August 1984, while the Nahdatul Ulama, the hitherto most resistant constituent member of the PPP, followed suit at its annual conference in December.

Muslims thus denied the possibility of placing the concept of an Islamic state upon the political agenda have been forced back onto the defensive. Increasingly, violence has been seen by frustrated Muslims as the means to draw attention to their grievances. Indeed, in the wake of the Tanjong Priok uprising (termed an instance of "embryonic guerrilla warfare" in the official media), Jakarta and other centers in East and Central Java were flooded with pamphlets exhorting the faithful to defend Islam by arms.[51] Again, the spate of bombings unleashed between October and December 1984 by extremist Muslim groups, and coming soon after the Tanjong Priok event, brings into sharp focus the role of Muslim fundamentalism as the cutting edge of extralegal opposition to the regime. The choice of targets, while bound to incur public outrage, was nevertheless apposite. These included such Suharto-Army-*abangan* (Javanist-Muslim) symbols as the Buddhist stupa of Borubodor, the Kraton or Javanese court in Solo, as well as the property of the most notorious *cukong* (capitalist crony) partner of Suharto, Liem Sioe Leong. As the most informed outside commentator of these developments, Susumu Awonahara, has commented, "The cleavage between institutionalized Islam, largely led by the well-to-do Muslims in towns and countryside, and the growing, unorganized, Islam of those who have little to lose has almost certainly widened, with the latter being politicized and radicalized."[52] Those netted in the wake of the bombings are drawn from a variety of backgrounds. They include Abdul Qadir Djaelani, former chairman of the banned Indonesian Islamic Youth Movement, Marwadi Noor, Yayan Hendrayana, and Tony Ardie (described by *South* magazine as leading Muslim zealots), A.M. Fatwa and H.M. Sanusi, both members of the Petition of Fifty group (establishment critics of the Suharto regime), and Dharsono, a former ASEAN Secretary-General.[53]

In a separate report, Awanohara writes that Iranian influence on Islamic youth in Indonesia is no longer ruled out by the regime. Some of these youths see certain similarities between the Suharto regime and that of the Shah of Iran. Evidence of this, he contends, is seen in the current popularity in Indonesia, especially among students and young intellectuals, of Ali Shariati, the Sorbonne-educated Iranian revolutionary, especially his critique of the well-to-do and corrupt *ulama*.[54] As one authority on the subject has written, Shariati's ideals of social justice and Islam have done more than any other form of religious indoctrination to make Islam the sole ideology of struggle in contemporary Iran for vast numbers of militant young people, who would otherwise have been attracted to secularist, left-wing doctrines.[55]

South reports that the previous Iranian Ambassador in Jakarta was issued warnings over alleged interference in Indonesian affairs while domestically, the activities of Muslim cells and study groups are under close surveillance. According to the same source, up to 30 Indonesian students are being trained in "subversion" in Libya (although we have no evidence of this; indeed foreign students in Libya are invariably gainfully enrolled in higher education).[56]

Indonesia through the eyes of the Islamic Republic of Iran

Iranian sources mention four factors which work to prevent Indonesian Muslims from grasping the realities of the Islamic world. These are (1) the cultural heritage of Dutch colonialism; (2) the present domination of the political, economic, and cultural network by global imperialism; (3) the alignment of the present regime to the United States; (4) the policy of repression and other measures taken by the Suharto regime, (5) and the country's relative distance from the center of the world of Islam. According to this account, those *ulama* who have a better understanding of their religious role are either in prison or in exile, while government *ulama*, who are paid by the Ministry of Religious Affairs, are deemed incapable of countering the wrongdoings of government officials. The goals of Indonesian Muslims, then, according to the Khomeini press, are to "counter the irreligious government," fight the conspiratorial expansionism of other religions," and "seek to unite under the Islamic movement."[57]

Viewed historically, according to the Iranian source, the problem began with the "excessive nationalism" of Sukarno who, in a historic blunder, passed over the opportunity to establish an Islamic state by reverting to "an undeveloped system of European humanism and liberalism ... grafted ... to simple traditional values and procedures." The due implementation of the Pancasila doctrine thus provided the "Western enemy with an opportunity to cunningly strengthen the Christian elements and gain wider influence" Sukarno then began to eradicate Muslim fighters who were "seeking an Islamic government" (a reference to the Darul Islam movement of East Java of the early 1950s). But, as the account continues, the New Order regime of General Suharto is even more prepared to impose Pancasila as a political, ideological, and national philosophy at any cost. On a prophetic, if ominous note, the source draws a parallel between the contemporary situation in Indonesia and that of Iran prior to the Islamic Revolution, particularly the lack a middleclass of substance in the country, the prevalence of bribery and discrimination, and the dependence of the country on the U.S.[58]

In summary, then, Khomeini's Iran is expectant that the Islamic restoration Aceh will be followed in other far-flung quarters of the Malay world. Viewing Aceh as the stronghold of Islam in the region and the symbol of unity of the *umma* in Southeast Asia, it holds, in the Iranian interpretation, that the rest of the region will naturally follow Aceh's example in restoring the unity of the *umma* in the manner of the historic spread of Islam in Southeast Asia.[59]

Again to accept a holy war-fanatic-fundamentalist-extremist image or stereotype of the Muslim opposition, as frequently alluded to by the official Indonesian media, is to accept a distorted truth. If the call by the Iranian side for *jihad* finds resonance among the *pesantren* (devout Muslims) of Aceh and indeed elsewhere in the archipelago, then it probably says more about the process of Pancasila democracy in Indonesia.[60] The creation of martyrs *à la* Amir Biki and the detention of liberal critics of the regime's excesses *à la* Dharsono thus appear as more a symptom of the participation crisis than the reaction of a regime confident in direction and accommodating of the pluralist and ethnic diversities of the country. Thus in the wake of the bombings, the myth of Middle Eastern bogeymen (Libya-Iran) fills the void created by the now long-departed PKI, in their separate ways both anathema to the pro-Western order of General Suharto.

Muslim separatism in the Philippines: origins and development

Viewed in historical perspective, the Moros problem can be seen as the dire creation, first, of the Spanish conquistadores who first confronted Muslim power in the Philippines from the sixteenth century; and second, the American "pacifier" who intervened directly in Muslim affairs in the south in the opening years of the century. Having emerged in the late thirteenth century as a separate hegemonic entity to that of Brunei, the Sultanate of Sulu then proceeded to extend its maritime tribute, collecting networks northward. In the face of the aggressive Christianization strategy pursued by the Spanish, however, the Muslim peoples turned to the rhetoric of *jihad* as an ideological counterforce. By 1920, in a change of tack, the America administration of the Philippines transferred effective control over the southern islands to Christian Filipinos. The struggle of the Moros then took on the additional burden of not only upholding their religio-cultural identity, but of resisting Filipinization. But the arrival after the Second World War of large numbers of Christian Filipinos, including forcibly relocated ex-Huks and families, injected a decisive element of competition for land and set the scene for the struggle for autonomy of the Muslim peoples of the south on a modern footing.[61]

Observers have traced this to the formal establishment of a Muslim Independence Movement proclaimed on 1 May 1968, the occasion on which a "manifesto" was issued declaring the creation of an independent Republic of Mindanao and Sulu. Moore, a student of this subject, has described the reaction of the Christian families in the south to this event as first "panic" and then the initiation of raids upon Muslim settlements. The indifference of fence-sitting Muslims, Moore explains, changed when the government decided to send troops to Mindanao to restore law and order. By 1972, when martial law was declared by the Marcos regime, the conflict had extended to Sulu.[62] Indeed, at the time of the author's visit to Mindanao and Sulu in 1974, the situation was that of open warfare. This climaxed in the Battle of Jolo (the de facto Muslim capital of the south), a tactical victory for the Philippines Armed Forces but a strategic politico-military defeat for the Marcos government in view of the internationalization of the conflict. Now under the banner of the Moro National Liberation Front (MNLF), the guerillas went from strength to strength in the face of Army excesses. As witnessed by the author in Mindanao in 1974, this included the burning of mosques. By this point, support—including arms and funds—were flowing to the Moros from various official Muslim sources, including the governments of Libya and Saudi Arabia. Again, as witnessed by the author, the eastern seaboard of the East Malaysian state of Sabah provides a "natural" base for the operations of Filipino Muslim emigres in the Sulu region. Tacit Malaysian government support for these refugee groups cannot be discounted.[63]

According to Cooley, in a cut-and-paste chronicle of Libyan terrorist activities around the world, Marcos, in November 1976, concluding that Gadaffi was the main backer of the MNLF and therefore the figure that could best solve the Moros problem, dispatched his wife Imelda to Tripoli in an attempt to extract pledges from the Libyan leader.[64] Aijaz Ahmad, by contrast, contends that the Islamic Conference, responding to Libyan prodding, was finding it "increasingly difficult not to support the MNLF in the face of escalated terror." The pressure was thus on Marcos to open negotiations. One month later, as it happened, Philippine government emissaries, Islamic Conference envoys and MNLF representatives led by Nur Misuari met together and drew up a preliminary peace accord and ceasefire (the so-called Tripoli Agreement).[65] Back in Manila, Marcos pledged concessions for the south in the way of regional institutions. A Marcos-proposed referendum for the south, however, was rejected out of hand by the MNLF. A second round of negotiations in Tripoli broke off on 3 March and again Imelda proceeded to Tripoli to extract concessions over the question of autonomy for the south. The ensuing referendum, held on

17 April and duly won by Marcos, was boycotted by the MNLF, who claimed that the first Tripoli Agreement had not provided for it. So despite further efforts by the Marcos regime to reinitiate talks, the Islamic Conference members including Libya blamed Marcos' departure from the original agreement in Tripoli. Misuari, who in the event stayed on in Tripoli, revealed that the MNLF had abandoned compromise efforts.[66]

According to Cooley, a split in the MNLF into first two factions and then three was the main reason for an apparent falling away of Libyan interest in the Moros question. This is a reference to the emergence of two factions which split over the issue of Misuari's commitment to military victory. The first of these is moderate Cairo-based faction led by Hashim Salamat while the second has links with Saudi.[67] Aijaz Ahmad points out that in fact Marcos has attempted to exploit factionalism among the Muslim rebels. To this effect he cites documentary evident that proves complicity of a rival so-called Bangsa Moro Liberation Organization headed by "one of the biggest landowners in Mindanao with the Army and intelligence agencies." More damagingly for the unity of the struggle on the ground, various ethnic and regional groups in the south have lined up with one or other of the contending foreign-linked factions.[68]

In May 1977 Nur Misuari announced that the MNLF was returning to its original goal of secession claiming, correctly, that Marcos had failed to respond positively to the MNLF's autonomy formula. This followed a period of internal struggle in the MNLF, leading to the defection/expulsion from the MNLF mainstream Salamat in February 1978. As Aijaz Ahmad explains, this intra-factional struggle has to be viewed against the background of Libyan versus Egyptian, Saudi, American, and Marcos-regime machinations. Misuari, of urban professional background, was exposed during his long sojourn in Libya to "secularist currents and left-wing liberation movements," while Salamat, an Al 'Azhar-trained cleric, became beholden to his respective conservative Middle Eastern patrons. Indeed, at the Islamic Conference Minister's Conference in Dhaka in December 1983, Misuari described Salamat as a "traitor" and as an "instrument of colonialism and the Marcos regime," [70] a reference to the known collaboration of the latter with Philippines ambassadors and government officials.

Thus, as far as the international Islamic connection is concerned, most recent indications are that the center of gravity has swung to the 43 nation Saudi-based Islamic Conference Organization (ICO), leaving Libya with reduced influence of the Moros on the ground. Indeed, the last-reported instance of direct Libyan intervention in the Moros question goes back to March 1979 when the Libyan Ambassador to the Philippines personally intervened to obtain the release of an American missionary seized by Muslims. But in negotiations to obtain the release of a kidnapped foreigner in January 1985, the ICO collectively became involved, and the Sulu Sultan Jamalul Kiram blandly commented on the kidnapping, "It's a way of showing the MNLF still exists today."[71]

According to a report published in the pro-Marcos *Daily Express,* a notorious biased source in consideration of opposition politics in the Philippines, yet another Muslim resistance group surfaced in late 1984, thus raising to four the number of MNLF factions. Numbering between 100 and 2,000 guerillas, this group is believed to have an estimated 20,000 sympathizers. Known as the Philippine Democrat Revolution, it is apparently led by a former ranking member of the MNLF.[72] Dalton, a Manila-based journalist, contends that while front members receive military and ideological training in Sabah, the real patron of this faction remains to identified. Since 1983, Dalton states, initiative on the battlefield has been taken by the so-called "reformist group" of the MNLF headed by Dimas Pundato, who in turn has the backing of local field commanders and many radical groups in the region.[73]

But against this background of splittism and intrigue, the voice of Nur Misuari has again emerged, taking advantage of the publicity surrounding the ICO Foreign Ministers' meeting at Dhaka in December 1983. At this forum, Misuari laid claim to an armed strength of 30,000 for his movement and spoke of a broader-based support for his movement from the Maoist New People's Army (NPA)-linked National Democratic Front and a group called the Philippines Democratic Socialists. As with the leadership of the Libya-based Patani resistance group, Misuari rejected the allegation of complicity with the communists: "We don't have any coordination nor do we sanction this.[74] Misuari who, intriguingly, had entered into negotiations with the Filipino opposition leader Benigno Aquino in Saudi Arabia on more than one occasion, rejected out of hand further negotiations with the "murderous regime" of Marcos in the wake of the exiled opposition leader's killing.[75]

If, in the wake of the assassination of Aquino, the Muslim resistance in the south expanded in tandem with the actions of church groups, students, businesspeople and labor, it is certainly the case that the Marcos government sought to step up its repression of the Muslims. In the words of the *Kayhan* reporter, "answering them with napalm and chemical bombing in Lanao del Sur in Mindanao." Further, Filipino Muslim leaders have requested the Islamic world to cease aiding the Marcos government whose military repression, they assert, "merely hardens the convictions of Muslim leaders who want to establish a Muslim republic.[76] Indeed, according to one expert witness, Iranian influence has already established a beachhead in the city of Marawi in Mindanao,[77] suggesting (but not necessarily establishing) a broader impact throughout the Muslim south.

As in Patani, the origins of the Moro question predate contemporary intervention by external actors, thus believing government propaganda that the problem is wholly imported (as implied by Imelda Marcos' travels to Tripoli in search of a solution). What remains to be analyzed—although this is not our project in this essay—is the degree to which the injection of foreign technology into Mindanao in the form of capital intensive agribusiness has served the government's pacification of the region, thus inflaming the costly Moros wars. As in Patani, a secularist Libya-backed secessionist front competes for the hearts and minds of the local Muslim peoples with conservative Middle Eastern patrons. While the progressive MNLF, on the one hand, finds itself squeezed by co-religionist factions on the right—many of them otherwise class enemies of the Moro peasants and fisherfolk—it appears, on the other hand, that the Maoist NPA is making even further inroads in Mindanao at MNLF expense. Clearly the MNLF has not been able to capitalize upon the crisis besetting the Marcos government. Nor has Libya maintained its pivotal role over the destiny of the secessionist struggle of the Moros people, as established during the early years of the martial law regime. Again the wild card appears to be Iran, but to what extent Iranian propaganda has been internalized—suggesting a deeper degree of religious commitment on the part of the Muslims the Sulu archipelago in their struggle for cultural, social, economic, and political autonomy—remains to be established.

Conclusions

1. With respect to the domestic wellsprings of Islamic resurgence in Southeast Asia, one should not ignore the phenomenon of religion serving to mask deeper social divisions and social stresses. The hallmark of the Iranian revolution—the return to the fundamentals of religion in the face of the stresses of fast-paced modernization and Westernization—is not lost upon either the National Front government in Malaysia or the Indonesian New Order. While the former his attempted to present itself— by coercion as much as inducement—as more holier than the fundamentalist, the latter has revealed itself—at least according to radical Acehnese spokesmen—as worthy successor to the Dutch colonial order. By diluting Islam as a political force, the Suharto regime has at one stroke driven a wedge between collaborating Muslim parties and personalities and the ever-righteous *umma* at large. The Aceh, the Moro, and the Patani cases, we have shown, stand out as case studies of peoples, Muslim peoples of the broadly defined Malay world, marginalized not only as a concomitant of the expansion of core capitalism over the colonial periphery, but as the object of internal colonialism of, respectively, Jakarta, Manila, and Bangkok. The grievance of these peoples, we have seen, have antedated contemporary external (Middle Eastern) interest and, by all indications, may well postdate it, such are the historical roots of the problems. Indeed, the fact that these three peoples have separately taken up arms against their respective governments

suggests that the charge of intervention by outsiders is more than often an ideological smokescreen thrown out by the regimes concerned to stifle real debate as much as to advance the myth of foreign bogey.

2. While internationally Libya and Iran (along with Syria) have drawn closer in their pan-Islamic endeavor, as revealed by the Southeast Asian example, there is no evidence that their respective versions of Islamic internationalism (or for that matter, "nonalignment") coincide. Libya, for one, has gone further than Iran in cementing state-to-state relations (Malaysia), upholding state to state dialogue (Philippines over the Tripoli Agreement), and has been more sensitive to the responsibilities flowing from membership in international fora along with the Muslim countries of Southeast Asia. Indonesia, for example, has actively participated in higher OPEC councils along with Libyan delegates, while Malaysia has frequently been drawn into dialogue with Libya in sessions of the Islamic Conference. But, as with a number of conservative Arab states, Libya has gone further than Iran in actively succoring Muslim liberationist fronts in Southeast Asia. Indeed, as shown above, Libya has matched rhetoric with largesse in consideration of officially approved projects (Malaysia). Iran, on the other hand, with its rhetoric of *jihad*, Islamic social welfarism, anti-Westernism, anti-communism, and the unity of the caliphate, has eclipsed the Libyan *dakwah* project in Southeast Asia from the fundamentalist right by reaching an audience in the *madrasah* (prayer houses) and mosques and even apparently the schools beyond the purview or under the noses of the invigilators of official Islam. While for reasons of state, Iran has moved to cement links—especially trade links—with other states (Malaysia), it continues to direct vitriolic invective against those states which depart from its own version of "true" nonalignment vis-à-vis the superpowers (Indonesia, the Philippines).

3. What should not be ignored in the discussion of external (Middle Eastern) drives of radical Islam in Southeast Asia is the question of domestic restraints. In Libya, as one analyst has pointed out, "it is the issue of oil that is the real measure of Libya's success in foreign policy and revenues depend on Western

willingness to purchase Libyan oil."[78] Suffice it to say that Libya's leverage in the international arena—including the Middle East—has diminished as a result of shrinking oil revenues. Likewise, preoccupation with its own domestic crisis serves to stymie Iran's pan-Islamic project. Nevertheless, while Khomeini is expectant that his Islamic Revolution at home will spontaneously ignite the passions of believers throughout the Islamic world, regardless of sectarian differences (Sunni or Shiite), Gadaffi's proclivity to intervene on the international stage reveals itself as a much more controlled if unpredictable affair, shifting interest (as matched by rhetoric) and investment (as matched by guns and funds) in anti-imperialist (anti-U.S.) as well as Islamic causes from continent to continent, ocean to ocean according to his own calculus of domestic, Arab, pan-Islamic, anti-Zionist and anti-imperialist need.

4. Finally, it is axiomatic that the various appeals of the Muslim peoples of Southeast Asia to the Libyan and Iranian versions of Islamic universalism—Islamic socialist on the one hand and Islamic fundamentalist on the other—as much as the endeavor of these two Middle Eastern states to promote their respective social utopias globally, are bound to come into conflict with the Western-derived principles of international law, to which the Southeast Asian states purport to adhere.

Notes

1. Eg, see *Monthly Review*, 36, 3 (July-August 1984): *passim*. While finding areas of convergence between Christianity and the left in certain settings, this volume has nothing to say about the role of Islam in opposition to dictatorship, much less its "liberationist"versus obscurantist potential.

2. E. Mortimer, *Faith, and Power: The Politics of Islam* (London: Faber and Faber, 1982): 279.

3. Muammar Al Qadhafi, *The Green Book: The Social Basis of the Third Universal Theory* (Part Three),Tripoli (1979): 1.

4. Ibid: 10.

5. R.B. St. John, "The Ideology of Muammar Al-Quadhafi: Theory and Practice," *International Journal of Middle East Studies*, 15, (1983). In this study St. John comments that even with the

publication of the three parts of *The Green Book,* Gadaffi has "still not provided a logical, in depth, systematic discussion of his thought," p.472.

6. *Jamahiriyah Mail,* 16 June 1984.

7. Mortimer, *Faith and Power:* 282.

8. *The Green Book.*

9. A.H. Ferdous, "Khomeini and the Fadayanis Society and Politics," *International Journal of Middle East Studies,* 15 (1983): 244.

10. Mortimer, *Faith and Power:* 282.

11. R.K. Ramazani, "Iran's Islamic Revolution and the Persian Gulf," *Current History,* (January 1985): 5.

12. *Kayhan International,* Teheran, 10 February 1985.

13. *Kayhan* (editorial), 3 March 1985.

14. Ramazani, "Iran's Islamic Revolution...,": 7.

15. M. Ladd Thomas, *Political Violence in the Muslim Provinces of Southern Thailand,* (Singapore: ISEAS Occasional Paper, No. 28, April 1975).

16. Pitsuwan Surin, "Islam and Malay Nationalism: A Case Study of the Malay Muslim, of Southern Thailand," unpublished Ph.D. thesis Harvard University, 1982.

17. CIA Research Reports, Southeast Asia, 1946-1976, "Security Situation in Thailand."

18. Thomas, *Political Violence:* 17-19.

19. J.McBeth, *Far Eastern Economic Review* (*FEER*), 20 June 1980. Most recently official Thai spokesmen put the number of PULO separatists to 250 broken up into groups of 10 to 15 each *(Bangkok Post,* 9 March 1985).

20. *Mimbar Socialis,* 3, 8 (October 1976).

21. See Thomas, *Political Violence* and Pitsuwan Surin, "Islam and Malay Nationalism..." for basic data on the three fronts. The reader should be cautioned, however, that there is a tendency in the literature on the Muslim insurgency to recycle uncritically data originating from Thai intelligence sources, a criticism from which the last cited author is not immune.

22. Interview by author, Benghazi, April 1984.

23. *Mimbar Socialist.*

24. Interview.

25. *Bangkok Post,* 20 April 1985

26. Thai Supreme Headquarters, Bangkok Home Service, 27 January 1985, Foreign Broadcast Information Service, 4 February 1985.

27. Paisal Sricharatchanya, *FEER,* 23 May 1985.

28. *Bangkok Post,* 19 March 1985.

29. *New Straits Times,* 17 and 18 January 1980.

30. *Malaysian Digest,* 31 January 1984.

31. *South,* February 1985.

32. R.S. Milne and D.K. Mauzy, "The Mahathir Administration in Malaysia: Discipline Through Islam," *Pacific Affairs,* 56, 4 (1983-84): 643.

33. R. Tasker, *FEER,* 6 December 1984.

34. R.S. Milne and D.K. Mauzy, "Malaysia: Politics and Leadership," *Current History,* (December 1984): 429.

35. AFP report carried in *The Australian,* 14 Sept. 1984. According to one Malaysian press report, derived from a Thai press source, a link existed between former PAS President Datuk Asri Muda and Muslim separatists in the south of Thailand. The ABIM (Malaysian Muslim Youth Movement) was seen as recruiting volunteers in support of the rebels. Although denied by Asri at the 1973 Islamic Conference meeting in Kuala Lumpur, he nevertheless pledged his support to Muslim rebels in Thailand and the Philippines. *The Star* (Penang) 31 December 1980. (My thanks to S. Barraclough for drawing attention to this source.)

36. S. Barraclough, "Managing the Challenges of Islamic Revival in Malaysia: A Regime Perspective,"*Asian Survey,* XXVI, 8, (August 1983): 961.

37. K. Das, *FEER:* 13 October 1983.

38. *Malaysian Digest,* 31 January 1984.

39. J. Clad, *FEER,* 9 August 1984.

40. *FEER,* 21 February 1985.

41. *Kayhan,* 13 January 1985.

42. *Keesings,*16-23, 11364, (January 1954).

43. *Kayhan,* 13 January 1985. See the spirited letter by Tengku di Tiro published in *FEER,* 10 January 1985. Here he states, "I have only one message to give to your readers: the Javanese can never protect Western interests outside Java against the power of the indigenous peoples once they are aroused and organized against Javanese colonialism. And that is inevitable."

44. *Keesings,* 29 July 1977.

45. *Keesings,* 29074 (7 July 1978).

46. *Keesings,* 32257 (July 1983).

47. G. Sacerdoti, *FEER,* 10 April 1981.

48. *Kayhan,* 13 January 1985.

49. J. Van der Kroef, "Indonesia: Prophylactic Murder and the Legacy of Gestapo," *Solidarity,* 99.

50. Known to the author during a two month sojourn in Tanjong

Priok in 1968, Amir Biki revealed himself as one who had already
distanced himself from the reactionary ideology promoted by KAMI-
KAPI the anti-Sukarnoist student movement to which he belonged.
It was apparent to the author that Amir Biki's concern with the glar-
ing contradictions of power, wealth, corruption and poverty, as symbolized by the overcrowded harbourside city, had brought him into
deep conflict with the KKO/Angkatan Laut (Army-Navy) and the
criminal gangs who ruled the port as a private fiefdom. This throws
scepticism upon some published reports that Amir Biki was in the
pay of Indonesian intelligence.

51. D.E. Weatherbee, "Indonesia in 1984: Pancasila, Politics and
Power, *Asian Survey,* (February 1985): 187.

52. Susumu Awonahara, *FEER,* 25 October 1984 and see articles
published by this author during late 1984 and early 1985 on the general subject of Islam and politics in Indonesia. Also see, M. Lane,
"The Tanjong Priok Incident," *Inside Indonesia,* (4 March 1985).

53. *South,* January 1984 and M. Lane, ibid. Although Sanusi, a
Muslim politician and Minister of Light Industries under President
Sukarno was subsequently charged by the State with masterminding
the explosions and was duly sentenced to 19 years in prison, his
connection with radical Islam remained "obscure" and no apparent
charges of foreign intervention were laid (see L. Kaye, *FEER,* 23
May 1985 and Reuter report SCMP, 16 May 1985).

54. S. Awonahara, *FEER,* 24 January 1985.

55. H. Enayat, *Modern Islamic Political Thought,* (London:
Macmillan, 1982): 155.

56. *South,* January 1985.

57. *Kayhan,* 18 November 1984.

58. *Kayhan,* 23 September 1984.

59. Ibid.

60. On this question, see Chapter 1.

See *Tapol Bulletin, no.* 50 March 1982. According to Adnam
Buyung Nasution, the Indonesian human rights lawyer who set up
the first Legal Aid Institute in Jakarta over thirteen year ago, Muslim
groups in Indonesia (as distinguished from their co-religionists in
Thailand and the Philippines) have not even developed strong Pan-
Islamic links. In a further turn of the screw on 31 May 1985,
Indonesia's parliament adopted a law proscribing any social or
religious organization from receiving unauthorized foreign funds.
Muslim, Christian, environmentalist groups as well as the Legal Aid
Institute, among others; sections of society, expressed firm opposition
to this legislation (AFP in *South China Morning Post,* 1 June 1985.)

61. See R.L.P. Moore, "Women and Warriors: Defending Islam in the Southern Philippines," unpublished Ph.D., University of California (1981): 63-83, and see a Aijaz Ahmad class and Colony in Mindanao," *Southeast Asia Chronicle,* 82, (February 1982): 4-10.

62. Moore, ibid.

63. If in the past the government of Sabah under the chief minister, Tun Mustapha Harun had provided succor to MNLF element, successive administrations have been bound to degrees, by the constraints imposed by Kuala Lumpur. Willingness on the part of Manila to set aside the issues pertaining to the Sabah dispute—in the interests of ASEAN unity—can be perceived as a quid pro quo for non-interference on the past of Malaysia in the Muslim insurgency in the Philippines.

64. J.K. Cooley, *Libyan Sandstorm,* (Holt, Rinehart and Winston, 1982): 225-227.

65. Aijaz Ahmad, "The War Against the Muslims," *Southeast Asia Chronicle,* 82 (February 1982): 19.

66. Cooley, *Libyan Sandstorm.* For details of the provisions of the Tripoli Agreement as well as MNLF perceptions of government goals with regard to the Muslim South plus MNLF historiographical treatment of the problem, see P.G. Gowing, "Contrasting Agendas for Peace in the Southern Philippines," *Kabar Seberang,* 8/9 (1981) passim.

67. Cooley, ibid.

68. Aijaz Ahmad, "The War Against the Muslims..." Geographically, Nur Misuari derives support from the Zamboanga and Tawi Tawi area, Hashim Salamat from Davao and Cotabato and Dimas Pundato (a third faction leader) from the Lanao area.

69. Aijaz Ahmad, "The War Against the Muslims..."

70. S. Kamaluddin and R. Tasker, *FEER,* 22 December 1983.

71. *Kayhan,* 27 January 1985. According to a letter issued by a Saudi-based spokesman of the MNLF published in *FEER,* 21 March 1985, the release was achieved by Nur Misuari in deference to the ICO.

72. *Daily Express,* cited in *Kayhan,* 6 January 1985.

73. J. Dalton, *The Australian,* 5-6 January 1985.

74. Kamaluddin and Tasker, *FEER,* 22 December 1983.

75. *Kayhan,* 18 November 1984.

76. Ibid.

77. R.K. Ramazani, "Iran's Islamic Revolution...,": 5

78. G. Henderson, "Libya: Redefining the Revolution," *Africa Report,* 29 (November-December 1984).

5. Death and the State in Malaysia

The murder/execution of two Australians convicted of narcotics trafficking by the Malaysian state on 7 July 1986 has not only concentrated the minds of thinking Australians and Malaysians on the question of capital punishment but has focused international attention on that country's judicial system, its political processes, and its human-rights image. Termed a matter of "national security" by the National Front Government of Mohammad Mahathir owing to the generalized nature of drug trafficking and drug addiction in the country, such cases as that of Chambers and Barlow are by definition never clear-cut civil cases but owing to their internationalization, are of the nature of political trials. A travesty of natural justice on any count, the specter of the victims may well return to haunt the National Front Government, in much the way that the viciousness of colonial orders in the Third World spelled their eventual undoing at the hands of the oppressed. Pudu prison in Kuala Lumpur as much as Pulo Condor/Con Son prison in Vietnam are visible symbols of this truism.

As I see the matter, three lies are central to the Malaysian Government's case in support of capital punishment, all of which have—to degrees—been echoed or magnified by the semi-official Malaysian press as well as the "autonomous" Australian press. Government propagandists would have the rest of the world believe, first, that there is no domestic opposition to capital punishment; second, and this is for domestic consumption also, that capital punishment meted out to the smallest cogs in the narcotics trade is a righteous act that cleanses society of evil and corruption; and third, that civil justice is done in a system where erosion of the autonomy of the judiciary is a hallmark of the administration.

In the following I will expose these lies, arguing that the

Malaysian Government, in inheriting the formidable apparatus of state repression of the not-long-departed colonial administration, has proven itself a worthy successor of the latter in social control, in maintaining social hierarchies, and in denying natural justice to the masses. If the threat of the Red Menace (CTs or communist terrorists in the official jargon) no longer appears as a plausible prop to a repressive state, then the social menace represented by the narcotics epidemic serves as a convenient surrogate to achieve the same end among an erstwhile acquiescent populace. I will argue that, compounding the problem arising from this myth-making, the National Front Government does not approach socio-economic problems in a holistic fashion; rather, it eschews a therapeutic approach to the narcotics problem, and it declines to adopt a punitive approach to the big wheels of corruption within and outside the administration.

It is clear that in mid-1986, faced with a convergence of crises political, economic and, social, Malaysia faced a watershed. Already, as revealed by Mahathir in an interview on the Australian Broadcasting Commission (ABC)'s "Carleton-Walsh Report" on 28 May, the Government has been obliged to backpeddle on one of the more controversial planks of its social engineering program, namely the New Economic Policy (although this has not been allowed to be publicized in the local Malay/English language press). The new direction involves holding in abeyance the scheme of positive economic discrimination in favor of the Malays *(bumiputras)*, which otherwise seeks to eradicate poverty and to redistribute wealth. But while the fetters on production across the ethnic spectrum have been lifted—in the face of declining world commodity prices—and in the interest of co-opting Chinese financial capital, the regime has in no way abandoned its communalist rhetoric and policies. While the National Front Government has achieved stunning successes in co-opting its former political enemies— even former political detainees—it has shown no signs of dismantling the edifice of the apparatus of state repression of which capital punishment is the cornerstone (as indeed it was under the colonial order). What, then, constitutes a capital offense in Malaysia?

Narcotics trafficking stands as one of at least several crimes punishable by death under the Malaysian Penal Code. These include:

1. waging war against the Government (section 121);
2. intending hurt or death to or restraint of the head of state (212A);
3. perjury resulting in the execution of a person indicted on a capital charge (194);
4. abetting suicide of certain categories (305);
5. kidnapping for murder (364);
6. certain offenses relating to mutiny in the armed forces (132).

In September 1975 the imposition of the death penalty on persons found possessing firearms, ammunition, or explosives in an area declared a security area was added to this list.[1]

The full weight of the penal code can only be understood alongside the Internal Security Act (ISA) of 1960 and the Essential (Security Cases) Amendment Regulations (ESCAR) of 1975. This is not the place to spell out the details of these notorious acts, well documented in the human rights literature. Suffice it to say that in combination, they bring to bear on the population the full weight of the state's dissuasive and repressive powers while denying the individual the minimum of rights underwritten in international human rights covenants.[2] Indeed, in commenting upon these regulations the International Commission of Jurists observed that they appear to go beyond what is strictly required for protecting the "life of the nation" as opposed to the "life of the government in power." [3] As a Malaysian critic of the ISA, Azmi Khalid has stated, "the only protection for the rights of individuals rests upon the unfettered discretion of executive officials."[4]

Trafficking in narcotics in Malaysia was first proclaimed a capital offence in April 1975 when an amendment to the Narcotics Act was approved by Parliament. Prior to this amendment the maximum penalty under the Narcotics Act was seven years' imprisonment. But as one student of the Malaysian human rights scene, John Lent, has written, the first hangings in Malaysia, after a lapse of eleven years, occurred on 6 January 1976.

However, it was not until September 1977, when the death sentence was meted out to a 14 year-old charged with the illegal possession of a firearm, that the alarm was raised in both domestic and international circles.[5] Indeed, such was the public outrage, especially from within the boy's community, that it might be said that the event triggered the opening salvos of the anti-capital punishment movement within Malaysia.

At a more formal level, the anti-capital punishment banner in. Malaysia has been variously taken up by a diversity of groups. These include the multiracial, nonpartisan social reform movement Aliran (which publishes a journal of the same name); the Young Christian Workers; the Environmental Protection Society; the United Chinese Schools Committees Association; the Young Buddhist Association of Malaysia; and the Muslim reform group, ABIM.[6] To these might be added the Consumers' Association of Penang, the Malaysian Bar Association, and the leading opposition party, the Democratic Action Party. Other voices include political exiles, Malaysian students abroad (albeit gagged if they received government scholarships) and concerned individuals at home.

Internationally, Amnesty International has spearheaded the campaign against the use of the death penalty in Malaysia and has likewise expressed concern about the continuing long-term detention without trial of about 160 people under the ISA (a number of whom it has nominated as prisoners of conscience). Growing international concern around the world at the number of executions carried out in Malaysia prompted a visit to Kuala Lumpur in 1982 by the Paris-based International Mission of Lawyers. *Inter alia,* their duly issued report called for the repeal of ESCAR and, in recognition of the substantially improved security situation in Malaysia, the release of detainees held under the ISA.[7]

In what could only be described as an unmitigated act of state vengeance, the Mahathir Government declared in 1983 that the possession of more than fifteen grams of heroin or 200 grams of cannabis was punishable by a mandatory death sentence Singapore and Brunei Darussalam soon followed suit. In relative terms these laws are as hypocritical as they are draconian. In most Western countries, fifteen grams of heroin would be considered a non-traffickable amount, merely enough to satisfy an addict's habitual use. In communist Laos, to strike a regional comparison, marijuana is still publicly sold and consumed as soup seasoning, which, no doubt. was the case in Malaysia in its pre-colonial past.

In 1984 an amendment to the ISA gave wide-ranging and arbitrary powers to police officers and the Minister concerned. It provides for detention without trial and, equally disturbing, provides for detention on the basis of suspicion. Even the reasons for detention are not open to judicial review. Although a detainee can make representation to an Advisory Board, its decisions cannot be called to account.[8] In cold terms, as domestic Malaysian critics of the Act have observed, Malaysia stands alone in the world in investing its government with the power of detention without trial to deal with the drug problem. As the Penang-based social reform group Aliran has commented, existing laws, namely the ISA, the Emergency Public Orders and Prevention of Crime Ordinance 1969, can also be employed to detain drug traffickers without trial. As Aliran acerbically comments, this just reveals the "limit of legalistic solutions" (to the drug menace in the country) and is symptomatic of the Government's approach "to lump power upon power unto itself."[9]

Since 1975, the year that the Narcotics Act was introduced, nearly forty offenders have been hanged (including six non-citizens) and over 100 await trial or appeal. Aside from narcotics cases, several other capital punishment cases in Malaysia merit attention.

For example, the case of Tan Chay Wa, who was hanged on 18 January 1983 under the provisions of ESCAR and notwithstanding an offer by the Government of Belgium to grant him political asylum should he be allowed to leave Malaysia. A known political dissident in Singapore, he was apprehended soon after his arrival in Malaysia for possession of a pistol. Despite the discrepancy between the gun he was alleged to have possessed at the time of his arrest and the number presented as evidence at his trial, he was duly executed.[10]

A second incident worthy of mention also concerns a case

involving firearms, which along with narcotics cases provide the
majority of those sentenced to capital punishment. In this
instance, the condemned, a local farmer, was found guilty for
possession of a single bullet and executed accordingly. If the
punishment seems disproportionate to this crime, then the
government crossed one more hurdle in both its repressiveness
and in its preparation of public opinion by the hanging of a
foreign national, a Thai taxi driver, found in possession of two
pistols and ammunition.[11] Yet another threshold was crossed with
the hanging of the first woman, who along with her husband was
found in possession of hand grenades.[12]

The lie to the government's propaganda that its imposition
of capital punishment is unchallenged by the community was
demonstrated in 1982 when the mandatory death sentence as a
penalty for possession of a firearm (ISA S57(1)) was challenged,
albeit unsuccessfully, in the Federal Court as contravening
articles of the Constitution relating to the deprivation of life and
liberty and other clauses.[13] This is but one of numerous rearguard
actions on the part of the judiciary to stem the erosion of its
autonomy vis-à-vis the executive arm of government.

The dispensation of justice Malaysia-style was pointed up
by the country's first political murder trial, which started on 12
October 1982. The bizarre case involved the murder of the
speaker of the Negri Sembilan State Assembly at the hands of
his political rival, the then Minister for Culture, Youth and Sport,
Datuk Mochtar Hashim.[14] Although duly convicted for murder,
the death sentence imposed on the Minister was commuted by
the Pardons Board. According to Amnesty International, the
Minister is "the only prisoner sentenced to death to have had
his sentence commuted by a Pardons Board in recent years."[15]

As a sequel to this tale one ISA detainee, Sim Kie Chin,
gathered the attention and support of several groups, namely
opposition parties, Aliran and the Malaysian Bar Council. They
argued that while the Pardons Board had commuted the death
sentence for the Minister, it refused it for Sim. On 10 September
1985 the vice-president of the Malaysian Bar Council, Param
Cumaraswamy, was arrested under the Sedition Act for a press
statement he made in July asking the Pardons Board to

reconsider its refusal to commute Sim's death sentence. In his statement Cumaraswamy evidently questioned the manner in which the Pardons Board had exercised its duties.[16] As a result, the human rights lawyer was acquitted by the High Court.

In October 1977 the "usually docile" Malaysian Bar Council passed a resolution calling on lawyers to boycott trials under ESCAR as "oppressive and against the rule of law." But to circumvent the lawyers' boycott, the Legal Profession Amendment Act of 1977 was introduced. As Lent reported, the Bar Council saw this Act as a deliberate attempt to muzzle the Bar.[17] In another measure to interfere with the independence of the judiciary, further amendments were made in August 1983 to the same Act. Over the protest of the Bar Association, the Attorney General (legally qualified although not a member of the Bar) has been made the approving authority with respect to rules pertaining to practice, etiquette and discipline.[18]

Commensurate with the assault on the judiciary from within has been the erosion of the system from without. This is seen in the way in which broader public support for the maintenance of the jury system in Malaysia has waned. While formerly restricted to capital charges and while never existing right across the board in Malaysia, the jury system is now effectively restricted to murder trials. (Trial by jury has been abolished for capital drug offenses.) The case against the maintenance of the jury system has been succinctly expressed by a former Solicitor General, Taii Sri Datuk Mohammed Salleh bin Abbas, who pronounced, "The only merit I can see of the jury system of trial is that it operates in favor of the accused person." One student of the question, Leong, mentions two reasons for the prevailing anti-jury attitude in Malaysia; first, the "lack of social or civil responsibility," and, second (as in Singapore), "changed public mood."[19] The argument that British and Malaysian social climates are variant and do not necessarily support the same social institutions (such as the jury system) may be intrinsically appealing to Malaysian nationalists, but proponents of the rule of law in the country, such as the Bar Association, have not shown signs of willingness to capitulate completely to constitutional tampering and executive fiat.

The righteousness of the National Front Government in prosecuting the draconian anti-narcotic laws in the effort to net (fearlessly?) the smallest pusher has unfortunately not been matched in rooting out big corruption in the Administration and commercial world. Rather, it thrives in scandalous proportions, sapping public morale, business, and even the stock exchange. By 1979, annual corruption complaints had reached 8,500, resulting in 128 people being arrested and charged. Of these, eighty-six were public servants. In 1980, 178 arrests were made and again the majority were public servants. In 1983 even the top administrator of Malaysia's Anti-Corruption Agency was among those convicted on an anti-corruption charge.[20] The fact that token efforts have been made to address the problem does not absolve the government from responsibility. A case in point is the Bank Bumiputra scandal concerning questionable investments in a Hong Kong investment fund. This touches the highest echelons of the United Malay National Organization (UMNO) component of the National Front Government. Another case is the scandal involving Tan Koon Swan, President of the Malaysian Chinese Association (MCA) component of the National Front Government, who is currently facing charges in Singapore of cheating, bribery, etc, on a massive scale.

The broader question of corruption in Malaysian society was brought into focus at a dialogue session hosted by Aliran in September 1984, which gathered together various oppositionist groups. At this meeting a declaration was promulgated which identified corruption as "a social scourge" and "one of the main causes for the declines and destruction of societies." A call was also made for liberalization of the press to allow further exposure of corruption. Linked to this was the call for greater government accountability to the public through such legislation as a freedom of information Act.[21] In practice, the flow of information from government to public was further eroded in 1983 by the amendment to the Official Secrets Act 1972 to make it an offence to receive and disseminate government information. In fact, the original act was modeled upon British legislation drafted and passed on the eve of World War II as a guard against espionage.[22]

If narcotics corruption cases involving officers of the state have not figured notably in convictions arising out of corruption cases in general, then it is because the networks are too pervasive. As the two condemned Australians pathetically revealed to the media, narcotics—and hence corruption—infuse the fabric of the prison system. Indeed, as the government concedes, only some 10 percent of the narcotics flowing south of the Thai border are intercepted despite the *cordon sanitaire* thrown up on the Malaysian side.   This means that the other 90 percent of non-intercepted narcotics are circulating through Malaysia with or without the connivance of officialdom. As I will demonstrate below, symbiotic links in Malaysia between traffickers and officers of the state, the police, the prison officials, customs officials and local authorities with a stake on the squeeze have been organically established since colonial times.

The most publicized capital punishment case in Malaysia has undoubtedly been the case of Chambers and Barlow, the first Westerners to be executed in Malaysia since colonial times and the first Australians hanged since 1967. The mood in Australia is against capital punishment and the Labor Government has long had an anti-capital punishment stand. Apart from intense media interest, certain features of this case set it apart. First, the dubious manner of judicial process. Second, unsuccessful pleas from the Prime Ministers of Australia and the United Kingdom to their Malaysian counterpart to intervene in the case on the side of clemency. One disturbing feature of the judicial process, at least according to a non-Malaysian witness, was the suppression of incriminating evidence, namely informers' evidence, thus making the Prosecution's case appear to rely on circumstantial evidence. Neither were the drug habits of the accused mentioned, as clearly this would have weakened the Prosecution's case further by exposing the endemic heroin trade within the Malaysian prison system.[23] The last step in this *danse macabre* was the signing of the death warrant while the High Court dispute was pending in answer to the plea that the Penang

Pardons Board had contravened natural justice by admitting to its hearing only the prosecution and no defense lawyers.

While Chambers and Barlow's defense lawyers in particular have been critical of the Australian Government for not making more forceful representations to the Malaysian side, in fact the Australian Foreign Minister Bill Hayden commenced formal representations to the Malaysian Government immediately after the failure of appeals to the High Court in December. These calls were repeated in March and with the Prime Minister lending his voice in the run up to the execution date. On the same day, the Australian Labor Party National Conference, then in session, passed a resolution expressing "extreme regret at the hangings." The Prime Minister himself termed them "barbaric." The assistant director of the Australian Institute of Criminology termed the hangings not only grotesque and ineffectual but an act of "legalized murder." As the Melbourne *Age* editorialized, "Nothing was achieved by this ritual killing, apart from the agony of innocent relatives, some possible momentary political advantage to certain people in Malaysia and an excuse for indignant headlines and mawkish television in Australia."[24] What, then, are the roots of the narcotics problem in Malaysia?

As in Thailand and French Indochina, the British in Malaya and the Straits Settlements derived substantial state revenues from the sale of opium through licensed outlets and accruing to the state Opium Monopoly. So too, via special arrangements, did such key local collaborators as the Sultan of Johore. For instance, in 1938 in the Johore state of British Malaya alone, some 197,367 tahils of opium were sold, down from 225,211 the preceding year and bringing in state revenues of 2,146,329 Straits dollars. According to a colonial report the decrease in consumption was due not only to economic causes but also to a reduction in the number of (licensed) smokers admitted to a register of addicts on the production of medical certificates. In that year, 153 tahils of illicit *chandu* (opium) were seized along with sizeable quantities of dross. Jealous of its monopoly, the colonial state in Johore recorded 477 convictions under the Opium and Chandu Enactment.[25] Thus while the worst human abuses of the drug trade were mitigated by a register of addicts (which included Europeans, although Chinese were predominant), breaches of the system, as implied by the number of convictions, were already rife.

With the outbreak of war, the system of state monopolies was interrupted. Overall, the addict population of Malaysia and Singapore had declined from a prewar figure of 186,000 to a figure of 40,000 by the late 1960s.[26] But by then the drug trade was privatized and illicit profits were flowing into the hands of the *towkay* of the West Coast Chinatowns in arrangements best dubbed "AliBaba relationships," sealed by political deals and consummated in mahjong games. Needless to say, the alcohol and tobacco business, the bane of a "true" Islamic order, continues to flourish as a licit activity.

An insidious counter-trend was at work, however, and had its regional origins in Thailand: the creation of demand for heroin (there was no parallel to the Japanese wartime trafficking in morphia in Southeast Asia, as was the case in China). In 1950, opium produced five and a half million U.S. dollars' revenue for the Thai state. But with the enforcement of a prohibition on opium sale in Thailand in 1958, traders and consumers turned to heroin, easy to manufacture from the local poppy and more portable than opium. As the anthropologist Geddes has written, while the coming of heroin in the region may have been inevitable, "the legislation designed to reduce the incidence of drug taking, may well have had the effect of increasing it."[27] Writing of the anti-opium legislation enforced in Laos under U.S. prodding some ten years later, the psychiatrist Westermeyer arrived at similar conclusions.[28]

All governments in the region share the view endorsed by the United Nations that prohibition is necessary to control narcotics consumption, and accordingly have taken measures to police the trade. Yet in all Southeast Asian countries, including Hong Kong (perhaps communist Laos is an exception here), the suppression of opium smoking over the past two decades has only been matched by a drastic rise in heroin addiction. At the same time, the profile of the addict has changed—from the elderly Chinese as predominant user to people of working age, of all ethnic groups, as predominant users. With the exponential rise in the cost of supporting a habit, so the incidence of crime has risen. While this is a familiar story around the world and requires no elaboration, the point is that the solution is as complicated as the problem is intractable.

Conclusion

We have seen above that opposition to capital punishment from across a broad spectrum of the Malaysian community coincides with a popular stand against big corruption reaching into the ruling party and coincides with a principled defense of civil liberties and the autonomy of the judiciary from within and without the legal world.

As Aliran has stated the matter, "the various restrictive labor laws, the Universities and Colleges Act, the Societies Act, ESCAR, the validation of emergency legislation" are proof of the authoritarian trend in Malaysia over the past ten years.[29] Indeed, to these measures might be added attempts to tamper with the Constitution, the tightening in 1984 of the Printing Press and Publications Act, the amendment in 1983 of the Official Secrets Act, thus stifling the flow of information from Government to public, the gagging in 1983 of sponsored Malaysian students abroad and the threat to vernacular instruction in schools which the Education Act poses. Again, as Aliran states, "the executive is so powerful that it even exercises powers over the legislature and some of the rights of the judiciary."

Nevertheless, subtle transformations of the political landscape suggest that the Malaysian state may yet meet its nemesis. One straw in the wind is the emergence of a Civil Rights Committee (CRC) formed of twenty-seven Chinese clans, education and community groups, critical of big corruption and seeking to challenge National Front political hegemony. According to one commentator, CRC poses a real threat to UMNO by openly allying itself with the leading Malay opposition party, PAS.[30]

If anything good were to come out of the case of Chambers and Barlow, at least for the Australian side, it would be a stimulus to proposals now being canvassed by the Australian Government to enter into bilateral extradition treaties for prisoners. Indeed, Washington has urged Pakistan to enter into such a treaty in the case of narcotics offenders. As Malaysia demonstrated with grotesque finality, the assertion of sovereignty and legal jurisdiction over foreign nationals cannot be easily challenged, especially when the political credibility of the regime is at stake. In Malaysia, of course, the victimized Chinese community would reject political favors to outsiders denied to themselves.

With the central validating myth of the "Communist Emergency" nullified as the armed remnants of the Communist Party of Malaya either surrender or become marginalized, the National Front Government faces either alienating its increasingly angry, cynical and politically conscious middle-class constituency completely, or having to tighten the screws of repression even further in order to maintain its political hegemony and silence its critics.

Notes

1. Amnesty, *Report of an Amnesty International Mission to the Federation of Malaysia*, 18-30 November 1978, (London: Amnesty International British Section, 1979).

2. See Ibid., passim.

3. Quoted in Hua Wu Yin, *Class and Comunalism in Malaysia* (London: Zed Press, 2nd ed., 1983): 183.

4. Azmi Khalid, "Law and the Decline of Freedom in Malaysia," in H.M. Scoble and L. S. Wiseburg, *Access to Justice* (London, 2nd ed., 1985): 89.

5. John A. Lent, "Human Rights in Malaysia," *Journal of Contemporary Asia,* 14, 4 (1984): 445.

6. *Far Eastern Economic Review* (Hong Kong) 26 November 1983.

7. *Human Rights Internet Reporter* (Washington; 8, 2/3 December 1983.

8. Anon, "Hanging Law: Another Light of Freedom Put Out," USAHA, Malaysian Student, Organization, UNSW, 1985.

9. Ibid.

10. *Human Rights Internet Reporter*, 8, 4 & 5, April-June 1983.

11. ABC Radio News Report, 20 January 1983.

12. ABC Radio News Report, 2 February 1983.

13. Param Cumaraswamy, *Lawasia* I, 2 (January 1983).

14. *Far Eastern Economic Review,* 22-28, October 1982.

15. Amnesty International Urgent Action, ASA, 28 May 1985, 76, 1986.

16. Asia Yearbook 1986, *Far Eastern Economic Review.*

17. Lent, *"Human Rights in Malaysia,"* : 445.

18. Cumaraswamy, *Lawasia,* II, 2, (January 1984).

19. A. P. B. Leong, "Jury Trial in Singapore and Malaysia: The Unmaking of a Legal Institution," *Malaysian Law Review,* 25 (1983): 85.

20. *Far Eastern Economic Review,* 12 May 1983.

21. *Human Rights Internet Reporter,* September-December 1984.

22. AFP in *South China Morning Post ,* 21 November 1985.

23. L. Mackay, *The Australian,* 23 June 1986.

24. *The Age,* 8 July 1986.

25. *Annual Report,* Johore, 1938, (London: H. M. Stationary Office, 1939).

26. Alfred McCoy, *The Politics of Heroin,* (New York: Harper & Row, 1972).

27. William Geddes, *Migrants of the Mountains,* (London: Claridon, 1976).

28. Joseph Westermeyer, *Poppies, Pipes and People: Opium its Use in Laos* (Berkeley: University of California, 1982).

29. *Aliran,* "The Constitutional Crisis and Democracy," Penang.

30. C. Murray, *Sydney Morning Herald,* 5 July 1986.

6. The Image of Brunei in Western Literature

In his classic study of the relationship of the West to the East through literature, Edward Said arrives at a new gloss upon the term orientalism. This he describes as "a way of coming to terms with the Orient that is based on the Orient's special place in European Western experience" (Said 1978: 1). The Occident-Orient relationship is not equal but is "a relationship of power, of domination, of varying degrees of a complex hegemony..." (Said 1978: 5). Intellectually, orientalism emerged as a "dynamic exchange" between individual authors and in turn, academic interpreters of the "intellectual and imaginative territory" shaped by the great British, French, and American empires (Said 1978: 14). The legacy of orientalism, then, according to Said, is the distribution or translation of this geographical sense into "aesthetic, scholarly, economic, sociological, historical, and philological texts..." (Said 1978: 12). Since the publication of Said's *Orientalism*, it is not possible to view Western writings on eastern themes but through a colonial optic. Said's method of textual deconstruction of erstwhile orientalist texts has not only changed academic perspectives on colonial literature but has challenged the assumptions of the academic status of so-called area studies. It also provides a clear-sighted optic through which the *indigènes* can first view and then recover their own history. Consistent with the broad philological method outlined by Said, this chapter looks to the systematic textual deconstruction of the genre of Western writing on one geographical area, namely Borneo/Brunei.

Western writing or "literature," loosely defined includes the works of early Western explorers, adventurers, naturalists, administrators—their cartographers and scribes included—and

writers who sojourned or resided in this area and recorded their
impressions in the form of short stories or novels. But who were
the audiences of these texts? Clearly, audiences differed through
time but were—and still are—largely metropolitan and Western.
Another audience in the modern period is the burgeoning Eng-
lish-speaking Asian middleclasses who have assumed certain of
the attitudes and prejudices of the West. Westerner, however,
implies a colonial or imperial vision otherwise distinguishable
from Arab, Chinese, or Indonesian perspectives to degrees
deemed part of a local tradition and therefore of a qualitatively
different order.

We would do well here to bear in mind the words of D.C.R.A.
Goonetilleke, the Sri Lankan author of *Images of the Raj: South
Asia in the Literature of Empire,* who cautions us on "the com-
plexities of the relation between the world of imagination and
the world of historical, political and biographical facts," the
facile confusion between the "ways of the artist with the method
of the historian" (Goonetilleke 1988: 6). Nevertheless, the selection, the ordering of facts as much as the imposition of se-
quence or chronology is also the method of the historian and to
which we adhere in the structuring of this chapter.

Brooke, Borneo and the image of the White Rajah in the fiction of Joseph Conrad

Arguably, few figures in the history of British imperialism could
rival that of the White Rajah of Borneo, James Brooke, not only
in extending the frontiers of empire, but for offering up the image
and symbol of the white man (the *orang putih*) as natural leader.
In Victorian imagination Brooke stood for empire, enterprise,
adventure, and progress over tyrannical oriental despotism,
slavery, piracy, and obscurantism and as the otherwise benign
protector of a misguided and oppressed native populace. In
commenting upon the contradictory role of Brooke as civilizer
and colonizer, Victor Savage remarks that Brooke
counterbalanced a pragmatic streak which realized the huge
economic potential of north Borneo with a romantic perception
of the native people as "noble savages." In this latter role, Brooke

saw himself as protector of the Dyak (Iban) from the materialism and immorality of Western civilization. For Brooke himself, Borneo offered "a battlefield, playground and theater" (Savage 1984: 284).

As Brooke rationalized in 1841, some two years after his first visit to Sarawak in a characteristic Victorian missive that would find no contradiction between missionary noblesse oblige and colonial capitalist opportunity:

> ...my object [sic] are to call into existence the resources of one of the richest and most extensive islands of the globe; to relieve an industrious people from oppression, and to check and, if possible, to suppress Piracy and the Slave Trade which are openly carried on within a short distance of three European settlements, on a scale and system revolting to humanity.

> ....Convinced as I am of the good that must result both to Malays and Dyaks from even my own endeavours, and resolved to persevere in them (as if I fail in all I propose I shall at least pave the way for future improvements, and leave, I trust, a favourable impression of English character)... (Brooke 1842).

Notwithstanding the view of Brooke as a benign civilizer and protector it was also the logic of colonialism—and Brooke rule was no exception—to lean more heavily upon the more entrepreneurial and active races, namely immigrant Chinese, than the indigent native. In other words, Brooke could afford to preserve the man-nature relationship of the (Dyak) Iban of the interior while getting on with the real business of civilization and colonization in the major coastal zones of exploitation.[1]

Undoubtedly, however, the Borneo fiction of Joseph Conrad more than any other body of English fiction has given imaginative meaning to a Western audience of the peoples of the "Land below the wind." *Almayers's Folly* (1895), *An Outcast on the Islands* (1896), *Lord Jim* (1900), and *The Rescue* (1920) were all based upon impressions derived between August 1887 and January 1888 when Conrad served as chief mate of the *Vidar,* which plied a route between Singapore and Dutch Borneo.

But it is *The Rescue*, regarded as one his less successful novels, and one that took Conrad more than twenty years to complete, that plausibly stands as his "Brunei novel." While more than one Conrad scholar has remarked upon the interest of Conrad in the history and figure of the Brooke family (cf. Gordon 1963, Baines 1971, Parry 1983), scholarly attention on the Brooke characterization has obscured the very real Brunei dynastic situation which Conrad weaves into the novel.[2]

Conrad's use of Brookiana in the writing of *The Rescue* has long been acknowledged by Conrad scholars. Indeed, as Conrad wrote to the Ranee, the wife of the descendant of Rajah Charles Brooke:

> The first Rajah has been one of my boyish admirations, a feeling I have kept to this day strengthened by the better understanding of the greatness of his character and the unstained rectitude of his purpose. The book which has found favour in your eyes has been inspired in great measure by the history of the first Rajah's enterprise and even by the lecture of his journals as partly reproduced by Captain Mundy and others (letter dated 15 July 1920 quoted in Watts 1969: 210).

This led one Conrad scholar, Watts, to suggest that Conrad's reading of the Ranee's *My Life in Sarawak* may conceivably have encouraged Conrad to resume work on the incomplete manuscript of *The Rescue* (Watts 1969: 210). Besides Brookiana, Conrad read and used such works as Wallace's *Malay Archipelago* and Keppel's *Expedition to Borneo*. All became sources for *Lord Jim* and *The Rescue* (Baines 1971: 308).

In a nutshell, *The Rescue* is a novel set in the Malayan archipelago in the 1860s. Subtitled *A Romance of the Shallows*, the novel deals—palpably—with the "enactment of cataclysmic events within a confined and isolated space" (Parry 1983: 142n). The protagonist, Captain Tom Lingard, otherwise known as the Rajah Laut, sails onto a "Shore of Refuge" where his friend Hassim, an exiled chieftain, waits for help to recover his kingdom. But divided loyalties enter into the picture when Lingard has to choose between his roots and his obligations when confronted with the need to release European travellers captured by a local chieftain when their yacht is grounded in the shallow waters of the islands. In the bargain the plebeian Lingard also sells his class to Travers, capitalist and man of affairs. The price of this moral betrayal is the death of Hassim and Immada and the loss of Lingard's soul. In the words of Parry, "The ultimate defection of a protagonist who is both betrayer and betrayed signify that larger crisis endemic to the European presence in the other hemisphere" (Parry 1983: 41).

As one Conrad scholar, Baines, has commented of *The Rescue,* in the creation of the characters of Hassim and Immada and faithful retainer, Jafar, Conrad draws directly upon the real historical events that transpired in Brunei in 1846 as graphically recorded in Spenser St. John's *The Life of Sir James Brooke: Rajah of Sarawak: From his personal papers and correspondence* (1879) (Baines 1971: 308 & 502-3). Although this author fails to make the specific Brunei connection and while Conrad never visited Brunei or any north Borneo port in his sailing career, *The Rescue* nevertheless offers up some very plausible images of the Brunei/Borneo Sultanate.

What plausibly did Conrad derive from his reading of St. John that would lend a Brunei verisimilitude to *The Rescue*? At least four elements of the fiction suggest themselves. First, Conrad's sense of place or the fictionalized geography of the novel. Second, characterization and plot, especially relating to the Malays. Third, the historical figure of Brooke so much admired by Conrad and, overarching all, Conrad's commentary on imperialism.

The Darat-es-Salam or Shore of Rescue of the novel is a composite of any Borneo Sultanate. Located 400 miles from the Straits of Malacca, "It has no specific name on the charts, and geography manuals don't mention it at all..." (Conrad 1985: 61). But as the narrative suggests, this was the coast of Borneo swept by the squadron of Sir Thomas Cochrane "some years ago" (Conrad 1985: 30). Indeed, as soon as the news of the murder of the Raja Muda Hassim reached Kuching, Brooke immediately called for help from Rear Admiral Cochrane's fleet and which, in an exercise in gunboat diplomacy, annihilated Brunei's defenses, effectively ending Brunei's independence. It also put an end to the piratical raids of the Illanun and who preyed upon English ships. In a revealing letter to William Blackwood, his publisher and editor, Conrad admits that the "paraphernalia of the story are hackneyed," that the yacht, the shipwreck and the coast had been used before. One such shipwreck, that Conrad knew of was that of the French Brig *"Amitié"* stranded on the coast in 1866 and attacked "by some vagabonds belonging to a certain Haji Saman" (Karl & Davies 1983: 382).

In the novel, Prince Hashim emerges as a composite of Hassin/Bedrudin. But how was Brunei evoked by Spenser St. John? What is the Brunei historical context upon which Conrad draws to elaborate the plot and characterization? In his book, St. John describes a situation which arose in the capital of Brunei in 1846. This relates to the return to Brunei of Muda Hassim and his brothers, who had otherwise facilitated the installation of the Brooke regime in Sarawak. When Muda Hassim forced the Sultan to recognize him as heir, he immediately became the victim of conspiracies. Eventually, the Sultan assented to the plot to get rid of Hassim and his followers. In a secretly planned assault, the attackers overwhelmed the Princes, including Prince Bedrudin. Bedrudin, wounded in the melee, managed to make contact with his sister as well as a slave-lad, Jafar. The latter he commanded to take his signet-ring and give it to Brooke as a sign of his loyalty. Jafar duly escaped but, rather than submit to the hand of their enemies, Bedrudin and, in turn, Muda Hassim destroyed themselves. Of Bedrudin, St. John writes, "Brave, courteous to a degree even to be remarked by the most punctilious of a punctilious service, ready to be influenced by a foreign civilisation, and wanting near him but a wise and appreciative European to render him a superior ruler" (St. John 1879: 108-111). Indeed, the scene in the novel when the slave, Jafar, brings the ring belonging to the Malay prince, Hashim, invokes this incident directly (Conrad 1985: 75). The ring becomes the symbol of trust and loyalty across the chasm of culture and race, although that too is perverted.

But it is in the figure of Lingrad, the "lone and uprooted Englishman," pitting his courage and wits against Dutch power in the struggle over the spoils of the archipelago, that we find a fictionalized and "plebian counterpart" to the aristocratic Rajah Brooke, so evidently admired by Conrad (cf. Parry 1983: 44). In the narrator's words:

> ...a true adventurer in his devotion to his impulse - a man of high mind and of pure heart, lay the foundation of a flourishing state on the ideas of pity and justice. He recognized chivalrously the claims of the conquered; he was a disinterested adventurer, and the reward of his noble instincts is in the veneration with which a strange and faithful race cherish his memory.
> Misunderstood and traduced in life, the glory of his achievements has vindicated the purity of his motives. He belongs to history...But there were others...obscure adventurers... (Conrad 1985: 15).

Parry writes that this passage is placed at the start of the book with the status of a thesis whose axioms are to be invalidated by the action of the novel (Parry 1983: 44).

Indeed, Lingrad/Linguard was a familiar figure to traders and travelers alike in Singapore in the late nineteenth century (cf. Warren 1977: 6-7). For example, the naturalist Burbidge, who passed through Singapore in the 1870s, remarked that while the trader-Captain Linguard was known by the natives of the Coti River region of southeast Borneo as the Rajah Laut, another maritime celebrity of the era was Captain Ross owner of the trading vessel *Cleater*, which plied the Singapore, Labuan, and Brunei route (Burbidge 1880: 19). Another was an Englishman named Wyndham at the court of the Sultan of Sulu and whom Conrad mentions in his letter to Blackwood (Karl & Davies 1983: 382). St. John describes Wyndham as:

> ...one of those adventurous spirits to be found in almost every outlandish place. He had been an officer under the command of the famous Admiral Cochrane...a short broad-shouldered fellow...His had been a life of adventure; and if rumor did

not belie him, all was fish that came to his net. Our arrival
did not please him, as he was devoted to the Spanish cause;
but blood was thicker than water, and he soon lent his hearty
assistance (St. John 1879: 150).

In fact, Wyndham's persona was written into an original
manuscript version of *The Rescue*. His homilies on race relations were, however, written out in the final version, even though
an ethnic exclusiveness theme is retained around the question of
the colonialist posture (Parry 1983: 48-9). Another composite
of the Lingard characterization is mentioned by Conrad in his
letter to Blackwood, namely in the form of a lone adventurer
with "occult influence with the Rajah of Bali," a disinterested
meddler—apparently also dealing in arms—but greatly respected
by the natives. As Conrad writes, "Thus facts can bear out my
story but as I am writing fiction not secret history, facts don't
matter" (Karl and Davies 1983: 382).

As Parry has written, "*The Rescue* harks back to times when
colonialism was still innocent of the concerted thrust later or-
ganised by international finance capitalism". Nevertheless, the
novel succeeds in parodying the official rhetoric of this earlier
era (Parry 1983: 43). Parry continues that:

> In the body of Conrad's fictional engagements with the im-
> perialist experience, this work is conspicuous for honouring
> and refuting colonialist myth, since the narrative discourse
> laments the ignominious failure of these noble impulses it
> set out to celebrate...

As such it is a work of:

> ... an enlarged and disenchanted historical imagination, re-
> viewing representations of an era that had already been con-
> stituted as history (Parry 1983: 40).

Ultimately, then, in the searing critique of Parry, *The Rescue*
distances itself from his earlier works, which can be read as
illuminations on imperialism (*Allymayer's Folly* and *An Outcast
of the Islands*) and becomes a "critical reflection on the corporate

consciousness of imperialism," "an elegy on a legend it had offered as a fit subject for eulogy" (Parry 1983: 58-9).

The image of Borneo in adventure fiction

It is perhaps trite to suggest that Conrad had literary precursors on the Borneo/Brooke theme just as it is trite to suggest that Conrad has spawned emulators on this genre of "adventure" fiction. But these early works of popular fiction reached an even wider audience than Conrad. They offered no critique of colonialism but were, rather, resonant with imperial overtones matching the then stereotyped views of race and empire that became standard fare lingering on, notably, in Western children's fiction on the Orient until the present.

Possibly the first exemplar of Western adventure fiction on Borneo was the novel of James Greenwood, *The Adventures of Reuben Davidger: Seventeen Years and Four Months Captive among the Dyaks of Borneo* (S.O. Beaton, London, 1865). The hero of this work is a castaway at the end of a long voyage from England, not on a desert island but in the pirate lair of some Dyak tribe of interior Borneo. As seen by the rescue of the hero, British pluck prevails over native turpitude, enlightenment over piratical excess and disorder. If the palpably Bornean setting of the novel owes to a received version of the Brooke fantasy, the story line owes more to Daniel Defoe's figure of Robinson Crusoe.

The Defoe/Selkirk/Crusoe castaway angle also has echoes in the tale of high adventure by Captain Mayne Reid, *The Castaways: A Story of Adventure in the Wilds of Borneo* (1870). Rescue for the castaway heroes of this story occurs at the end of a cross Borneo escape by looking out from the summit of Mount Kinabulu beyond "the strange old wooden-walled of Bruni" to the British Colony of Labuan and "the glorious old banner of Britannia" (Reid 1870: 252).

The powerful *Boys Own* image of the White Rajah undoubtedly persists in Western imagination, indeed one of the more enduring images of the Raj. Echoes of the Brookes and Conrad together, for example, are found in the *The White Rajah*

(1961) by Nicholas Monsarrat, a writer of popular full-blooded adventure stories in exotic locations. The scene for this novel is Makassang, a fictionalized island in the Java Sea. The protagonist of this novel is Richard Marriott, "adventurer and pirate, disinherited son of a British aristocrat enlisted by the Rajah of Makassang to put down rebellions on his island kingdom." As stated in the blurb, Marriott's problem was "How Makassang was to be led from its feudal barbarity, from its centuries old habits of treachery and despotic vengeance, and made fit to take its place in the expanding world of the nineteenth century...". The novel is structured in three parts, "The Heir 1850," "The Pirate 1860," and the "White Rajah 1861" each adding to the Borneo verisimilitude and offering a highly romantic embroidery upon the Brooke/Lord Jim legend.[3]

Colonial administrators, agents and sojourners

Aside from dutiful compilation of official records and the writing the annual reports, the various Residents and Assistant Residents of Brunei appear not to have been of reflective or literary bent, at least not alongside certain of their contemporaries in the Malayan Civil Service; the Frank Swettenhams, the Hugh Lows or the Hugh Cliffords or even the Brookes.[4]

Indeed Sir Hugh Clifford, who sojourned in Malaya and Singapore between 1883 and 1929, visited Brunei in 1902. Clifford, who later in his career became successively Governor of the Gold Coast, Nigeria, and Ceylon, visited Brunei in his capacity as Governor of the Straits Settlements. As such he was one of a group of key Victorian colonial officials responsible for the establishment of British rule in Malaya, and on occasion made policy rulings touching on Brunei. Evidently unlike many of his fellows he explored the country, learnt the Malay language and customs, and reveled in the simplicity of Malay peasant life. As Savage remarks, while Brooke idealized the Dayak as "noble savages," Clifford romanticized the Malay as "noble peasants." But by romanticizing medieval Malay society (Roff 1966: x-xii), he was not against pouring scorn upon the Malay ruling class (Wicks 1979: 66). For Clifford, the implied obscurantist postures and conventions of the Malay ruling classes would wilt with the extension of British influence in the Peninsula (cf. Savage 1984:287). But if the qualities Clifford admired in the common peoples of Malaya were being destroyed by the onward thrust of British imperialism in Malaya, and of which he was a key agent, then this led to an inner turmoil in the man—a gap between public and private life—and which he may never have resolved (Wicks 1979: 72).

The tension is nowhere more explicitly expressed than in a piece Clifford penned on Brunei called "A Dying Kingdom," and published in *Macmillan's Magazine* in 1902 following a visit to the land some years earlier on the official steam yacht:

> The sights which are presented by modern Asia seem specially fashioned for the purpose of stimulating the imagination. They are compact of strange paradoxes and unlikely contradictions. Here is a land of darkness under sun-glare, of idyllic simplicity and virtue cheek by jowl with vice, treachery, wickedness unspeakable, cruelty that is satanic, tyranny, misrule, oppression; a land in which barren places sprout into a new strong life suddenly at a whisper of the white man's will, and kingdoms old in story decay and putrefy in unsightly abjectness and squalor. It is the battleground of the new and the old; the spot where modern things and things very ancient meet in the death-grapple; where antiquated notions of right and wrong, of fitness and unfitness, die hard, as old things are wont to do, and new ideas spring into being and flourish with the heartless insolence of youth. We white men know the good from the bad. Our theories are the result of centuries of self-discipline, of education, of deep thought. The customs and the kingdoms of Asia fall down before our trumpet-blast as did the walls of Jericho of old; and if we did leave a train of broken things behind us, who among us shall dare to doubt that old; and if we did leave a train of broken things behind us, who among us shall dare to doubt that our revolutions tend to the greatest good of the greatest number.

Such Jeffersonian effusions were undoubtedly confirmed by Clifford's audience with the Sultan (Hashim Jalil-ul-alam

Akamudin), during whose reign the British Residential system was introduced. Echoing the sentiments of a legion of European predecessors to the Court of Brunei, he describes "disgust, horror, contempt, repulsion and an unreasoning feeling of contamination" at viewing the decayed kingdom, the result not of war, famine or pestilence but "vice, consistent avarice, short-sighted folly....self indulgence, lack of self restraint, and loss of self-respect." Even the people of Brunei, he opined, "have lost their ancient arts together with their ancient greatness" (Clifford 1902: 106-114).[5] Hashim, who died in advanced age in 1906, was reputed to have had thirty concubines and well over a hundred sons and daughters (*State of Brunei Annual Report 1963*, 1965: 226). In *Heroes of Exile* (1906), Clifford made Brunei the setting of at least one of his fictional recreations on the Malay world.

Author of *On the Fringe of the Eastern Seas: The City of Many Waters*, published in 1924, Peter Blundell offers a perspective on Brunei from the standpoint, not of the ubiquitous visitor or transient, but of a resident Englishman, a *Tuan Besar*. Blundell, a pseudonym for Frank N. Butterworth (1875-1952), was a sometime seaman turned engineer who found himself employed as manager of the Island Trading Syndicate's cutch factory in Brunei between 1905 and 1913. As such, Blundell/Butterworth found himself one step removed from colonial officialdom and its social conventions.[6] No less, he was well positioned to observe not only the commercial life of the colony, but the everyday life of Bruneians at work, at play, in a state of crisis (a cholera epidemic), in ceremonial mood (Hari Raya), at weddings, coronations, and in a multiplicity of settings. Although not beyond such crude orientalist stereotyping of Brunei women as "very highly sexed," "fond of port wine," overall his portrait of the Brunei Malay—Malay fishermen, the Malays who stripped the bark of the mangroves to supply the raw material for the cutch factory, the craftsmen of Kampong Ayer, and Malay women—was not unsympathetic: "...the average Brunei citizen of the lower class is a decent, honest fellow and a hard worker." This is not a sentiment that readily springs from the pages of colonial writings on Malaya, especially from the commercial classes. Indeed, Blundell was more scathing of those British officials who staffed the Eastern Services: "of obscure antecedence, no morals and great ambitions." An exception was his friend Godfrey Hewett, the Labuan-based British Consul for Brunei. Given the low caliber of British officials he encountered in Brunei, his preference overall was for the absorption of Brunei into Sarawak, where he believed the Brooke administrative model was altogether superior. Perhaps it was publicly expressed sentiments like this as much as, I suspect, his flauting of colonial social conventions that necessitated him to find an American publisher for his work. In any case, we cannot ignore this work, described by one bibliographer of Bruneiana as "virtually the only pre-Second World War book in English on Brunei" (Francis 1990: 8).

W. Somerset Maugham and Brunei

Images of Brunei in the West also appear refracted through the Borneo essays of the British writer Somerset Maugham. Maugham traveled to Malaya and Borneo including Brunei in 1929. His two-week sojourn in Brunei was recalled by William Doughty (1886-1971), a long-time resident and a former engineer in the cutch factory. Maugham apparently derived the prototype of the District Officer in such stories as "The Outstation" and "Virtue" from the figure of Eric Pretty, then Resident of Brunei and cultivated by Maugham in the course of a number of bridge-playing sessions. Although Pretty denied any link with "The Outstation," he admitted to being the model for the diligent government servant in "Virtue" (de Frietas 1975 intro.).

Maugham also published impressions of his 1929 visit to Brunei in *A Writer's Notebook* (1951). In a cameo piece reminiscent of the descriptions by Victorian travelers of the harem, Maugham offers an evocation of an audience with the Sultan (Ahmed Tajudin Akhazul Khairi Wadin b.1913), still a boy in his teens. Maugham also offers caricatures of the employees of the cutch factory and the club which Maugham evidently patronized. British civil servants concerned with policy in Brunei were likewise not spared Maugham's sarcastic wit. Maugham describes the Resident Counselor stationed in Labuan, as:

...conscientious and hard-working, but stupid....the kind of official who is always afraid of doing the wrong thing, and bound up in silly prejudice and red-tape. Though he has been here for thirty years, he speaks little Malay and takes no interest in the country...his concerns are purely local and are confined to the club and the comings and goings of people in his district (Maugham 1951: 186-189).

With few exceptions Maugham concerned himself with Europeans in colonial situations, many of them identifiable. As Anthony Burgess remarks, these were the only people he got to know and therefore cannot be blamed for sidelining the "natives" in his literary works (Burgess 1969: xvi).[7] Less blameless, however, was Maugham's ignorance of changes taking place in native attitudes—what today we would call responses to colonialism—as opposed to his awareness of the more obvious changes that had taken place in the lives of expatriates in such colonial outposts as Borneo, such as rendered by modern communications:

The countries of which I wrote were then at peace. It may be that some of those peoples, Malays, Dyaks, Chinese, were restive under the British rule, but there was no outward sign of it (Maugham 1951: 7).

Willy nilly, war put an end to this idyll. Brunei Town and old Labuan were destroyed utterly by the Allied bombing deemed necessary to dislodge the Japanese occupier. As it happened, it was the parenthesis opened up by the Japanese interregnum that gave pause to—indeed, gave stimulation to—a select cadre of Brunei Malay intellectuals, offering a new way to apprehend their relationship with the colonial powers.

Brunei in the image of post-war British novelists

Post-war Brunei became the fictional setting for at least three English novelists, two of note, namely the plebian Anthony Burgess and the aristocratic Alec Waugh. Known for his iconoclastic contributions to English letters, Anthony Burgess first achieved minor prominence as author of *The Malayan Trilogy* (also known in the American edition as *The Long Day Wanes* (1964). Described by one critic as "the clearest literary reflection of the end of Empire..." (Ford 1983: 70), this work drew upon his experience in such outposts of empire as Gibraltar (1943-46), colonial Malaya (1954-57), and Brunei (1957-1960). In Malaya he taught at the Malay College in Kuala Kampar, "the Eton of the East," and subsequently in Kota Bharu in the state of Kelantan. In 1957 and following a sojourn in England, Burgess moved to Brunei, where he taught history and phonetics in the Sultan Omar Ali Saifuddin (SOAS) College in Bandar Brunei.

A highly ribald account of Burgess' sojourn in Malaya and Brunei from the time of his arrival in August 1954 to his forced repatriation from Brunei in 1960 appears in his autobiography, *Little Wilson and Big God: Being the First Part of the Confessions of Anthony Burgess* (1987). As Burgess explains, while teaching school in the mornings, he spent the afternoons writing and proofing parts of *Trilogy* then in press. He also began two new novels while residing in Brunei, *The Right to an Answer,* which he finished in 1960 and published the same year, and *Devil of a State*. As he explains:

> This novel was, is, about Brunei, which is renamed Naraka, Malayo-Arabic for hell. Little invention was needed to contrive a large cast of unbelievable characters and a number of interwoven plots. Though completed in 1958, the work was not published until 1961 when, for what it was worth, it was made a choice of the Book Society. Heinemann, my publisher, was doubtful about publishing it: it might be libelous. I had to change its Borneo setting to an East African one. Heinemann was right to be timorous. In early 1958 *The Enemy in the Blanket* appeared, and this at once provoked a libel suit.

One can only surmise, but the fact that the libel suit was dropped goes far in explaining Burgess' loyalty to Heinemann. This publisher, it would appear, obliged Burgess to shift the Brunei backdrop of *Devil of a State* from its Southeast Asian setting to somewhere between Mombassa in Kenya and Dar-es-Salaam in Tanganyika. Still, as Burgess would have us believe, he, not Graham Greene, wrote the Malay novel and he, not even Conrad, spoke Malay. To be generous, we can say that Burgess revealed a talent at consulting the Winstedt dictionary of Malay.

Devil of a State, according to one Burgess scholar, Samuel Coale, "reads like his Malayan trilogy in miniature," albeit an extremely comic gloss on the fuller and richer Malayan works. Plots and subplots abound into which characters and episodes are interwoven. But the underlying theme of the novel is rebellion. As Coale explains: "It exists on all levels of society, in the family, in politics, in social customs, and in religious matters." But ultimately, rebelliousness is checked by "older, traditional values like marriage, family loyalty, and political good manners that are still valid and important" (Coale 1981: 44). Written and published prior to the 1962 Azahari rebellion, Burgess was evidently alert to the political stirrings of nationalism in Brunei. The character of Patu, the nationalist leader, is a likely take on Azahari himself. The meeting turned riot in the Chin Chin Cinema is feasibly a prose version of meetings convened by Azahari's political party in the Bolkiah Cinema. The futility of political self-determination expressed in the novel appears to match the strong reservations of the Brunei government—then and now—as to multi-party democracy.

Not appearing in any of this country's public libraries, *Devil* is clearly too close to the mark. Coale, writing from the perspective of the literary critic, opines that the work may be "too comic and too shrill." He continues that "the cheap shots at the characters seem almost a caricature of satire and comedy, a too-easy 'put-down' of the 'little world of the misled'..." With this novel, according to Coale, Burgess is poised to expand his literary scope and range and move on to better things (Coale 1981:47). In literary terms, that is undoubtedly the case, yet it is clear that Burgess took some time to work the Brunei experience out of his mind. Brunei figures again—highly irreverently—in his 1976 novel *Beard's Roman Women,* but only as a fictional device and then in part as a hallucination or reverie upon a stint at working for Radio Brunei, a conduit he exploited to bruit some highly unsavory doggerel on SOAS and Brunei at large.[8]

But, as an "end of Empire writer," where did Burgess stand apropos colonialism? Certainly he lived through an era of change, witnessing at first hand the stirrings of Asian nationalism, the challenge of communism, and the transition to a new order rid of the old colonial hierarchies of which he was both part and which he so evocatively satirized. Another Burgess scholar, Carol M. Dix, writes:

> Burgess is a social realist, or perhaps pessimist, and he drops no hints of a better, more united future. Yet he believes in imperialism seeing the conflict it creates as good for society (or for novelists at least (Dix 1971).

Still, the plebian Burgess offers a positively relativist view of a plural society alongside the Eurocentric and class-conscious offerings of Alec Waugh (1898-1981). Although gaining some reputation as both travel writer and novelist in the United Kingdom, Waugh lived in the shadow of his more celebrated brother Evelyn. The setting of Waugh's 1960 novel *Fuel for the Flame* is unmistakably Brunei and identifiably matches the oil town of Seria. Some pains are gone to in an author's note to state that place and characters are imaginary. Nevertheless, Waugh evidently visited Brunei to research the novel, as he offers an indebtedness to the management of Royal Dutch Shell in "Borneo" as well as in some other countries where he sojourned to research oil-towns. As stated in the publisher's blurb:

> In this novel Alec Waugh returns to the theme of the motives and passions of European men and women in the tropics. Using as his locale the imaginary island of Karak in the South China Sea, he portrays the social and domestic relationships of the white colony against the wider issues of political intrigue.

Karak had maintained itself as an independent monarchy though with British advisers, throughout the days of militant colonialism and though the discovery of oil introduced prosperity as well as foreign interests, the traditional life of the Karakis continued to exist side by side with British social conventions. But now, as this novel opens, the stresses and unrest produced by warring ideologies cast their baleful shadow over the little tropical kingdom, bringing a testing time for all whose lives and fortunes are involved."

As with Burgess' *Devil of a State,* this novel is only explicable against the political backdrop of the times, namely, the Azahari Rebellion. An air of verisimilitude is injected into the words of one of the protagonists, who explains that the young Prince (Rhya) who returned from England with an English girl as his intended wife remains "the chief obstacle to our peace of mind. During his father's lifetime, we have no cause to worry: afterwards, anything may happen."[9] If the background of this novel revolves around the foibles of the colonial caste system of a company town in an exotic tropical setting, the subplot concerns the machinations of a nationalist agent provocateur. In the words of Colonel Forrester of British intelligence:

> It's a very simple story in essentials. There is a strong group of military men and industrialists who want to take over the country, maintaining the throne as long as the old king lives, establish a Republic when he dies; they want to nationalize the oil. They have backing in New York and also, I believe, in London. They believe that the best way to seize power was by creating a Communist bogey, there is no real Communist Party in Karak, though there are a few disaffected elements who would join one if it were properly organized.

One might assume that Waugh himself was close to British intelligence, as the Indonesian-backed Azahari rebellion which broke out in 1962 cannot have been completely unpredicted. Matching the socially introverted life of company expatriate society and his own aristocratic values, Waugh's study of British social conventions relegates the natives at best to background noise. Waugh's life and that of his protagonists is a dizzy round of cocktail parties, lunch parties with the Resident, and hobnobbing with the Prince Rhya, heir to the throne. All in all, in the in the words of Krause and Krause, this novel adds up to a set of "superficial essays on oil, government and modern colonialism" (Krause & Krause 1988: 160).

Two more novels by British authors see in Brunei/Borneo a backdrop for intrigue and adventure. These are Gavin Black's (pseudonym of Oswald Wynd) *You Want to Die, Johnny!* (1966) and Tom Lilley's *The K Section* (1972). The setting of *You Want to Die, Johnny!* is an imaginary Sultanate, Bintan, the last surviving British protectorate in Borneo. At the center of the action is the British Resident and his associates who find themselves up against organized crime and international intrigue. Once again the turmoil surrounding the 1962 rebellion provides the backdrop for this novel of suspense and adventure. *The K Section,* set in a less identifiably Borneo location, "somewhere east of Singapore" in an imaginary British colony, is another example of the genre of the east as backdrop and the natives as distractions to the real-life activities of colonials. Such props as the Queen Elizabeth Hotel and the Gurkhas lend an element of familiarity, reassurance, and verisimilitude to a Western reader. To the extent that the natives appear in this novel, they are woodenly depicted as communists or as members of a liberation front (the Bajau), or at best, as auxiliaries of the European-dominated Special Branch. The context is palpably the British endeavor in north Borneo in the early sixties to neutralize the activities of Sukarnoist forces infiltrating from Indonesia, a broader operation that saw actions against the Chinese communists in Sabah/Sarawak, and in 1962, the surgical operation mounted by the British to put down the Azahari rebellion in Brunei. In commending this first novel, a reviewer for *The Times* mentioned the special quality of "authenticity," suggesting author participation in the events.

Conclusion

As seen through the optic of various texts and literatures, Western images of Borneo/Brunei were, after Said, very much part of an "imaginative territory" bounded and shaped by empire. Unlike the Occident-Orient relationship between, say, Napoleon and

Egypt, or even the Fifth French Republic and Cambodia, two
Asiatic civilizations of prodigious monumental splendor, Borneo
was home to no obvious relics or reminders of great indigenous
civilization. On the contrary, here was a darkness lightened only
by the perceived nobility of its savages. Even the highly exotic
flora and fauna invoked a Darwinian sense of struggle between
lower and higher forms of life. Here was a *terra incognita*
waiting for discovery—indeed, waiting to be charted, pacified,
civilized, missionized and colonized. The Islamic Sultanate of
Brunei, however, appeared as an historical enigma to the early
travelers, soldiers and missionaries, at once both threatening and
obscurantist. As colonialism primordially dealt with political
structures, not pagan tribes, the Sultanate of Brunei became the
prime object of attention of outside powers in the north Borneo
geographic region. Accordingly, it was the political center of
Brunei that came to be condemned by the unequal distribution
between East and West of economic, military, and social power.

To be sure, though, as Sweeney remarks of Said, he has
offered much not only on the assumptions and attitudes of the
Orientalist mind set but, by inference, the pioneers of Malay
studies in the West, the Windsteds, the Wilkinsons as well as
the St. Johns and the Cliffords, and who, for all their prejudices,
errors and biases after all laid the bases for a critical examination
of a culture and to which natives and non-natives alike necessarily
have to enter into a dialogue (Sweeney 1987: 15).

Philologically, a similar imbalance between East and West
opened up. As Silverstein found of Burma through the prism of
Western novels, the subject matter and themes are those that
interest non-native writers. The issues and problems raised are
those of the Westerners (and Japanese) in a strange and distant
land. Few of the writers were familiar with the local language;
hence there was little empathy with local history or culture. The
jibe holds for Conrad as well. After all, as Parry remarks,
Conrad's primary audience were subscribers to *Blackwood's* and
New Review and "still secure in the conviction that they were
members of an invincible imperial power and a superior race"
(Parry 1983: 1).

As Silverstein found of the Western writers on Burma, so in

Brunei, there were those who emphasized the triumph of Western culture and Christian values. In Brunei as much as Burma the great historical event was the Pacific war, although in the case of Brunei this was not so much reflected in Western fiction as in the stimulus it gave to a national Brunei fiction. While in Borneo/Brunei there was no insider critique of colonialism as of George Orwell's experience in Burma—unless that can be read into the writings of Conrad (cf. Silverstein 1985: 129-139)—it was inevitable that locals would rise to the occasion. Literature was one of the weapons, indeed one of the few weapons in a colonial situation.

Overall, then, this clutch of British "end of empire" novels on Brunei/Borneo, palpably written for metropolitan audiences, echo Said's comment on the writings of Albert Camus apropos Algeria, namely that in both *L'Etranger* and *The Plague*, Camus highlights an entirely French civil society and an entirely French agenda vis-à-vis the sovereignty issues waged against colonialism by Algerian Muslims (Said 1990: 93). Although underdeveloped, modern travel writing on Borneo, it might be said, tends to represent the replay of colonial fantasies, modern travel, at least as refracted through the optic of travel guides plausibly represents a replay of the fantasies of Victorian travelers and their more recent emulators.

What has not been discussed here, indeed, a separate project, is in Said's words the "sustained reaction and response to the metropolitan literature" comprising "great stonelike slabs, the masterpieces that constitute the canon or great tradition..." Thus, the importance of *The Tempest* to Carribean writers, Kipling to Indian writers, and Conrad to African writers mentioned by Said (Said 1990: 83) finds its Brunei/Borneo equivalent again in Conrad, but also in less prosaic form in the works of Clifford, Maugham, and Burgess, not to mention the great and lesser explorers and administrators. In Brunei the critique of colonialism was muted and in any case, as shown below, came to be expressed in culturalist-defensive forms.

Notes

The author is particularly obliged to Simon Francis, bibliographer of Brunei, as well as former colleagues in the Department of History, Universiti Brunei Darussalam.

1. Specifically on Conrad's interest in the history of Brooke of Sarawak, see J.D. Gordon, *Joseph Conrad: The Making of a Novelist* (London: Russell and Russell 1963) (1940).
   On the Borneo inspiration for Conrad, see Jerry Allen, *The Sea Years of Joseph Conrad* (London, 1967).
2. In 1888 Charles Brooke, the second Rajah of Sarawak, obtained the mining license to Brunei's coal deposits in Muara, Named Brooketon Colliery the mine was a kind of extra territorial area protected by contract until 1924 when it was found to be unprofitable and closed down. Output varied between 10,000 and 25,000 tons per annum (cf. Franz 1980).
3. The White Rajah myth has also gained some stimulus of late from the White Rajah himself or at least his descendant, Anthony Brooke, the Rajah Muda. Ruler of Sarawak from 1939 until just prior to the Japanese invasion, Anthony opposed the post-war cession of the State to the British crown. Today, from exile, he fights for the rain forests of Borneo and their forest dwellers, a stand which meets with studied derision from both the Malaysian Federal government and the State government of Sarawak (cf. David Stamp, "White Rajah back to do Penans good," *Borneo Bulletin*, 6/7 July 1991: 125.).
4. One exception, perhaps, was G.E. Cator, Resident of Brunei between May 1916 and March 1921 and who published his impressions of an enthronement ceremony in Brunei in *Asian Review* (1939).
5. It is perhaps apposite to mention the Clifford-Conrad connection. Undoubtedly a shared experience in the Malay world brought the two together. Clifford initially incurred Conrad's pique, however, over his criticism of Conrad's use of language and lack of knowledge about Malays. A happy reconciliation and the start of a life-long friendship was reached after Conrad favourably reviewed a book of Malaya impressions by Clifford. It is clear that each read each other's works although it was Clifford who benefited from the master's detailed advice on the preparation of his writings (cf. Baynes 1971: 252-53).
6. Blundell, a pseudonym for F.N. Butterworth, was also a prolific writer of fiction. At least a dozen of his books have a Malaya and/or

Borneo flavor and much of it full of ironic humour. Among those with a specific Borneo or palpably Brunei setting are *The Jungle Trail: A Story of Borneo* (1923), *Mr. Plodd of Borneo* (nd.), *The Kidnappers* (nd.), and *Morals for Matilda* (1927).

7. A parallel here might be the writings of Albert Camus on Algeria. Edward Said writes that in both *L'Etranger* and *The Plague*, Camus highlights an entirely French civil society and an entirely French agenda vis-à-vis the sovereignty issues waged against colonialism by Algerian Muslims (Said 1990: 93).

8. A no less perverse example of "expatriate" literature is that of George J. Fernandez, *Abode of Peace* (1975). As plot as summarized in one bibliographical study of Brunei concerns:

the survival story of a young Indian teacher and his family who lived for four years in a highly hypocritical and capitalistic society, and an international community in Brunei (Krause & Krause 1988: 60).

A non-Westerner, this Asian author nevertheless reaches through English a burgeoning middle-class Asian audience in the Singapore/ Malaysia area, themselves new bearers of Orientalist attitudes in a post-independence situation.

9. In 1967, the ruler of Brunei, the Seri Begawan Sultan Omar Ali Saifuddin (1916-86), resigned in favor of his son, the present Sultan Hassanal Bolkiah.

Bibliography

Allen, Jerry, *The Sea Years of Joseph Conrad,* (London, 1967).

Appell, G.N. and L.R. Wright (eds.), *The Status of Social Science Research in Borneo* (Ithaca: Cornell, 1978).

Baines, Jocelyn, *Joseph Conrad: A Critical Biography* (London: Pelican, 1971).

Beccari, Odoardo, *Wanderings in the Great Forests of Borneo,* (London: Archibald Constable and Company, 1904).

Beeckman, Daniel, *A Voyage to and from the Island of Borneo,* (1718), (Reprinted: Folkestone: Dawsons of Pall Mall, 1973)

Belcher, E., *Narrative of the Voyage of H.M.S. Samarang, During the Years 1843-46,* 2 Vols. (London: Reeve, Benthan & Reeve, 1848).

Belfield, H. Conway, *Report upon the present condition of affairs in Labuan and Brunei,* (FMS Government Press, 1905).

Bellwood, Peter, "Trade patterns and political developments in Brunei and adjacent areas AD 700-1500," Paper for the *Tenth International Congress of Anthropological and Ethnological Sciences* (New Delhi, 1978).

Black, Gavin, *You Want to Die, Johnny!* (London: Collins, 1966).

Blundell, Peter, *One the Fringe of the Eastern Seas: The City of Many Waters* (New York: Robert M. McBride and Co., 1923).

Bock, Carl, *The Headhunters of Borneo: a narrative tale of travel up the Mahakkam and down the Barito; also Journeys in Sumatra, 1881* (Reprinted: 1985).

Broek, Jan O.M., "Place names in 10th and 17th century Borneo," Department of Geography, University of Minnesota, mss., 1959.

Brooke, Charles, *Ten Years in Sarawak* (London, 1886).

Brooke, James, *Letter from Borneo with Notices of the Country and its Inhabitants addressed to James Gardner Esq.* (London: L. and G. Seeley, 1842).

P.M.B., "Five days in Brunei" in *Blackwood's Magazine,* 214, (1778): 529-536.

Burbidge, F.W., *The Gardens of the Sun: or a naturalist's journal of the mountains and in the forests and swamps of Borneo and the Sulu Archipelago* (London: Murray, 1880).

Burgess, Anthony, *Time for a Tiger* (London: Heinemann, 1956).

Burgess, Anthony, *Devil of a State* (London: Heinemann, 1961).

Burgess, Anthony, *Maugham's Malaysian Stories* (London: Heinemann, 1969).

Burgess, Anthony, *Beard's Roman Women* (1976).

Burgess, Anthony, *Little Wilson and Big God; Being the First Part of the Confessions of Anthony Burgess* (London: Heinemann, 1987).

Carey, T.F., "Two Early Muslim Tombs at Brunei", *Journal of the Malaysian Branch of the Royal Asiatic Society*, 11,2 (1933): 183.

Cleary, Mark and Francis Lian, "On the Geography of Borneo," *Progress in Human Geography* 15, 2 (1991): 163-177.

Clifford, Hugh, "A Dying Kingdom," *Macmillan's Magazine* (1902).

Clifford, Hugh, *Heroes of Exile* (London: Smith, Elder and Co., 1906).

Clifford, Hugh, *In Court and Kampong* (London: Grand Richards, Second Edition, 1927) (First published: 1897)

Clutterbuck, Walter J., *About Ceylon and Borneo* (London, 1891).

Coale, Samuel, *Anthony Burgess*, (New York: Frederick Ungar, 1981).

Collingwood, Cuthbert, *Rambles of a Naturalist on the Shores and Waters of the China Sea: being the observations in natural history during a voyage to China, Formosa, Borneo, Singapore, etc.*, (1868).

Conrad, Joseph, *The Rescue, 1920* (London: Penguin, 1985).

Crawfurd, J., *History of the Indian Archipelago*, 3 Vols., (Edinburgh: Archibald Constable, 1820).

de Crespigny, C.A.C., "On Northern Borneo," *Proceedings of the Geographical Society*, 16 (1872): 172-183.

de Frietas, G.V. (intro), *Maugham's Borneo Stories* (Singapore: Heinemann Asia, 1975).

Dalton, Bill, *The Indonesia Handbook* (Vermont: Moon Publications, 1978).

Dalrymple, Alexander, *A Plan for Extending the Commerce of the Kingdom*, 1769.

Dix, Carol M., *Anthony Burgess: Writers and Their Work* (London: Longman, 1971).

Earl, G.W., *The Eastern Seas; Voyages and Adventures in the Indian Archipelago in 1832-33-34* (London: William Haller, 1837).

Fell, R.T., *Early Maps of Southeast Asia* (Singapore: Oxford University Press, 1988).

Flemich, C.O., "History of shifting agriculture in Brunei: 1906-1939," *Malayan Agricultural Journal*, (1940).

Ford, Boris (ed.), *The New Pelican Guide to English Literature No.8: The Present*, (London: Penguin, 1983).

Forrest, Thomas, *A Voyage to New Guinea and the Moluccas from Salambangan* (London: G. Scott, 1779).

Francis, Simon, *Borneo in History: A Catalogue of Books in the Borneo Collection of the University Library Describing Borneo Before 1960,* (Brunei: Universiti Brunei Darussalam, 1990).

Franz, Johannes C., *The Sultanate of Brunei: Oil Wealth and Problems of Development* (Wirtschafts und Sozialgeo-graphisches der Friederich Alexander Universitaet Nuernberg (1980) (trns. from German by Michael Schmitz and Alistair Sharp, Universiti Brunei Darussalam, 1990).

Forbes, F.E., *Five Years in China, from 1842 to 1847 with an account of the occupation of the islands of Labuan and Borneo by Her Majesty's Forces* (London: Richard Bentley, 1848).

Goonetilleke, D.C.R.A., *Images of the Raj: South Asia in the Literature of Empire:* (London: Macmillan, 1988).

Gordon, J.D., *Joseph Conrad: The Making of a Novelist* (London: Russell and Russell, 1963).

Greenwood, James, *The Adventures of Reuben Davidger: Seventeen Years and Four Months Captive Among the Dyaks of Borneo* (London: S.O. Beaton, 1865).

Guertz, E.P. "British North Borneo," *JSBRAS* 14, (1884): 333-335.

Guillemard, Francis, H., *The Cruise of the Marchesa to Kamchatka and New Guinea: With notices of Formosa, Lui-Kui, and various islands of the Malay Archipelago* (London: J. Murray, Second Edition, 1899).

Harrison, Thomas H., *Borneo Jungle: an account of an Oxford expedition to Sarawak* (London: Lindsay Drummond, 1938).

Harrison, Thomas, H., *Background to a Rebellion,* Singapore: Straits Times, nd.

Harrison, Thomas, H., (with B. Sandin), "Borneo Writing," Special Monograph, No.1, *Sarawak Museum Journal,* (1966).

Harrison, Thomas, H, *Prehistoric Wood from Brunei,* Monograph of the Brunei Museum Journal, 2, (1974).

Harrison, Thomas and Barbara Harrison,"Kota Batu in Brunei," *Sarawak Museum Journal,*11, 8 (1956): 283-318.

Harvey, W.S., "Note on the N.W. coast of Borneo, from Pulau Labuan to the entrance of Maludu Bay," *Royal Geographical Society Journal* 16 (1846): 292-294.

Haynes, H.S., "A List of Brunei Malay words," *Journal of the Singapore Branch of the Royal Asiatic Society* 34 (1900): 39-48.

Hino, Iwao and S. Durai Raja Singam, *Stray Notes on Nippon-Malaisian Historical Connections,* (Kuala Lumpur: Kuala Lumpur Museum, 1941).

Horton, Anthony V.M.,"The Development of Brunei during the British Residential Era: 1906-1959: A Sultanate Regenerated," (Ph.D. thesis, Hull University, 1985).

Horton, Anthony V.M., (ed.), *Report on Brunei in 1904 by M.S.H. McArthur* (Athens: Ohio University Center for Southeast Asian Studies, Monographs in International Studies, Southeast Asia Series No.74, 1987).

Hallet, H. Hughes, "An Account of a berhantu ceremony called 'perakong' by the Orang Belait of Brunei," *Journal of the Malay Branch of the Royal Asiatic Society,* 16,1 (1938): 102-108

Hallet, H., Hughes, "A Sketch of the History of Brunei," *Journal of the Malay Branch of the Royal Asiatic Society,* 17, (1940): 23-42.

Johns, W.E., *Biggles in Borneo,* (London: White Lion, 1943).

Karl, Frederick R. and Laurence Davies, *The Collected Letters of Joseph Conrad,* Vol.7.1: 1861-1897 (Cambridge: Cambridge University Press, 1983).

Keppell, H., *The Expedition to Borneo of H.M.S Dido for the Suppression of Piracy: with Extracts from the Journal of James Brooke, Esq, of Sarawak,* (London, 1846).

Keppell, H., *A Visit to the Indian Archipelago, in H. M. Ship Maeander. With portions of the private journal of Sir James Brooke, K.C.B.,* 2 Vols. (London: Richard Bentley, 1853).

Kong, Lily and Victor Savage, "The Malay World in Colonial Fiction," *Singapore Journal of Tropical Geography,* 7,1 (1986): 40-52.

Krausse, Sylvia C.E. and Gerald H. Krausse, *Brunei,* World Bibliographical Series, Vol. 93, (Oxford: Clio Press, 1988).

Lai Nam Chen, *Images of Southeast Asia in Children's Fiction* (Singapore: Singapore University Press, 1981).

Lee, Francis, *Secret in Sabah* (Singapore: Heinemann, 1967).

Time Out in Sabah (Singapore: Heinemann, 1967).

Leach E.R., *Social Science Research in Sarawak: A Report on the Possibilities of a Social Economic Survey of Sarawak presented to the Colonial Social Science Research Council HMSO,* 1950.

Leyden, John, "Sketch of Brunei," *Singapore Chronicle* (1837).

Leys, Peter, "Observations on the Brunei political systems, 1883-1885; with the notes by Dr. Robert M. Pringle," *Journal of the Malay Branch of the Royal Asiatic Society* 41, 214 (II) (1968): 117-130.

Logan, J.R.,"Traces of the origin of the Malayan Kingdom of Borneo proper with notices of the condition when first discovered by Europeans and at later periods," *Journal of the Indian Archipelago* and East Asia, 11,8 (1848): 513-527.

Low, Hugh, *Sarawak; Inhabitants and Productions: being notes during a residence in that country with H.H. The Rajah Brooke* (London, 1848) (Reprinted: 1988).

Low, Hugh, "Selesilah (book of descent) of the rajas of Brunei", *Journal of the Singapore Branch of the Royal Asiatic Society*, 5, (1880): 1-35.

Marryat, Frank S., *Borneo and the Indian Archipelago: with drawings of costume and scenery*, (London: Longman, Brown, Green and Longmans, 1848).

Matheson, Virginia, "Studies in Borneo: An Overview and Bibliography," *Kabar Seberang*, 16, (1985): 100-139.

Maugham, Somerset W., *A Writer's Notebook* (London: Heinemann, 1951a).

Maugham, Somerset, W., *Collected Short Stories*, Vol.7. 4, (London: Heinemann, 1951b).

Mayne, A.C., "Summary of explorations in British Borneo," *Proceedings of the Royal Geographical Society* 10, 3, (1888): 134-146.

Menon, Kunnikrishnan, "Negara Brunei Darussalam: from Protectorate to Statehood: The Ceaseless Quest for Security," (unpublished Ph.D. dissertation, Victoria University, Wellington, 1988).

Monsarrat, Nicholas, *The White Rajah* (London: Cassell, 1961).

Moor, J.H., *Notices of the Indian Archipelago, and Adjacent Countries: being a collection of papers relating to Borneo, Celebees...*, (London: Frank Cass, 1837) (Reprinted: 1968).

Muller, Kal, *Indonesian Borneo Kalimantan* (Berkeley: Periplus, 1990).

Mundy, Rodney, *Narrative of Events in Borneo and Celebees, Down to the Occupation of Labuan: from the Journals of James Brooke, Esq. Rajah of Sarawak, and Governor of Labuan. Together with a narrative of the operations of H.H.S. Iris*, 2 Vols., (London, 1848).

Nicholl, Robert (ed.), *European Sources for the History of the Sultanate of Brunei in the Sixteenth Century Brunei* (Brunei Museum, 1975).

Nishimura, Juko, *Kuraki Nichirin*, (Tokyo: Bungei Shinju, 1979).

Pg. Omarali bin   Pg. Anak Hashim, "Bibliography: Brunei in the Sarawak Gazette," *Brunei Museum Journal*, 6, 4 (1988).

Parry, Benita, *Conrad and Imperialism: Ideological Boundaries and Visionary Frontiers* (London: Macmillan, 1983).

Pomeranty, Charlotte, *The Day They Parachuted Cats on Borneo* (Mass.: Young Scott Books, 1971).

Pringle, Robert, *Rajahs and Rebels: The Ibans and Sarawak Under Brooke Rule: 1841-1941* (Ithaca: Cornell University Press, 1970).

Reid, Mayne, *The Casteways: A Story of Adventure in the Wilds of Borneo* (London: T. Nelson and Sons, 1870).

Roff, William R. (ed.), *Stories by Sir Hugh Clifford* (Kuala Lumpur: Oxford University Press, 1966).

Said, Edward W., *Orientalism* (London: Routledge and Kegan Paul, 1978).

Said, Edward W., "Narrative, Geography and Interpretation," *New Left Review,* 180, (1990).

Sanib Said "The Development of Brunei Historiography: a survey and evaluation," *Tenth Conference of the International Association of Historians of Asia,* (Singapore, October 27-30 1986).

Savage, Victor, *Western Impressions of Nature and Landscape in Southeast Asia* (Singapore: Singapore University Press. 1984).

Silverstein, J., "Burma through the Prism of Western Novels," *Journal of Southeast Asian Studies,* 16,1 (1985): 29-139.

Singh, Ranjit, *Brunei 1839-1983: the Problem of Political Survival* (Singapore: Oxford University Press, 1984).

St. John, Spenser, *Life in the Forests of the Far East,* (London: Oxford University Press, 1988) (Original: 1862).

St. John, Spenser, *The Life of Sir James Brooke: Rajah of Sarawak: From his Personal Papers and Correspondence,* (Edinburgh & London: William Blackwood and Sons, 1879).

Sweeney, Amin, *A Full Hearing: Orality and Literacy in the Malay World* (Berkeley: University of California Press, 1987).

Takeyama, Michio, *Harp of Burma* (Tokyo: Tuttle, 1966).

Tate, D.J.M., *Rajah Brooke's Borneo* (Hong Kong: John Nicholson, Hong Kong, 1988).

Treacher, William H., "The genealogy of the Royal Family of Brunei," *Journal of the Straits Branch of the Royal Asiatic Society,* (1885).

Treacher, William H., "British Borneo: Sketches of Brunei, Sarawak, Labuan and North Borneo," *Journal of the Straits Branch of the Royal Asiatic Society,* 20:13-74; 21, (1889-90): 19-122.

Wallace, Alfred Russel, *The Malay Archipelago: the land of the orangutan, and the bird of paradise. A narrative of travel, with studies of man and nature* (New York, 1869).

Warren, Jim, "Joseph Conrad's Fiction as Southeast Asian History:

Trade and Politics in East Borneo in the late 19th Century," *Brunei Museum Journal* 4,1 (1977): 21-33.

Watts, C.T. (ed.), *Joseph Conrad's Letters to R.B. Cunninghame Graham,* (Cambridge: Cambridge University Press, 1969).

Waugh, Alec, *Fuel for the Flame* (London: Cassell, 1960).

Wheatley, Paul, *The Golden Khersonese* (Kuala Lumpur: Penerbit Universiti Malaya, 1980).

Wicks, P.C., "Images of Malaya in the Stories of Sir Hugh Clifford," *Journal of the Malay Branch of the Royal Asiatic Society,* 52, 235 (1) (1979): 57-72.

Winstedt, Richard 0. *"A Brunei code,"* Journal of the Singapore Branch of the Royal Asiatic Society 1,1, 1923: 251.

Yamazaki, Tomoko, *Sandakan Hachiban Shookan Teihen Joseishi Joshoo* (Tokyo: Chikuma Shooboo, 1972).

Young, Gavin, *Slow Boats to China* (London, Penguin, 1987).

7. Rentier Capitalism in Negara Brunei Darussalam

The smallest, least-populated,[1] and probably least-known state in Southeast Asia, Brunei only resumed full sovereign status from its former protecting power, the United Kingdom, in 1984. Upon independence, Negara Brunei Darussalam, as it became officially known, assumed full responsibility for its defense and foreign affairs, joined the United Nations, the Association of Southeast Asian Nations (ASEAN) and the Organization of the Islamic Conference (OIC).

From 1906 until 1959, with the exception of the Japanese interregnum, executive power had been in the hands of a British Resident; Brunei did not experience a complete loss of sovereignty, especially in matters relating to local customs and religion. Nevertheless, as in the Borneo states and in Malaya itself, the British protectorate system laid down the fundamental administrative, legal, and judicial armature. While the Sultan effectively replaced the British Resident as the source of executive power in 1959, and while representative institutions and a constitutional form of monarchy were set down in a constitution in 1959, a state of emergency imposed in the wake of an unsuccessful rebellion in 1962 has not been lifted nor have representative institutions been permitted to take root.

As a consequence of the discovery and exploitation of its oil resources, commencing in 1928, Brunei is today, in per capita terms, one of the richest states in the world (US$15,200 in 1989). Indeed, more than one observer has remarked upon parallels between Brunei and Kuwait, namely wealth, size, population density, religion, economic management, defense and security, and political system—an analogy made all the more graphic by the high profile achieved by Kuwait in the Gulf War of 1990-91

(Dasse 1991). Prior to a discussion of the political economy of Brunei, a brief analysis of the Sultanate's political system will suggest this Middle Eastern analogy.

Organization of political power in Brunei

It is a statement of fact that Brunei today remains one of a handful of absolute monarchies in the world reigned over and simultaneously ruled over by the hereditary ruler, the Sultan and Yang Di-Pertuan, Sultan Hassanal Bolkiah, who succeeded his father, the late Sultan Omar Ali Saifuddin in 1967. As such, the Sultan holds the office of Prime Minister and Minister of Defense and wields full executive authority. Other immediate members of the royal family and key appointees control commanding positions in the government and in economic management. Prince Mohamed Bolkiah, the eldest of the Sultan's three younger brothers, is Minister of Foreign Affairs. The Sultan's youngest brother, Prince Jefri Bolkiah, is Minister of Finance and thus in ultimate control of the powerful Brunei Investment Agency. While formally assisted by four constitutional councils, the Sultanate has been ruled by decree since 1962 when key provisions of the 1959 Constitution were suspended, most notably the electoral process.

As in Kuwait, the monarchical structure of government in Brunei and the concentration of power and wealth in the hands of a ruling family suggest rule by oligarchy. But unlike the situation in Kuwait, where a National Assembly provided for under a constitution inaugurated in 1962 became an increasingly vocal force in Kuwait politics prior to its dissolution in August 1976, the legislature in Brunei has never been other than a rubber stamp. Indeed, Brunei has yet to take the step adopted by Kuwait two months prior to its invasion, namely allowing the formation of a National Council or rump parliament. Where post-invasion Kuwait promises elections, there is no announced timetable for the restoration of the electoral process in Brunei, nor, indeed, for the lifting of the state of emergency. Thus, whereas in Kuwait one can speak of a shadowy parliamentary opposition crystallized around political parties, the very concept of an opposition is not officially accepted in Brunei. The possibilities of the single surviving sanctioned political party in Brunei actually entering the political process looks remote at the present juncture.

Commencing in 1986, however, the cabinet system of government in Brunei was strengthened by increasing the number of ministries from seven to eleven and with the addition of deputy ministerial positions. While such an arrangement, along with a further cabinet reshuffle taking effect in January 1989, offers a more technocratic profile to the "regime," it has become something of a pastime among observers of the Brunei scene to identify among the Ministers and advisers those who tend to ideological or Islamic solutions to the country's development and those who come down on the side of a pragmatic accommodation with modernization and development. Usually identified as heading the "ideologues" is the kingdom's senior religious official, the State Mufti, along with the powerful Minister of Education, Pehin Abdul Aziz. Also included in this camp are Pehin Badaruddin, Permanent Secretary to the Prime Minister (the Sultan), and with various responsibilities spanning information and religion, and the Minister of Religious Affairs, Haji Mohammad Zain. Those who are considered more pragmatic in their vision are such Western-educated confidants of the court as the Special Adviser to the Sultan in the Prime Minister's Office, Pehin Dato Isa, and the Minister of Industry and Primary Resources, Pehin Dato Haji Abdul Rahman. While the Sultan and Prince Mohamed have traditionally been perceived as pro-Western or at least pragmatic, increasingly they are obliged to straddle or play off the two camps or tendencies, an increasingly difficult act, for, as few would deny, today it is the "ideologues" who are in the ascendancy with the technocratic or pragmatic group on the defensive (Weaver 1991: 56-93).

But if official Islam is in a sense manageable in a country where the Sultan is considered the secular head of the faith, there is no doubt that the Sultan is alert to the dangers of a Nasserite-type putsch from within as much a challenge from without. From the political standpoint, the role of praetorian guard is ensured by a 1,000-strong battalion of Ghurkhas recruited by and dependent upon the Sultan. But sensitivity to challenges was also shown up by a major restructuring of Brunei's armed forces in September 1991. In this move, three services were effectively created where hitherto there had been one. In announcing this shakeup, which also involved a rotation of key personnel, the Sultan not only cautioned vigilance against the possible eruption of regional disputes à la Kuwait but also doubted the reliability of leadership within the otherwise professionally encadred and British-trained armed forces; in the words of the Sultan (quoted in *Borneo Bulletin* 15 October 1991) "Senjata makan tuan" (weapons could be turned against oneself).

Rentier capitalism in contemporary Brunei

The foundation of the country's wealth, it is clear, stems from the exploitation of the country's hydrocarbon resources, which began in the third decade of this century. Unlike the Asian Newly Industrialized Countries (NICs), whose economic development is based upon the manufacture and export of manufactured goods for Western markets, Brunei's economy is almost entirely dependent (98 percent) on the export of oil and gas. For all intents and purposes Brunei's economy conforms to those less diversified economies of the Middle East also dependent on high-income-earning natural resources. Such economies—at least as mediated by forms of state control— are typically beneficiaries of substantial amounts of royalties or external rentals on a regular basis. In the literature on the petroleum-based economies of the Middle East, such states have been termed rentier states supported by rentier economies. What are the acknowledged features of rentier states and rentier economies?

The rentier state concept, or the notion that states based upon external sources of income are substantially different from states based on domestic taxation, was first proposed with reference to such Middle Eastern economies as Iran by Mahdavy (1970) and Libya by Mabro (1969) and First (1974), although clearly the concept of rent (and ground rent) can be traced back to Marx and before him, Adam Smith. More recently, Colclough (1985) has proposed the relevance of the rentier state model to Brunei, albeit speculatively. In general terms, as recipients of substantial foreign rents, the economies of rentier states are extroverted in the sense that the key industry—export of oil and gas—has very little to do with the production processes of the local economy. Typically, producer states have appropriated sufficiently large shares of the rents that accrue to the oil companies as profits to embark upon large public expenditure programs "without resorting to taxation and without running into drastic balance of payments or expenditure problems" (First 1974: 148). In a situation of rising oil revenues, the government or at least the public sector becomes the dominant factor in the local economy. This gives rise to a special form of *étatisme*. Specifically, if most of the oil royalties or rentals are used to import consumption goods, then the productive sectors of the economy will be untouched beyond that worked by foreign enterprise. In such a rentier situation, there is no "nexus between production and income distribution," since revenues accrue directly to the government not through any production, but from oil taxes, which come from outside the economy. Consumption patterns become geared to the use of imported commodities: "There are no links between the proceeds of production, effort, and incentive" (First 1974: 149-50). Further, Beblawi (1987: 52) has drawn distinctions among a rentier state, rentier economy, and rentier mentality. *Inter alia*, a rentier state is a special version of a rentier economy in which the defining feature is the "externality" of the rent origin. But such an economy also creates a rentier mentality, implying a break in the work-reward causation and where reward or wealth is not related to work and risk taking.

In theory, as Colclough has written of rentier economies in general, the state could live off the dividends by managing investment portfolios. Up against the high-technology extractive industry, the social base of the country remains backward; agriculture and other domestic industries tend to stand still or wither. Typical of "enclave" economies, linkages between the oil sector and other sectors are very limited, downstream industries nonexistent as the product tends to be exported in crude or refined form. Rather, in an inversion of the development process, the rentier economy supports the development of the service sector almost exclusively as the employer of an army of foreign technicians and laborers. Typically, also, the legacy of colonial education policies is a severe skill restraint. In a situation in which the government is obliged to pay generous consumption benefits to nationals in the way of housing, education, medical benefits, and social services, it is entirely rational for national workers to remain unemployed rather than take jobs outside government. Often a situation of over-expansion of public sector employment also arises (Colclough 1985: 29-32).

In development terms, the rentier state pre-empts a shift to the producer state. The generation of wealth, albeit abundant, throws up the paradox of a state of a high-technology industry in an otherwise backward economy (cf. First 1974: 150). Along-side all these features of the rentier state, additional barriers to a transformation to a producer state economy or the diversification of the economy are the inflated cost structure and an in-flated currency. Almost anything can be imported more cheaply than it can be produced at home (Colclough 1985: 31). As will be discussed later, rentier states also characteristically privilege political considerations over strictly economic considerations. This has profound implications for state-society relations and the form that *étatisme* entails. How applicable, then, is the rentier state/rentier economy paradigm to the Brunei situation? What specific forms does *étatist* control over resources take in Brunei? How is the state-society relationship in Brunei mediated in an erstwhile rentier state situation?

In the following section, I shall trace the dynamic of economic development in Brunei, the making of an oil-dependent economy, and the constraints this imposes upon industrial diversification— the full transition to the import-substitution stage and other indices of industrial deepening, namely domestic capital accumulation.

The dynamic of colonial economic development

One approach to modern Brunei economic history would be to discuss the economic incorporation of the state to sub-regional,

regional, and global economic networks, according to chronological stages of both economic and political development. This broad world-systems analysis, however, would have to be modified, to take into account the legacy of powerful local tributary forms of surplus accumulation and their culturally expressed correlates in the form of patrimonial distribution of rewards. Thus, to give credence to local forms of economic activity—not inconsiderable in the case of Brunei before the Protectorate—it is important to outline such pre-colonial forms of production and exchange as the development of craft manufacture, as well as the central role of the Sultanate in mediating regional and long-distance trade and exchange. Only then can we understand the economic forms surviving into the colonial period.

A discussion of the Brunei economy under the Protectorate, then, would necessarily address not only the emergence of new forms of production, consumption, and exchange, but would equally account for the "dissolution" effects of monetization on the traditional economy, the development of a standardized currency, the imposition of new forms of taxation, and the creation of colonial monopolies. Central here—and in common with other economies on the colonial periphery—is the creation under colonial auspices of "extroverted" forms of economic activity—namely, in the Brunei example, the development of new extractive industries. This is not just a question of elucidating modern versus traditional economy or a restatement of economic dualism, but a question of tracing the complex evolution of, subsumption of, and coexistence of new and old forms of economic activity through time, and in response to broader regional and international political and market forces and demands.

As the British historian A.V.M. Horton has written, such was Brunei's integration or actually subsumption into a colonial economy with Singapore as sub-metropole that, by the opening years of this century, the capital city and surrounding districts were described in a British report as producing almost nothing and dependent on imports for all necessities except for a small amount of locally produced rice. Hence the establishment of the British Residency in Brunei in 1905-06 resulted in a reorganization of the fiscal regime, effectively leading to the abolition of a "feudal" system of administration, taxation and land tenure based on crown, ministerial, and "feudal" *(tulin)* lands with serf tenure. Under the new dispensation, aside from a civil list, all other revenues would go to the state. For the first decades of the century, the program of buying up *tulin* rights left the state heavily indebted. Through to the 1930s, then, Brunei was actually subsidized by the Federated Malay States and the Straits Settlements (Horton 1990: 26-32).

The first of Brunei's resources assayed by British merchant capital was coal. This resource was exploited until 1926 by the Brooke family in a special economic enclave at Brooketon in the Muara district. Another extractive industry developed under the auspices of colonial capital was cutch, a by-product of mangrove trees, processed in a plant run by the Island Trading Company in Brunei Town until closed down in the early 1950s. Cutch was actually Brunei's most valuable export between the years 1906 and 1922. In the period before oil revenues guaranteed Brunei's solvency, only the timely establishment by British capital of rubber plantations in Brunei rescued the country economically. Production fell away during the Great Depression and only recovered in the postwar period, reaching a peak in production in 1960 before being allowed to decline (Franz 1990: 243-4). But with the exploitation of oil commencing in 1932, and the realization of super-profits through production-sharing arrangements with Royal Dutch Shell, even the vestiges of a traditional economy, paddy rice and fishing, have been permitted to run down. Not only did new oil revenues give a massive expansion to government revenue, but by 1936 Brunei was able to clear its national debt (Horton 1990: 26-32). As a general statement, then, agriculture, fishing, and forestry activities in the Residency period ranged from the lowest level of self-sufficient subsistence economy practised by certain tribal groups in remote areas to purely commercial farming without private consumption.

While at the outset of the Residential era the Sultan privately languished in a state of penury consistent with the sorry state of the Sultanate at the hands of such local agents of British mercantile imperialism as the Brooke family and the North Borneo Company, by 1934, Horton (1990: 26-32) estimates, the Sultan was gaining a private income in excess of a handsome income received from the government. In the postwar period, however, Civil List expenditure rose to £35,000 annually, double that figure again by 1961. Together, as discussed below, the expanding revenue base along with a strengthened monarchical system served to define the nature of the evolving rentier economy.

A special form of *étatisme*

Visibly, Brunei has undergone rapid structural change in the postwar period, from an overwhelmingly agrarian society to what Franz (1990: 129-31) has described as a service sector society. Thus while in 1947 more than 50 percent of the population was employed in the primary sector, by 1971 the figure had declined to just over 10 percent. In the same period, the tertiary—here understood as service-sector grew from around 30 percent to over 50 percent, while the secondary sector remained at the same level.

But even as urbanization has progressed in Brunei, the development from an agrarian to a tertiary sector society has not followed the conventional pattern of developing countries. Rather, Brunei has moved towards a tertiary society without developing the secondary linkages. Even the growth of the secondary sector from the early 1970s onward has been entirely due to the expansion of the construction industry and therefore does not signal any kind of industrial deepening (Franz 1990: 131). Thus today, in place of such commercial agricultural activities as rubber plantations, it is the state which supports large-scale farm projects—the Mitsubishi Corporation Macfarm or model farm is one—in the attempt to reduce dependence upon foreign imports of basic foodstuffs. But as these operations are largely noneconomic or "showcase" operations, they should be seen more in terms of their political statements (Franz 1990: 209).

It should be clear, then, that Brunei's economy is almost entirely founded on its petroleum and gas resources, generating some 61 percent of GDP, relative to 32 percent generated by the service sector and 2 to 3 percent by agriculture. Some three-fifths of Brunei's petroleum and gas resources, which, as mentioned, account for almost all export resources, are directed towards Japan. Similarly, government revenue is derived primarily from its oil and gas interests and from company taxation, including that of Royal Brunei Shell. There is no income tax. There is also no trade deficit, no national debt, and the balance of payments remains in surplus (Hong Kong & Shanghai Bank 1988: 8).

A special feature of the oil industry in Brunei is the "privatized" character of ownership and operational control of the oil industry. Since 1913 the Shell Group of companies has dominated the search and exploitation of Brunei's hydrocarbon resources. Today the oil industry in Brunei is dominated by four companies belonging to Brunei Shell in each of which the state holds a 50 percent share. Dominating the energy sector is Brunei Shell Petroleum (BSP), responsible for exploration and production of oil and natural gas as well as oil refining and crude oil trading. Second in importance is Brunei LPG, a three-way tie-up between Brunei, Shell, and Mitsubishi Corporation, contracted in 1972 and concerned with liquefying the gas it buys from BSP. Brunei LPG sells the liquefied gas to a third company, Brunei Coldgas, which in tandem with a fourth company, Brunei Shell Tanker, arranges transportation and sale to Japanese customers. Central to the LPG operation is a twenty-year agreement—renegotiated in 1993—to supply the Tokyo Electric Power Company, the Tokyo Gas Company, and the Osaka Gas Company. Overall, the government derives an estimated 85 percent of all earnings of Brunei Shell Petroleum in the form of taxes and royalties (Economist Intelligence Unit 1990-91: 47).

In part as a conservation measure, the normal level of oil production has been held in recent years at 150,000 barrels per day, although this threshold was breached to take advantage of higher oil prices prevailing in late 1990 as a result of the Gulf crisis. Notably, in the period from 1986 onwards, Jasra Elf, a union of Brunei (meaning Royal family controlled) Jasra International Petroleum (Jaspet), and Elf Aquitaine Offshore Asia BV have made important offshore oil discoveries in Brunei, thus breaking into the Shell Groups' monopoly. Significant by world standards, the 1990-91 discoveries are bound to raise the threshold of known resources, albeit a closely guarded state secret. Although Brunei's large earnings from its foreign investments provide it with considerable immunity from oil price fluctuations, government spending is influenced by its hydrocarbon revenues. The construction sector in particular stands to benefit from higher state spending as do other non-oil economic activities (Economist Intelligence Unit 1991, no.1: 31).

It is of interest that Brunei has never been tempted towards nationalization of the oil industry, as for example has Algeria; nor has it allowed a state oil industry to develop along the lines of Malaysia's Petronas or Indonesia's Pertamina; nor, indeed, has Brunei chosen to join OPEC. The reasons are basically as much political as economic. Under British tutelage, pro-Western Brunei distanced itself from OPEC's radical posturing on pricing and production policies, but as a relatively small player in the international oil stakes, Brunei was able to take advantage of the spot market when opportune. Otherwise, though, Brunei shares the basic feature of the economies of oil-rentier states, namely the way in which the state emerges as the main intermediary between the oil sector and the rest of the economy.

Another special feature of *étatisme* in oil-rentier states stemming from the accumulation of windfall profits is the massive increase in public expenditure programs. While such infrastructural developments as housing, health and education figure in such programmes, so does spending on defense which has characteristically reached new heights.[2] Such spending and employment opportunities also constitute an important instrument of redistribution of oil revenues among various social groups, the political importance of which is obvious. This has been termed the "internal recycling of oil wealth." But, no less, the "external recycling of oil rent" reinforces the rentier character of the state, notably through overseas portfolio investment. Characteristically this throws up a "tripartite alliance" between the state (in Brunei this function is served by the Brunei Investment Agency), the new business elite (in Brunei, the *bumiputera* merchants, contractors and financiers alongside certain Chinese comprador interests[3]), and circles of international capital—the subject of wide speculation on the part of finance journalists in the case of Brunei (Abdel-Fadil 1987: 86).

The modus operandi of the Brunei Investment Agency, created in 1983 in order to manage the Sultanate's reserves and which in turn eclipsed the British Crown Agents who had traditionally performed this role, bears scrutiny. As explained in a recent and rare interview by its managing director, Dato Abdul Rahman Karim, also a Permanent Secretary in the Ministry of Finance, the Agency only handles 40 percent of the kingdom's foreign reserves which he estimates at US $27 billion. The remainder is divided among eight foreign (mainly Japanese and American) institutions, including Morgan Guaranty, Bankers Trust, Citibank, Nomura Investment, and Daiwa. From 50 to 60 percent of the Agency's money is in bonds and from 40 to 50 percent is in stocks and shares (such blue-chip companies as Mercedes, Siemens, IBM, and Sony, banks and real estate, all in all realizing two billion dollars profit per year (cf. Weaver 1991: 76-7).

Besides the role of the Brunei Investment Agency in "external recycling" we should add QAF Holdings, "a diversified concern with close links to the Royal family" and the second largest business operation in the country after Brunei Shell, and the Sultan, an active investor in his own right (Economist Intelligence Unit 1990-91: 43). As Beblawi (1987: 55) observes of oil rentier economies, "the distinction between public service and private interest is very often blurred. There seems to be no clear-cut conflict of interests between holding public office and running private business at the same time, and it is not infrequent to use the one to foster the other." Clearly, estimates of the Sultan's private wealth today turn on separating out national reserves from those under Royal control. Bartholomew (1989: 16) asserts that "Brunei is a private country run like a private possession. One is entitled to ask if the Sultan does not control the country's reserves, who on earth does?" Further, as Dasse has written of the switch by Brunei from sterling investments to dollars and yen: "The Sultanate acquired a form of direct political pressure on the U.S. and Japan who cannot ignore such an important investor." Yet another feature of the rentier state, as mentioned, is the existence of a "parasitic" consumer class in the absence of a producer class. Brunei has long enjoyed the highest per capita income in Southeast Asia and is in the same bracket as certain of the industrialized countries and the oil-producing countries of the Middle East. While evidence of prosperity is highly visible (for example, Brunei boasts one of the highest car-ownership rates in the world), as Franz states, income relativities—and, by inference, income inequalities—are difficult to gauge. By any measure, however, wages are higher than in neighboring Sabah, Sarawak, and Indonesia, made more attractive by the strength of the currency, the fact that such staples as rice and sugar are fixed and subsidized, and that the state can afford not to levy tax on income. Additionally, citizens—a restrictive category in Brunei—are beneficiaries of other benefits such as subsidized education and housing. But, as Franz notes, prosperity creates demands that cannot be satisfied with a low income. Demand is thus actually stimulated by the government practice of granting loans to local Bruneians at interest-free or low-interest rates. This has had the effect, at the obvious expense of savings, of stimulating the purchase of such luxuries as television sets, video recorders, and cars (Franz 1990: 135-40). Clearly, then, the Brunei consumer, not producer or risk-taker, is the apotheosis of the Brunei middleclass.[4]

Industrial diversification in the non-oil gas sectors

In what ways has the state sought to encourage industrial diversification so as to free Brunei from its erstwhile rentier state condition and push the economy along the path of domestic capital accumulation, as in the free-market economies of Southeast Asia? Rhetorically, at least, Brunei has long been committed to such a course. Such was the thrust of the nation's Fifth Development Plan (1986-90). Indeed, the creation in January 1989 of the Ministry of Industry and Primary Resources was heralded as ushering in the development of productive industrialization in the country. The year 1991 marks the end of the nation's fifth five-year plan and sees Brunei entering its sixth five-year plan. Although not yet formally announced, it is expected that the plan will focus on specialized infrastructural development such as industrial parks and export-oriented and capital-intensive industries, all in line with the drive to diversify the oil-based economy.

The prospects for sustained diversification of the economy in the non-oil and gas sectors are called into question by several factors. These include the inability to attract foreign investment, know-how, and partners; the inability of local business to compete with the state sector, the shortage of human resources and materials; and the minuscule size of the local market for potential local manufacturers.

The inability to attract foreign investment and expertise has not necessarily been for want of trying. For example, in March 1990 a high-powered Bruneian delegation visited the UK, the first ever—to Europe, to seek UK private investment in the Sultanate. Taiwanese, Australian, and Singapore businessmen have similarly been encouraged to invest in Brunei. Still, the perception exists that Brunei lacks the necessary infrastructure and skilled workforce, and is otherwise only half-hearted about its commitment. This not only concerns administrative obstacles thrown up against potential investors, but also a public attitude that sees outside influences in terms of cultural threats. Thus the results of the diversification drive to date are meager and include the establishment of several plants producing clothing for export, a soft-drink canning factory, and a steel roofing plant—all almost wholly reliant upon the import of raw materials. Only the embryo of an industrial import substitution policy has so far been created.

Emblematic of the problem of domestic capital formation is the demonstrable inability of *bumiputera* businessmen to compete with the state sector. This was revealed in the course of a well-publicized meeting in 1990 of over 300 local businessmen in the nation's capital to discuss the problem of delayed payments by government departments to private contractors. As reported in the local press, "the contractors were apparently not satisfied with the explanations provided by government spokespersons" *(Borneo Bulletin* cited in Economist Intelligence Unit 1990, no. 3). The result, in early 1991, was a "funeral procession" of local civil contracting firms and a "flood" of bankruptcies on the part of local and foreign contractors. While most of the large international consultancy companies attracted during the government building boom years have been able to leave behind a skeleton staff in the Sultanate, *bumiputera* building contractors have been victims of both "careless cash control" and cash flow problems *(Borneo Bulletin* 24 March 1991).

The labor shortage in Brunei is partly artificial, the result of cultural predilections on the part of locals, and partly real, the result of a dearth of skilled personnel. Characteristic of rentier economies, a relatively high percentage of the workforce is employed by the government. In Brunei, the public sector accounts for more than two-thirds of the indigenous labor force (57,700), and Brunei Shell Petroleum, for much of the rest. Indeed, as the Minister for Industry and Primary Resources has conceded, the government's campaign to lure the local workforce into the private sector has not been successful *(Borneo Bulletin* 14 April 1990).

It is clear that the demand for labor has been sustained in the eighties by the increased level of development, as laid out in the Fifth Development Plan and in various diversification policies. The increased demand for labor, both blue-collar and professional, however, has not been entirely left to market forces but is equally regulated through labor regulations, quotas and immigration controls (Thambipillai 1990: 15). In April 1990 the Minister of Industry and Primary Resources, Pehin Dato Haji Abdul Rahman, affirmed that Brunei's movement towards industrialization will open up 40 new jobs as it begins to implement some 2,000 industrial activities, half of which could be taken up by locals *(Borneo Bulletin* 14 April 1990). It would appear, however, that economies like Singapore, as opposed to Brunei, were poised to take advantage of these developments by exporting infrastructure engineering, professional consulting, building materials, technical support services, and information technology (Supplement, *Borneo Bulletin* 8 July 1991: V).

While a small but growing local underclass of detribalized Iban migrants from Sarawak and stateless Chinese has historically existed in Brunei, labor is almost entirely imported and drawn from the labor-exporting countries of Southeast Asia, especially such sources as low-wage and labor-abundant Thailand, the Philippines, and India, alongside traditional sources such as the Malaysian states of Sarawak and Sabah (Thambipillai 1990: 14-15). While Brunei is therefore a net exporter of remittances (itself an important feature of the growth economies of the region), it shares with rentier economies at large the luxury of paying no social overheads for its erstwhile dispensable, docile, and imported proletariat. This comprises some 30,000 expatriate workers mostly employed in the construction, petroleum, and service sectors. While union rights technically exist in Brunei (the *Trade Union Act* of 1961) they are honored only in the breach in the private sector, and contract labor in Brunei is exposed to the full gamut of otherwise documented risks and abuses associated with the intra-ASEAN and Middle East trade in labor.[5]

Overall, then, overdependence upon foreign labor stems from the small number of locals entering the workforce, the insufficiency of local skilled labor and a cultural predisposition for public sector employment. Otherwise, the main constraint on expansion in the non-oil sector, and particularly in construction, is the shortage of labor rather than capital (Economist Intelligence Unit 1990, no. 2: 9).

One of the clearest statements on Brunei's commitment to opening of the economy away from a pure rentier economy model and towards industrial diversification was made by the Sultan in July 1991. On the occasion of his 45th birthday, the Sultan outlined certain of the future lines of development he wished Brunei to pursue over the next twenty years, as contained in a twenty-year master plan on Brunei's development, which also cited obstacles to foreseen objectives. Indeed, the Sultan noted that while a small effort had been made by local companies in manufacturing (three companies involved in the export of clothing, a plastics factory, a plant manufacturing roofing materials), all relied upon imported materials and all were dependent on foreign labor. The desired direction for industrial diversification, he ruled, should be towards activities that give opportunities to locals. Brunei, alone among the ASEAN countries, he noted, does not produce consumer goods, is reliant upon imports of all basic commodities, and is entirely dependent upon the exports of one basic commodity group, oil and gas. The Sultan's prognosis was for Bruneians, especially the younger generation, to be *lebih cekal* (more determined) and *bersikap terbuka* (open in their attitude) to foreign advice and training. As a panacea he announced a new Technical and Vocational Education system to complement existing post-secondary institutions—which have already gone far in changing attitudes and preparing a younger generation for the workforce, especially, it might be noted, in winning acceptance for a role for women in the workplace. Matching the call for openness in attitudes towards science and technology was an announcement that Brunei would seek to operate a more "open" foreign policy in a post-Cold War situation, implying the establishment of diplomatic links with China and the Soviet Union *(Pelita Brunei* 17 July 1991). Similar pro-development sentiments were expressed by the Sultan on the occasion of the Fourth ASEAN Summit in Singapore on 27 January 1992.

Transitions from authoritarianism: changing ideology and culture

One measure of the transition from authoritarianism to a more participatory political culture would be the emergence of a civil society supporting such autonomous institutions as a free press, universities, political parties, civil rights, labor rights, and so on. But, as in certain of the Gulf states, British interest in the oil-rich Sultanate has always been proprietary; indeed, Britain retained control of Brunei's external policy until 1 January 1984, the date that Brunei became a sovereign independent country. Although the first elections in 1962 saw an anti-Malaysia and anti-British socialist party (the Azahari faction) swept to victory in the polls, only timely British intervention rescued the Sultanate from widespread rebellion mounted by the aggrieved party otherwise denied its seat in government. As mentioned, the state of emergency declared at the time has not been lifted and security obsessions (the parallel with British military support to the Sultanate of Oman is illustrative) have prevented a resurfacing of the experiment in representative government.

Singh (1988: 67) writes that in fact the reverse has taken place. In 1984, the appointed State Legislative Assembly was suspended and the power of the monarchy further strengthened. A relaxation in 1985, which saw the emergence of the "opposition" Brunei National Democratic Party and the loyalist National Alliance Party, did not prevent the subsequent banning of the former party and detention of the party's leadership following a call by its leaders (in Kuala Lumpur) for a lifting of the state of emergency, the standing down of the Sultan as prime minister, and the calling of elections. Originally launched with the Sultan's blessing, the Party had attracted an estimated membership of 3,000, mainly businessmen and professionals. The death in 1990 of the president of the outlawed BNDP, shortly after release from detention along with the party's secretary-general, just about put an end to this experiment in (albeit guided) representative democracy (Economist Intelligence Unit 1990, no. 3; Leake 1990).

Consonant with the language of nation-building and echoing the efforts of the other insular "Malay" countries of Southeast Asia, Brunei has chosen to elevate the orthodoxy to the level of a national ideology. This is termed Melayu Islam Beraja (MIB-Kingship), an amalgam of Islamic values grafted onto Brunei Malay culture linked with a sense of the monarchy as the "defender of the faith and an unbroken line of independent Brunei sultans." Unlike the more accommodative thrust of, say, Indonesia's Pancasila or even Singapore's avowed list of national values, MIB is "emphatically not multicultural" but carries strong anti-foreign (including anti-Western) overtones if taken too literally. As a correspondent of the *Far Eastern Economic Review* (15 November 1990) has written, by pushing the Islamic agenda, the secular course of political development has been held in abeyance (indeed, secular has become a pejorative term in the context of MIB). While the MIB concept crystallized prior to independence in 1984, there is no doubt, the report continues, that the current emphasis is driven by the conservatives in the Ministries, notably those restored to influential positions following the 1988 proscription on political parties. Indeed, concern over religious dissonance is matched by concern over political dissent and social discord. In 1989 the Sultan warned that "troublemakers" driven by jealousy and frustration were attempting to engineer a confrontation between the people and the government (Economist Intelligence Unit 1990, nos 2 & 3).

In what sense, then, is a civil society in Brunei supported by the existence of an autonomous press? Prior to the launching in 1953 of the longest running newspaper in the country, *The Borneo Bulletin,* Brunei had no tradition of a press. Originally a British-owned venture, the paper was sold in 1959 to the Singapore Straits Times Group. Even though a part share was acquired in 1985 by QAF Holdings, Brunei's first listed company, the paper's editorial outlook as well as advertising content continued to be shaped by the Straits Times Group. QAF Holdings, otherwise under Royal family control, acquired full ownership of the paper in early 1990 and in the following year relaunched the paper as a daily *(Borneo Bulletin 3* May 1991). Published in English and romanized Malay, the country's only local newspaper carries no editorial, one or two pages of local news, little or no analysis, and no investigative features of a political or administrative nature. Perhaps only a lively letter-to-the-editor column conveys a sense of spontaneity. Otherwise, the press in Brunei is seen as an outlet for advertising media and an instrument of nation-building (cf. *Borneo Bulletin* 3 May 1991). Aside from this newspaper and certain corporate publications (such as those of the Shell Group), there have been no books or magazines published in Brunei by private or commercial concerns since 1962. All other forms of print and electronic media are under state control. Foreign publications are subject to a gamut of legislation that dates back to colonial times and has been strengthened since independence, to censor material deemed subversive of the social, political, and religious order (cf. *Laws of Brunei Darussalam).*

As in other Islamic states Bruneian Muslims are torn between loyalty to nation and to the *ummat*, the Muslim community at large. National choices are, necessarily, mediated by religious affiliation. Brunei, as an active member of the OIC, politically tends to an Islamic consensus on international issues. In the tension between modernity and tradition, it is often religious priorities that take precedence in developmental decisions. As an Islamic state it is not surprising that since independence, the trend in Brunei has been towards strengthening public institutions commensurate with an Islamic ideal. This holds in education, banking, public administration, the legal superstructure, as well as in morality and public conduct. While other Southeast Asian states see themselves as repositories of Asian values, model Asian-style democracies, agents of development, potential NICs or a combination of all, Brunei sees itself, first and foremost, as an exemplary Islamic Malay *negara* state in Southeast Asia. The strengthening of the official political and religious orthodoxies in the country, however, leaves no leeway for those who would dissent from the official Sunni creed and who would—as the Sultan warned in 1990—defile Brunei's way of life, including Islam and loyalty to the monarchy. The matter was made more explicit in February 1991 when a Royal decree banned a Muslim movement known as Al Arqam on the grounds that it was spreading teachings contrary to Islam (Economist Intelligence Unit 1991, no. 2: 31). No crisis of authoritarianism, such as that identified by Pye (1990), has yet threatened to undermine the state. The ability of the state to co-opt, reward, and silence has neutralized or at least postponed those voices that would champion the idea "that no one has a monopoly on absolute truth."

Conclusion

In the literature on rentier states, Mahdavy (1970) has demonstrated the case of Iran, while Mabro (1969) and First (1974) have noted the applicability of the model to Libya. As shown above, Brunei fits the pattern exactly. Colclough (1985), in highlighting the barriers to diversification of the Brunei economy away from the "distortions" arising from a high-income-earning natural resource, sees Brunei as a potential or "qualified" rentier nation. But the vulnerabilities described and cautioned by Colclough are in fact symptoms of the condition, namely the "heavy dependence upon the productive activity of other people" in order to preserve consumption standards and the political and economic risk of converting capital into foreign financial assets.[6]

Whereas the phenomenon of the rise of the new middle classes has helped to define the production and consumption patterns of the populations of the NICs of Asia, no such middle class *qua* class has emerged in Brunei. That is not the same as saying that a new consuming class has not arisen in Brunei. As shown above it has, but whether this new class of consumers—in the absence of producers—is supported by the integuments of civil society matched by the emergence of truly autonomous institutions, that has to be answered in the negative.

It is no doubt the example of the ASEAN economies as much as Brunei's membership of ASEAN that has motivated Brunei to adopt this version of economic *perestroika* and the rhetoric of developmentalism.[7] But beyond the rhetoric lies the dead hand of tradition and history. In Brunei even development is mediated through the veil of cultural rationalizations. The implication for organization development, as one management consultant concluded from a controlled study of one Brunei work unit (a university), is that a profound tension exists between "a national policy designed to limit the extent and slow down the rate of cultural change *and* a development policy that advocates rapid educational and technological advancement" (Blunt 1988: 239). Indeed, as Abdel-Fadil (1987: 106-7) argues, the transitional path from one form of rentier economy to another, under the conditions of declining income from oil, is "highly unstable and surrounded by many uncertainties." He continues that it is "impossible" to draw safe conclusions about the capability of an oil-rentier economy to steer a transitional course to a self-sustained growth path.

Similar uncertainties surround the prospects in Brunei for the transition from authoritarianism to a more representative form of government. If the models are increasingly Middle Eastern, then we may say that historically Islam has not proven to be hospitable to democracy. In Brunei, unlike the case of Malaya, the British abrogated their responsibility to bequeath democratic institutions, and unlike the experience of other Southeast Asian countries, the populist nationalist push in Brunei was belated, misdirected, and botched. But neither in Brunei—anomalously perhaps—have the structural and demographic distortions wrought by developmentalism to a basically traditional polity found their corollary in demand for new political rights as in the manner of a Taiwan, a South Korea or, for that matter, a Kuwait. Brunei obviously fails to meet the basic cultural preconditions for democracy as set down by Huntington (1984). Anderson (1991: 1-15) has argued that contrary to conventional wisdom, the monarchies of the Middle East are in fact particularly well suited to the requirements of state formation. Among the advantages of legitimated absolutism, she cites the ability of monarchs to appeal to tradition "to hobnob with international bankers and ride horseback with presidents." Still, she would not refute Huntington's argument that "the monarchy is ultimately too brittle and restrictive to accommodate the political demands of new social groups." She would also concede that the half-hearted commitment on the part of the Middle Eastern monarchies to egalitarian values raises the question of who is to benefit from the transition.

In what way, then, does the Brunei example inform the debate on the transition to democracy? Overall the experience of Brunei would not appear to support the view that authoritarianism is a necessary and facilitating element in a country's social, economic and political transformation. As seen in the Brunei case, even alongside the ASEAN economies, the structures of authoritarianism are contradictory to the political and economic needs of an increasingly complex regional capitalist sub-system. As shown, the state in Brunei has actively sought to influence the ability of certain groups of capitalists to accumulate. For example, *bumiputera* businesspeople might be able to win contracts, but fetters have been imposed when the contracts are implemented. The overall privileging of citizens over non-citizens as a legal category has also imposed a serious obstacle to the operations of the important Chinese segment of capital. The subordination of labor, especially migrant labor, is another example of the ability of the state, under rentier capitalism, to distort the class and even demographic profile of the country. Yet another anomaly facing the Brunei state is that between a low skills base and the increasingly sophisticated information, knowledge, and management needs of industry, especially in the oil sector.

What has been argued in this chapter, then, is that the limits to a full-blown transition from "feudalism" to rentier capitalism to a mature capitalist economy are as much a function of the state in specific historical context and a country's particular subordination within the world-system as of the legacy of culture *per se*. However, it is true that culture, ideology, and tradition might become, under the auspices of the rentier state, a mask, a guide to action, and rationalization of the political, economic, and social status quo.

Thus, the argument has not been, after Huntington, to ascribe to culture either a determinant or independent role (Huntington 1984). Rather, after Cumings (1989), culture has been viewed as integral to the political and material levels of society, a function of time and global context. Accordingly, it has not been suggested, according to O'Donnell, Schmitter and Whitehead (1986), that it is necessary to separate out social, economic, and cultural elements but, rather—in line with a broad political economy perspective—it has been demonstrated that it is necessary to build socio-structural factors into explanations of regime formation and the processes of transition. However, as others have conceded, this is a very complex task. In this analysis, then, it is easier to delineate why a transition will not and cannot occur, especially in the absence of even the trappings of a bourgeois democratic culture (much less raw industrial capitalism), rather than predict how or when such an event will take place.

Notes

The author wishes to acknowledge a critical reading of a draft of this paper by Mark Cleary, although the author alone remains responsible for matters as they stand.

1. In terms of residential status, of the country's total population of 226,329 in 1986, 67.7 percent were Brunei citizens. A further 9.2 per cent were permanent residents, while 23.1 percent were temporary residents, including one to two percent transients or short-term visitors. Of the residents, the overwhelming majority were Malays. Chinese constituted the majority (61 percent) of the permanent residents and, while all the main ethnic groups were represented in the temporary resident category, 39.7 percent were Chinese (cf. Tong [n.d.]: 78).

2. In 1989 the UK concluded a £250 million arms deal with Brunei, under which Brunei is buying 16 BAe Hawk 100 fighter aircraft and three corvettes to be equipped with Exocet anti-ship missiles. Brunei already has a Rapier air defence missile system (Economist Intelligence Unit 1990, No. 3).

3. Notorious among Chinese comprador interests in Brunei was the former National Bank of Brunei, 70 percent owned by the Chinese tycoon, Khoo Theck Puat, and 30 percent owned by the Sultan. This was closed in September 1986 but not before Khoo absconded with some 650 million dollars. Otherwise the 66,000 Chinese in Brunei play a dominant role in private sector activity, as shopkeepers and in the service industry. Only 6,000 are thought to be citizens. Besides an anomalous legal status thus depriving a considerable percentage of the population of the country of 'rights' and citizen privileges, Brunei Chinese-erstwhile comprador capitalists-are also victims of state policy which massively favors *bumiputera* interests (cf. Economist Intelligence Unit 1990-91: 42).

4. Between 17-21 July 1991 the Brunei Malay Chamber of Commerce and Industry organized an "International Consumer Week." The rationale for this event was ostensibly the demand created by a more discerning Brunei consumer armed with "oil-powered purchasing ability." As the advertising blurb stated:

Never before seen under one roof in Brunei. This incredible variety of consumer products From costume jewelry, silver tableware, furniture, home hi-fi, crystal chandeliers, exercise equipment, electrical appliances, security systems, handicraft to holy water from Medina (*Borneo Bulletin* 8 July 1991).

Indeed, among Brunei's main imports are jewelry, precious metals, paintings, watches and furniture.

5. The matter was stated clearly by the Brunei Darussalam Commissioner for Labor, Awang Haji Zainal, who informed Japan's Vice-Minister of Labor in the course of a visit that the formation of trade unions is "redundant" owing to "the peaceful and harmonious relations between the employers and employees" in the country *(Borneo Bulletin,* 7 August 1991: 1).

6. Writing in 1985 he cites the case of the U.S. freeze on Iranian assets in 1979. The events of 1990-91 over the Gulf are no less indicative of the risks of this strategy (Colclough 1985: 29-32).

7. Illustrative of the way that Brunei is being drawn into a more technocratic superstructure via its links with ASEAN is a report alluding to an agreement signed by Brunei on behalf of ASEAN with the European Community, whereby Brunei will fund and site in Brunei a centre to develop business management skills *(Borneo Bulletin* 24 July 1991: 1).

References

Abdel-Fadil, Mahmoud, "The Macro-behaviour of Oil-rentier States in the Arab Region," in Hazem Beblawi & Luciani Giacomo (eds.) *The Rentier State* (London: Croom Helm, 1987).

Anderson, Lisa, "Absolutism and the Resilience of Monarchy in the Middle East," *Political Science Quarterly,* 106, 1 (1991): 1-15.

Bartholomew, James 1989, *The Richest Man in the World: The Sultan of Brunei* (London: Viking, 1989).

Beblawi, Hazem, "The Rentier State in the Arab World," in Hazem Beblawl & Giacomo Luciani (eds.) *The Rentier State,* (London: Croom Helm, 1987).

Blunt, Peter, "Cultural Consequences for Organisation Change in a Southeast Asian State: Brunei," *Executive* (The Academy of Management), 2, 3, (1988): 235-240.

Colclough, Christopher, "Brunei: Development Problems of a Resource Rich State," *Euro-Asia Business Review,* 4, 4, (1985): 29-32.

Cumings, Bruce, "The Abortive Abertura: South Korea in the Light of the Latin American Experience," *New Left Review,* 173, (1989): 5-32.

Dassé, Martial, "Brunei: the Kuwait of South-East Asia," *Defense National,* 47 (June 1991): 135-149.

Economist Intelligence Unit, *Country Report, Malaysia, Brunei,* (London: The Economist, 1989, 1990, 1990-91).

First, Ruth, *Libya: The Elusive Revolution,* (Harmondsworth: Penguin, 1974).

Franz, Johannes C. *The Sultanate of Brunei: Oil Wealth and Problems of development,* Universitaet Nuemberg, trans. from German by Michael Schmitz & Alistair Sharp, (Brunei: Universiti Brunei Darussalam, 1990).

Hong Kong & Shanghai Bank, *Business Profile Series: Brunei Darussalam,* Hong Kong: Hong Kong & Shanghai Banking Corporation, 1988).

Horton, A. V. M., "Aspects of Finance in Brunei During the British Residential Era, 1906-1959," *Borneo Research Bulletin,* 22, 1 (1990).

Huntington, Samuel P., "Will More Countries Become Democratic?," *Political Science Quarterly,* 99, 2, (1984), 193-219.

Leake, Jr, David, *Brunei: The Modern Southeast Asian Sultanate,* (Kuala Lumpur: Forum, 1990).

Mabro, Robert, "Libya: Rentier State?," *Project,* 39 (November 1969): 1090-1101.

Mahdavy, H., "The Patterns and Problems of Economic Development in Rentier States: The Case of Iran," in M.A. Cook (ed.) *Studies in the Economic History of the Middle East from the Rise of Islam to the Present Day,* (Oxford: Oxford University Press, 1970).

O'Donnell, Guillermo, Schmitter, Philippe C. & Whitehead, Laurence (eds.), *Transitions from Authoritarian Rule: Tentative Conclusions about Uncertain Democracies,* (Baltimore: The Johns Hopkins University Press, 1986).

Pye, Lucien W., "Political Science and the Crisis of Authoritarianism," *American Political Science Review,* 84, 1 (1990): 3-19.

Singh, Ranjit, "Brunei Darussalam in 1987: Coming to Grips with Economic and Political Realities," *Southeast Asian Affairs 1988* (Singapore: Institute of Southeast Asian Studies, 1988).

Thambipillai, Pushpa, "Foreign Workers and Development in ASEAN: The Brunei Context," Working Paper, Department of Public Policy and Administration (Brunei: Universiti Brunei Darussalam, February, 1990).

Tong Niew Shong, *Demographic Trends in Negara Brunei Darussalam,* (Brunei: Universiti Brunei Darussalam, Educational Technology Centre, nd).

Weaver, Mary Anne, "Our Far-Flung Correspondents: In the Sultan's Palace," *The New Yorker* (7 October 1991: 56-93).

8. Wartime Portuguese Timor: The Azores Connection

It is a little-recalled fact of history that the Portuguese colony of Timor was twice invaded during the Pacific War, first by a combined Australian-Dutch force on 17 December 1941 and by the Japanese Imperial Army two months later. The Australian guerrilla forces, pushed back to the mountainous hinterland of the island by the new invader, sought support from the Timorese people, until obliged to withdrew almost completely in 1943. While the sufferings of the Timorese in this internecine colonial struggle were enormous and while Australian guerrilla activities have entered Australian war history as mythology,[1] the broader gauged diplomatic wrangling over the wartime and postwar status of the Portuguese colony are less well known.

Portugal was a neutral in the war. Lisbon was an important listening post for the allies and Asia alike. Accordingly, Japan valued its relationship with Portugal and did not wish unduly to provoke a break. Thus, while Hong Kong was occupied by the Japanese during the war, the neutrality of the Portuguese colony of Macau was not in the main violated. No less consequential for the postwar status of Timor was Allied support for the restoration of Portuguese sovereignty in the territory. This was achieved via an act of high theater owing to the Australian presumption to take the Japanese surrender in both Dutch and Portuguese Timor over the objection of the concerned colonial powers.

In this chapter I seek to demonstrate that, notwithstanding the efforts of concerned Japanese diplomats, the Japanese army occupation of Timor became the leading issue troubling wartime relations between Portugal and Japan. Nevertheless, Japanese wartime rule in Portuguese Timor departed from the experience elsewhere under the Co-prosperity Sphere by its failure to succor an independence movement. Thus unlike the case of the Dutch East Indies (including Dutch Timor), where the colonial restoration was opposed both military and politically, no challenge arose in Portuguese Timor to the restoration of colonial power in the post-surrender period. Nor did the independence cause for Portuguese Timor attract outside attention. As this chapter demonstrates, the Portuguese Prime Minister, Dr António de Oliveira Salazar, was able to skillfully lay claim upon Anglo-American support for the maintenance of the Portuguese overseas empire (Timor included) in exchange for Allied access to the mid-Atlantic base facilities on the Portuguese controlled Azore Islands.

The roots of this arrangement are very deep. Portugal and Britain are party to an alliance of over four hundred years' standing. In a treaty of 1661, England promised to "defend and protect all conquests or colonies of Portugal." This promise was reiterated in the Anglo-Portuguese declaration of 14 October 1899.[2] Britain's involvement in Portuguese affairs deepened, however, commensurate with its Iberian economic and financial interests. Legacies of history in turn colored wartime relations between the two, especially when an Allied victory seemed assured. Most vital and consequential to the Allied cause was the Portuguese grant on 13 October 1943 of the Azores bases to both Great Britain and the United States. As part of the quid pro quo, the United States informed Portugal on 26 October 1943 that it "undertook to respect Portuguese sovereignty in all Portuguese colonies."[3] In fact, the American connection with Portugal goes back to the First World War when the U.S. gained its first access to a naval base in the Azores.

But as one analyst of America's overseas bases has written, the war was nearly over when Portugal agreed to an American request in 1944 to construct an air base on the island of Santa Maria in the Azores. Nevertheless, the U.S. bases in the Azores, which also included Lajis air base, became "important in other ways and in relation to other threats."[4] As shown below, the destiny of Timor and its people was directly linked with these developments. More than once in their troubled history the Timorese have been hostage to colonial and great power rivalry.

The diplomatic setting

In February 1941, Anglo-Australian military representatives met at the Singapore Conference with their Dutch counterparts to confront the menace of a southward Japanese thrust. But it was not until November 1941 that the Dutch acceded to Allied requests to dispatch forces to Ambon and Timor, as earlier agreed.[5]

In the interim, Australia had been involved in lengthy but unsuccessful diplomacy aimed at securing a "privileged" position in Portuguese Timor. Australia sought Portuguese acquiescence in an Australian military presence in the colony.[6] According to an official British source, it was the activities of Japanese submarines off Timor in early December 1941 that triggered these "urgent precautions." The report affirmed that both the British and Australian governments had arranged "in agreement with the Portuguese government" for the immediate intervention by a mixed Dutch-Australian force.[7] A certain diplomatic *leger de main* was involved here, as the Portuguese Prime Minister was less convinced that this government had acquiesced in a breach of its own neutrality. As the U.S. Minister in Portugal noted the day after the Dutch-Australian invasion of Timor on 17 December, Prime Minister Salazar addressed the Portuguese National Assembly, reiterating his country's principled stand in refusing to accept the explanations of the British and Dutch governments over the violation of Portuguese neutrality.[8] Indeed, the Portuguese Minister in Washington revealed in a conversation with the Under Secretary of State, Welles, that negotiations on the "proposed joint action by the British and Portuguese" had not been concluded at the time of the occupation.[9]

According to an internal U.S. government memo, the suggestion to occupy Portuguese Timor came from Admiral Thomas C. Hart, Navy Commander of General Wavall, Commander of the Allied Forces.[10] But this could have been no more than a suggestion, as the U.S. government was at pains to assure Portugal that "it had no intention of encroachment in any form upon Portuguese sovereignty over the Azores," while equally seeking assurances from Salazar that the Axis be kept at arm's length.[11]

Indeed, the Portuguese protest at the Dutch-Australian invasion was unequivocal. According to the official cabled response from Dili on the day of the invasion:

> The Governor of the Portuguese colony protests vigorously against the aggression, absolutely contrary to the principles of law, being carried out against this part of Portuguese territory, by Dutch and Australian forces, who claim to be acting in accordance with instructions received from the Government of the Netherlands Indies in agreement with the Government of the Commonwealth of Australia. [12]

The reply by the Australian Foreign Minister, Dr. Evatt, to the Portuguese Governor, Manuel d'Abreu Ferreira de Carvello, appears as a studied exercise in disingenuity: in order to defend against Japanese aggression it has been found necessary to prevent Japanese breach [of] neutrality. Further, he stated, Australia sought to assist "in every way possible regarding administration and economic life of the colony."[13] While this is hardly borne out by the historical record—especially in the postwar period—Evatt's vision of an Australian Monroe doctrine is less well known!

But neither had the Japanese been inactive in the area of prewar diplomacy in the South Seas. In 1938, the British authorities in Batavia learned from the Dutch that the Japanese were exerting pressure upon the Portuguese in Timor to relax legislation relating to Japanese economic concessions.[14] The signing of a Japanese-Portuguese Agreement in October 1941 relating to the establishment of an air service between the Japanese-mandated territory of Palau and Timor was thus met with apprehension by Washington. But no secret clauses were written into the agreement nor had the Portuguese capitulated to excessive Japanese demands.[15]

In Australia, one of the leading protagonists of intervention in Timor to meet the Japanese challenge was Hudson Fysh, founder of Qantas, who travelled to the colony to negotiate landing rights for the Darwin-Dili-Batavia Flying Boat Service.[16] In turn, Group Captain Ross, an Australian Civil Aviation official, arrived in Dili in April 1941 on duties connected with the Qantas service. He also reported on the political situation in the colony to the Australian Department of External Affairs. In September Ross was appointed as temporary British Consul when it was learned the Japanese intended to establish a Consulate in Dili. On 5 October 1941, Evatt appointed Ross as official representative in Portuguese Timor, although he was not formally recognized as British Consul by the Portuguese Government until 10 December.[17]

Inside Timor: 1942-45

As described by an official Indonesian source, Japanese forces won "glorious victories" (*kemenangan yang gemilang*) in their thrust into Dutch Timor in February 1942. This success was attributed to careful intelligence preparation by Japanese agents prior to the event, as much an adroit propaganda cultivation of an "older brother" image. In this version Japanese forces led by General Hayakawa met no native resistance to their 19 February invasion of the Portuguese enclave of Oecussi on the north coast of the island simultaneous with a landing on the south coast of Dutch Timor. Thus the major resistance effort, such as mounted at Penfui airport and in the interior of Dutch Timor, was by the Allied forces in situ.[18] Japanese sources reveal that advanced military planning for the operation involved both Navy and Army, although from the outset, it was determined that the Army would eventually be responsible for the defense of the island as a whole.[19] But unlike in Portuguese Timor, where the occupation Army gradually eased the Portuguese administration out of office and ruled via the gun, in Dutch Timor—as in the rest of occupied Netherlands East Indies— the symbols of Dutch colonialism were replaced by Japanese. Thus Dutch Timor became Timor-*ken* (or province) and was subsumed in an administrative setup that linked it to the Lesser Sunda command based in Singaraja, in turn answerable to Japanese Navy Command in Makassar.[20]

According to Japanese sources, the Imperial Army did not initially seek to take over the whole administration of Portuguese Timor. Rather, they were guided by local circumstances. They did, however, seek from the outset to control certain essential matters such as defense, "offense," maintenance of public peace, the "prevention of major incidents," and the requisition of goods and labor.[21] But as the Japanese record reveals, Portuguese-Japanese relations in Timor came under severe strain as the occupation progressed. Contrary to Australian military mythology, the Portuguese Governor upheld a stridently independent anti-Japanese line. Such was the Governor's obstructive behavior that his authority was bypassed and the colony's telegraphic communication to Lisbon was cut.[22] For example, a Japanese communication in June described the Governor as "obstinately uncompromising," having rejected Japanese demands to punish certain Portuguese officials and "servants" (ie, loyal Timorese) and for assisting the "invading army" (ie. Australia).[23] In short, the Governor was branded a "great hindrance to the carrying out of the air war and defense operations."[24] Accordingly, on 24 June, the Imperial Government presented to the Portuguese Premier a detailed list of hostile acts committed by the Portuguese authorities and Timorese alike. But two months later, the local Japanese authority detected no change for the better.[25]

Meanwhile, as the Japanese looked to native collaborationists to prop up their occupation, Portuguese-native relations—traditionally adversarial—began to unravel as well. On 24 October the Army decided that all 600 Portuguese in Timor would be concentrated in a designated place. The sole exceptions were the Governor and the Mayor of Dili, who were to remain in office. All Portuguese were to be disarmed. The Army's policy of sequestration of the community ("to the gratitude of the Portuguese") was ostensibly for their protection.[26] While the fund of "gratitude" on the part of the surviving internees was exhausted at war's end, the question of protection from the wrath of the people was possibly not without basis. As the Japanese Consul in Dili, Saito reported to Tokyo, the natives are now "turning up their noses" at the Portuguese who have otherwise looked down upon them.[27]

According to a Japanese Military report of 15 October—in studied contrast to standard Australian accounts—the native Timorese, far from being hostile to the Japanese presence, were positive in supplying information, in acting as guides, and in mobilizing to kill the enemy troops. Not only were they reported to be hostile to Australia but were seen as bitterly anti-Portuguese. Indeed the same report described a "simultaneous uprising" of the natives in two villages south of Dili on or about 20 August. Reportedly, some Portuguese and Chinese were massacred, thus leading to "extreme apprehension" in the Portuguese community. The cause of the uprising was unknown but was believed to have been incited by "a group of natives from former Dutch Timor who came forward to cooperate with the Japanese forces." Alternatively, the Japanese speculated, the rebels could have acted to settle "grudges against the Portuguese because of ill-treatment" in their moment of vulnerability.[28] The truth concerning this rebellion—no doubt an allusion to the infamous "Black Column"—lies somewhere in-between. Dunn's interpretation of the actions of the Column and the Japanese—intrigues to reopen the wounds left by the uprisings earlier in the century and exploitation of traditional tribal rivalries—thus appears as convincing.[29]

In response to these harrowing events, the Portuguese Governor sought to have all Portuguese temporarily evacuated to the offshore Portuguese island of Atauro and to this end petitioned Lisbon to send a ship.[30] The message duly delivered— and intecepted—by the Japanese, spoke of "constant native uprisings" and the "impossibility" of continued residence in Timor.[31] Of course, the requested vessel did not arrive and the move to Atauro did not transpire (although, ironically, this scenario occurred in the face of the Indonesian invasion some thirty years later).

But neither could the Allied bombing of Dili have cheered the population. According to a Japanese diplomatic dispatch in late 1942, two or three Allied planes bombed Dili about once a week, in November becoming a daily occurrence. As a result there were many casualties among the Chinese and Timorese. According to Japanese Consular reports, major targets included the Consulate (November 1942), the radio station (March 1943), a Portuguese vessel, and a hospital (February 1944). Thus by June 1942, Allied bombings had forced the Timorese population to flee the city for the countryside. Aside from the Army presence, only a few Chinese shopkeepers remained in the city.[32]

Life was made harder for the Japanese by the actions of Australian guerrilla forces who, through June 1942 at least, made night raids on the city. Japanese reports pay backhanded tribute to the estimated 300 to 400 Australians of the 2/2 Company whose actions were "to the considerable discomfort of our opposing forces."[33] Similarly, a report of April 1943 noted that "recalcitrant Portuguese and native forces in the hinterland still keep up opposition."[34] This is a reference to the "International Brigade" comprising a number of "*deportados*" exiled from Portugal for revolutionary tendencies.[35]

As explained by one official Indonesian source, while the Indonesian population initially welcomed the Japanese as liberators from Dutch colonialism, a sense of resentment against Japanese excesses developed, if short of armed revolt.[36] But perhaps the local Portuguese attitude towards the wartime experience at the hands of the Japanese is summed up by a participant who wrote with unconcealed bitterness of "three years living under Japanese tyranny in the Liquica-Maubara concentration camp."[37] As for the Timorese, the inter-imperialist struggle fought out in their homeland could hardly have been welcomed, although as clients of the respective armies or as "free agents" as in the case of the anti-colonial rebels, some may have seen marginal advantage in the turmoil. But these were primitive rebels, not yet men with a national program, as were the Fretilin independence fighters some thirty years on.

The Japanese-Portuguese dialogue on Timor

As decoded transcripts of official wartime Japanese communications unfold, Tokyo worked hard at mending the diplomatic damage with Lisbon that the Army wrought in its wasting campaigns in Timor between 1942 and 1945. No doubt, the insights afforded the cryptographers of the U.S. War Department "Magic" program assisted the Allies to stay one move ahead of their adversaries in the prosecution of the war in general. Timor, of course, being only one object of the Allied intelligence eavesdropping program waged in those years.

Thus, some months after the Japanese entanglement in Timor, the Japanese Premier, Hideki Tojo, counseled his diplomatic representatives in Dili and Lisbon alike to uphold a moderate policy in their dealings with the colony:

> Before we apply our power, viz: punishment, seizure, occupation etc., we should first do our best in their (Timor's) improvement and development.

But Tojo had more than the welfare of the Timorese in mind.

> As Europe will have a very important influence upon the future of the East Asia wars, we need to give close attention to our relations with Portugal.

Indeed, as the War Department analyst surmised, Tojo was mindful of the need for Portugal's support in a second front in Europe.[38]

Clearly, by early June, a state of impasse existed over the Timor crisis. While on the one hand, Salazar sought both an Australian and a Japanese evacuation from Timor, Japan on its part proposed that Portugal withdraw troops and instruct its civil authorities in Timor to cooperate with the Japanese. On its part, Portugal made an offer to Japan to disarm the Australian soldiers in Timor and hold them in custody until after the war, provided that Japan withdrew. But neither was this acceptable to Japan. Thus, in June 1942, a "conference for the betterment of relations" between Portugal and Japan was proposed by the Japanese side but thwarted, according to local Japanese interpretation, owing to British pressure.[39]

Meanwhile, Chiba, the Japanese Minister in Lisbon, kept up

the dialogue with Salazar. He reported of one such conversation during September 1942, that the Portuguese leader's attitude on the Timor question was "polite but firm." Indeed, he cautioned Tokyo that even infringing nominally on Timor's sovereignty could bring relations with Portugal to a "sudden crisis."[40]

Incredibly, Nazi Germany also weighed into the Timor affair, pleading unity between the Axis powers. As the German Minister in Lisbon told Morito Morishima, Chiba's successor:

> If as a result of the Timor difficulty, Japanese-Portuguese relations deteriorate, naturally Portugal's relations with Germany and Italy will be affected. Don't you think you had better try to find a way to settle the Timor problem?[41]

The Timor question was also a topic of discussion between the Nazi Foreign Minister, von Ribbentrop, and Oshima, the Japanese envoy in Berlin. At issue in Portugal's relationship with Germany, Ribbentrop lectured, was the value of Lisbon as an intelligence collection base as well as a source of supplies of wolfram. Tellingly, the Foreign Minister remarked, "It is very important that we do not in any way jeopardize his (Salazar's) political position."[42] Indeed, as an earlier report revealed, the Portuguese dictator had confided in Morishima that, following the fall of Mussolini, his own position had been made vulnerable by labor agitation and schemes to overthrow the government. News about Timor, censored rigorously in Portugal but entering the country via Portuguese escapees from Timor residing in Australia, only added to the sense of malaise at home.[43]

On 26 June 1944, Salazar informed Morishima that there was no longer any reason for Japan to hold Timor, since Japan was on the defensive and Timor had lost its value as a base to attack Australia. He further expressed concern at the "difficult international situation" which Portugal would face if Britain and America were to attack Japanese forces in Timor. Morishima, loyal servant of Tokyo, offered the two reasons why Japan could not remove her troops at that juncture. First, American victories in the Pacific notwithstanding, Japan reserved its prerogative to launch an offensive against Australia at any time. Second, even if Japan withdrew its forces, it was doubtful if Britain or the U.S. would respect Timor's neutrality.[44] While the Minister's first rationalization was entirely spurious given the Japanese reversals in the Pacific, the second was based upon sound logic in light of the precedent set by the Australian-Dutch invasion of December 1941.

As an intercept of 14 July makes clear, the Japanese believed that Salazar would eventually propose talks on the question of the Japanese withdrawal. Clearly, the risk for Japan was that a refusal posed a break with Portugal, especially if the Anglo-American side pressured Portugal into a joint dispatch of troops. "Sooner or later," Morishima cabled Tokyo, "Japan will have to decide whether it is more important to keep troops on Portuguese Timor or to maintain relations with Portugal." Yet, he observed, owing to Timor's importance as a base, withdrawal was unthinkable.[45]

The following month Morishima learned of an impending ultimatum served on Japan by the Portuguese government apropos Timor, namely to withdraw its occupation forces or face a rupture of diplomatic relations.[46]

As Salazar revealed in a meeting with Morishima, while the U.S. had not broached the subject of Timor directly, Britain had done so. When in October 1943 it obtained the Azores base rights, Britain reaffirmed her obligation to protect the Portuguese colonies. Specifically with respect to Timor, the U.S. had pressed Britain to apply the Anglo-Portuguese alliance. The Portuguese leader thus made it known to Morishima that in view of both the Anglo-Portuguese alliance and the Anglo-America alliance, it was inevitable that the U.S. would send troops to Timor if Japan declined to withdraw. As Salazar cautioned, in the advent of a U.S. intervention in Timor it would be impossible for Portugal to look on "with folded arms." Necessarily, Portugal would respond. It followed, according to this logic, that Portugal forestall such an eventuality by coming to a prior arrangement with Japan.[47] Clearly, the Japanese Minister's role in Lisbon must have appeared as unenviable as Tokyo's response was an unequivocal "impossible." On 26 August, Morishima received the following instruction from Foreign Minister Shigemitsu:

If the upshot is that Portugal breaks off relations or declares war on us because we refuse to move our forces it cannot be helped.

Yet, he continued, "make it appear that Japan is refusing Portugal's request." In other words, a total dissimulation was required of the unfortunate Morishima if pushed by the Portuguese side.[48]

So concerned did Morishima become regarding a threatened break between Japan and Portugal over the issue that he sought the Japanese Foreign Minister's approval for a plan to evacuate Japanese residents from Portugal to Madrid. This plan was opposed by the Japanese Consul in Madrid, Suma, who feared that in turn Japan's relationship with Spain would likewise "come to grief."[49]

Morishima further counseled an end to the "strategy of evasion" over the matter. He advised Tokyo that the general sense in Portugal was that the defeat of both Germany and Japan was inevitable. Accordingly, the Japanese envoy now counseled a policy of assenting to withdraw from Timor in principle while in practise doing nothing about it. What he envisaged—and this was consistent with Salazar's basic demand—was to stage a withdrawal only ahead of the disembarkation of a Portuguese occupation force. In this event, as the Minister sanguinely reminded Tokyo, the long distance of the colonial outpost in Southeast Asia from Goa and Portugal, not to mention Portugal's own shipping problems, worked in favor of the maintenance of the status quo in Timor.[50]

Japan wanted it both ways. It definitely did not want to break with Portugal but was obdurate in maintaining its military occupation of Timor. By early 1945, however, a sense of compromise emerged in Lisbon. Apparently Salazar had modified his line on the Japanese evacuation issue, believing that the time was no longer suitable.[51]

And conversely, Morishima went over to the view that Japan's interests would best be served by an immediate evacuation of its forces from Timor. As he counseled Tokyo, it was unlikely that America would occupy Timor even in the event of a Japanese withdrawal. Clearly, he argued, American priorities were elsewhere, namely China, Taiwan, and Japan itself. Moreover, he reasoned, the failure of Japan to evacuate Timor could be seized upon by the U.S. as a pretext to demand base rights in Macau. Portugal, he feared, might even raise the issue. The cost to Japan of a fallout with Portugal, he reminded Tokyo, was the loss of an important listening post in Lisbon. Finally, he implored, the military reasons for the occupation of Timor were now invalid.[52] Nevertheless, the Japanese Army and Navy thought otherwise, as the Foreign Minister signaled in his reply to Morishima. Quite simply, Japan could not accede to Portugal's request.[53] Probably the diplomats knew better than the generals, as Portugal's diplomatic break with Nazi Germany came the following month.[54]

The America-Portugal-Timor triangle

As demonstrated below, the centrality of Timor to the U.S. bases diplomacy with Portugal is borne out by the official American record. From a U.S. State Department memo dated 11 June 1945, we know that the Portuguese leader had requested the U.S. Ambassador in Lisbon for details of plans relating to Portuguese participation in the expulsion of Japanese from Portuguese Timor. Evidently this issue had been taken up by the U.S. in a note of 28 November 1944. Likewise, the British offered similar assurances to Salazar around the same time, relating to Portuguese participation in such a mission. As, the memo continued, "these assurances constituted practically the only consideration given us in exchange for the facilities at Santa Maria." Moreover, the Santa Maria facilities were of "incalculable importance." Tellingly, the memo stated, "the principal reason for the delay in obtaining Portuguese assent to the use of Santa Maria was our delay in giving the assurances as to Timor, which were denied by Dr. Salazar." The memo further counseled adherence to the plan to which the U.S. was already committed, namely the facilitation of the Portuguese restoration in Timor.

This is particularly important in view of impending negotiations for long term military rights in the Azores. The Department does not feel that it can start negotiations until the Portuguese are fully satisfied on the question of Timor.[55]

According to a follow-up Memo of 2 September 1944, the Combined Chiefs of Staff appointed an Anglo-American Military Mission to enter into discussions with Portuguese military authorities to discuss Portuguese participation in operations to expel the Japanese from Portuguese Timor. A Portuguese force strength of 4,000 (a regimental combat team) plus 400 native troops was felt to be an acceptable size. Portuguese offers of air units were rejected on the grounds of insufficient technical backup, although a request for supply of ammunitions was accepted. But having accepted Portuguese participation in the operation, the U.S. declined to formally commit itself to the taking of Portuguese Timor and declined to facilitate deployment of Portuguese forces elsewhere. In any case, the memo noted, military operations against Portuguese Timor had to await the completion of higher priority operations against the Japanese.[56] These broad recommendations were duly approved by the State-War-Navy Coordinating Committee (SWNCC) in Berlin. The necessary steps were then taken by the SWNCC panel sitting at Potsdam to inform the Secretary of State as to the above action taken by the Joint Chiefs of Staff. But, as this step was overtaken by events, delivery to the Secretary of State was not deemed necessary.[57] In short, the joint U.S.-Portuguese plan did not materialize; local circumstances dictated otherwise.

As U.S. State Department documents reveal, four broad objectives appeared paramount in U.S.-Portuguese relations at war's end. These were to maintain and improve existing cordial relations, to ensure continuation and development of the base facilities in the Azores, and to encourage Portuguese participation in efforts to achieve economic and military integration in western Europe as well as coordination in the North Atlantic area. Finally, it was hoped to assist the economic and strategic development of Portugal's African possessions. The same communication underscores the primacy of the Azores connection in the overall relationship between the two countries.[58]

As it happened, U.S. diplomacy bore fruit in the postwar period. On 2 February 1948, the U.S. obtained a five-year extension of an existing agreement for transit facilities for U.S. military aircraft at Lagens airfield in the Azores. In May 1948, the Portuguese extended facilities to the UK in the Azores identical to those accorded to the U.S. One should not neglect the postwar realignments that brought not only the U.S. and Portugal into partnership via the Azores bases, but also the Japan-America alliance that assumed a new importance with the outbreak of the Korean War in 1950 and the emergence of the Cold War. One lingering problem, however, beset postwar relations between Japan and Portugal; namely the question of war reparations stemming from the Japanese occupation of Timor. This was anticipated by the Japanese Minister in Lisbon in the immediate post-surrender period. As Morishima signaled Tokyo on 29 September 1945:

> It needs no effort of imagination judging from recent allegations of activities committed by our army–to suppose that killing and wounding did occur to some extent at the time of our occupation of Timor.

He suggested that as the matter of reparations was bound to be raised by Portugal sooner or later, the best approach was the offer of a cash payment in the equivalent of US$68,000.[59] Regrettably, no record of the Portuguese response to such a gesture—if formally offered—can be located.

So it was not until 1951 that "settlement of issues caused by the Japanese occupation of Portuguese Timor" during the war were facilitated by U.S. intervention. At least one intra-departmental State Department memo urged Japanese agreement to an "exchange of letters" with Portugal "in view of our current relations with Portugal re Azores."[60]

Post-Surrender Timor

In March 1944 the Japanese authorities were (again) alerted to rumors that troops leaving Portugal for Africa were in fact en route to Australia where they were expected to join with Allied forces in an attack on Timor. While the Portuguese leader denied this rumor when requested by Japanese officials, a similar story emerged via the German Consul General in Lourenço Marques (Maputo). The rumor was given further substance in July. The Japanese learned of a report in which Salazar explained how at a recent British Empire Conference in London, the Australian Prime Minister Curtin contended—apparently with the concurrence of other delegates—that the recovery of Timor was "imperative for the protection of Australia." An Anglo-American expedition to guarantee that objective was thus foreseen by the Japanese. But, it was speculated in Tokyo, should the Allies seek this objective without Portuguese concurrence, then necessarily they would refuse to restore Timor to Portuguese rule. In the light of this scenario, the Japanese surmised, Portugal might be compelled to dispatch its own forces to Timor to achieve its restoration of power.[61]

This intelligence assessment proved prophetic of future events, but it was not until the immediate pre-surrender period that Japan moved to diplomatically stymy the Allied advance on Portuguese Timor by restoring sovereignty to the neutral power.

As Premier Tojo made it known to Morishima in Lisbon in early 1945, Japanese policy in the southern areas involved evacuating "rear areas" first. Accordingly, such "front-line" zones as Timor would be left to the last. (The rationale of course was that retreat was an exceedingly difficult operation.) In the meantime, as Tojo instructed, the negotiating tack with Portugal was to check a fallout by approving the withdrawal as a matter of principle.[62]

On 16 May 1945 Tojo advised Morishima in Lisbon that there was no longer any objection to his entering into negotiations with Portugal over the terms of the Japanese troop withdrawal from Portuguese Timor. Conditions set by Tojo for an eventual withdrawal of Japanese troops were that first, Portugal remain neutral (an improbable demand, since Portugal was clearly by this stage pro-Allies), that Portuguese Timor not be reoccupied by the Allies (also an improbable demand, as Portugal could hardly call the shots on the matter), and that Portugal obtain a guarantee of safe conduct for the withdrawal of Japanese troops. In conversation with Salazar on 28 May, Morishima reported to Tokyo that the Portuguese leader intended to maintain neutral relations with Japan. Both parties were in agreement that the Japanese withdrawal would not occur before the arrival of the Portuguese forces. Such an event, the Japanese Premier advised, could lead to friction between the Portuguese and Japanese troops. Indeed Japan was hopeful that the Portuguese contingent would weigh up as more than just a token force so as to counterpoise the envisaged Allied occupation.[63]

On 15 August Morishima was informed by the Japanese Foreign Ministry that Japan was proceeding to restore Portuguese Timor to Portuguese control. In fact, just prior to receiving this message, Morishima cabled Tokyo imploring first, restoration of Portuguese sovereignty, second, the return to Portuguese control of their radio link (to Macau) and, third, the transfer of Japanese arms to the Portuguese authorities. Tokyo replied that while the arms transfer issue was stalled owing to its "delicate" nature, within the week the "military authority on the spot" would have been ordered to comply.[64]

But events were moving fast. On 5 September, the Japanese duly notified the Portuguese government that the colony was restored to Portuguese administrative control, and that radio contact would be re-established between Macau and Timor on about 10 August. Portugal further made it known via its Foreign Office that all Japanese officials and military personnel in Timor would be placed at the disposal of the U.N. If desired, Portugal would transfer them in her vessels to any port the Allies might designate.[65]

The following day the Portuguese Foreign Office made it known that it had informed the Allies, first, that Portugal viewed the occupation of Portuguese Timor by Allied troops "with disfavor," second, Portugal wished to settle the Timor question by direct negotiation with Japan and, third, that Portugal was in the process of negotiating with the Anglo-Americans for the dispatch of a warship.[66]

These facts appear to have been censored out of the public view. The transfer of sovereignty achieved by the Japanese on 5 September, at least, was conveniently sidestepped by the Allies, especially the Australians. Incredibly, Timor was destined to be "invaded" one more time before the Portuguese contingent could arrive. As shown below, the Allies were determined to "punish" Portugal for its "acquiescence" to Japanese demands.

The Portuguese, at least, must have been relieved that Japanese rule in Timor did not mirror the wartime occupation of such colonial possessions as French Indochina, the Dutch East Indies, or British Burma, where the Japanese had either cultivated or armed anti-colonial sections of the population (Burma, Indonesia), or where at war's end had in part turned their weapons over to insurgent nationalist forces (Vietnam). Indeed, a Portuguese Foreign Office spokesperson, Matias, had expressed such a concern. Specifically, he argued, that unless Japan transfer its weapons direct to Portugal then the colonial power may well have to contend with a "native uprising."[67]

Morishima, whose pro-Portuguese bias has been noted, reported in early September that the Portuguese were apprehensive lest Australian forces re-enter Portuguese Timor on some pretext or other. The Portuguese, he noted, were adamant that negotiations over Timor should not be held in Tokyo with the Allies. Rather, discussions by the Allies on the important question of arms transfers should be held in Lisbon, as far as the administrative authority of Portuguese Timor was concerned.

Accordingly, Morishima advised Tokyo not to discuss the Timor question with the Allies "before learning of the outcome of Portugal-Allies negotiations."[68] It is unlikely that even Morishima's sources in the Portuguese capital would have been au courant with the shadow boxing behind U.S. base diplomacy over the Azores, with Timor as the Portuguese ace.

On 13 September, in reflection of the real situation in post-surrender Japan, Foreign Minister Shigemitsu cabled his Minister in Lisbon that Japan awaited Allied instructions as to the terms of the arms transfer issue. Accordingly, he sought Portugal to gain Allied consent before issuing the arms transfer order. No reports of local surrender negotiations had been received by Tokyo, although it was well understood that radio contact had been established between Timor and Macau (thus signaling a resumption of Portuguese authority in the colony).[69] Intriguingly, a rare ellipse in the "Magic" record stamped "not releasable" carries strong implications for political sensitivity surrounding the transfer-of-sovereignty issue, not to mention the legality of the Allied role in facilitating the Portuguese restoration.

Australia, Timor, and the Japanese surrender

As we have seen, since early 1944 the Japanese authorities had expressed concern apropos Allied—especially Australian— intentions towards Timor. This concern was borne out by events. But it was not until the post-surrender period that Australia was in a position to act.

According to W.D. Forsyth, the senior Australian diplomat concerned, by August-September 1945 the Australian government was determined that an Australian—not Portuguese—force take the Japanese surrender on Timor. Originally, a separate surrender ceremony was envisioned for Kupang (Dutch Timor) as well as for Dili. Australian motives in pursuing this course, as expressed by Forsyth, were twofold; first, to mark the fact that it was the Australians alone who resisted the Japanese and, second, that the Portuguese, whose "neutrality had helped the Japanese to turn (Timor) into a base," should have no military part in the termination of hostilities.[70]

Hastings notes that on 28 August, Canberra cabled London requesting that no facilities be given to enable Portuguese forces to reach Timor and that the Japanese surrender should be to Australian forces only. But the British government rejected the suggestion of a second Australian occupation of Portuguese Timor. In any case, it was noted, Portuguese vessels could not be prevented from sailing from Colombo or Lourenço Marques.[71]

In fact, the Japanese learned of Australia's intentions on 7 September via an Australian press dispatch. As reported on that occasion, the Australian Minister for Defense Kim Beazley stated on 7 September that "arrangements have been made to accept the surrender of the Japanese in Dutch Timor while arrangements for the capitulation in Portuguese Timor will be made in cooperation with the Portuguese government."[72] No doubt the Japanese were still banking upon the arrival of Portuguese reinforcements to pre-empt the Australian advance. Indeed, a Domei report of 14 August revealed that the Portuguese units were assembled at Lourenço Marques, ready to stage a triumphant return to Timor.[73] Not surprisingly, perhaps, news of the Australian announcement of the Japanese surrender was censored in Portugal.[74]

As it happened, the Japanese surrender in Timor was accepted on behalf of Australia by Brigadier Lewis Dyke in Kupang on 11 September. The ceremony took place on the quarterdeck of the HMAS *Morseby*. As an Australian press account of the time notes, the failure of the Australian government to permit participating Dutch service representatives to sign the document met with expressions of "keen disappointment and concern" on the part of the Dutch authorities.[75]

According to Forsyth, the Australian cabinet decided on 19 September on a scheme for a separate ceremony at Dili. He notes that the exercise was "recognized to be primarily political." He describes his own role in the affair as finessing what amounted to an unprecedented involvement in "military tasks in peacetime on neutral territory."[76]

The Australian contingent departed Kupang for Dili on 23 September. The Commander of the Australian force, Dyke— as reported in the Australian press—congratulated the Portuguese Governor, Fereira de Carvalho on the restoration of Portuguese rule. The party established that there were no Australian POWs in the colony and that only 200 Japanese remained.[77] On this occasion, the governor was informed of the surrender in Kupang while he was briefed on arrangements to be made for the surrender of remaining Japanese forces.[78]

According to Wallis, an Australian journalist who witnessed the "restoration" ceremony it was "a short and simple affair, held in front of the landing stage from which the Portuguese ensign flew."[79] The haste with which the Australian contingent dispatched with ceremonials and the timing of the event were well considered. Indeed, the following morning (27 September), after much expectation and delay, the Portuguese sloops arrived. As Wallis coyly notes, they were welcomed in "another colorful ceremony."[80] Dunn writes that Portuguese rule resumed two days later with the arrival of a troop ship carrying a military expedition.[81]

What seems to be ignored in these Australian versions is that Portuguese rule had in fact resumed on 5 September when the Japanese informed Portugal of the occurrence. Clearly, as both the surrender ceremony in Kupang on 23 September and the "transfer" ceremony in Dili the following day suggest, the Australian side was adamant about bypassing both the Portuguese (and the Dutch) in their dealings with the defeated enemy. The haste with which the Australian expedition was dispatched to Kupang and Dili and the cavalier attitude towards complex questions of international law strongly point in this direction. Hastings has drawn attention to the political debates over the Timor question in the Australian parliament, which was probably the first major debate on international affairs in Australia after the war.[82] It is worth citing in full the Hansard record of the speech of the Australian Minister for Foreign Affairs, Dr. Evatt, as not only was he able to silence his critics by calling upon the need for a broader understanding of Allied (UK-USA) objectives, he was the first to make public the Azores linkages in the Timor equation. As Evatt stated the matter:

> The occupation and use of the Azores as an air-base by the USA and the UK were of supreme importance and an arrangement had to be made between Great Britain and Portugal. The Portuguese asked the British Government, as a part of the arrangements over the Azores, to ensure that the government of Australia should give an undertaking that in its postwar planning it would make no attempt to alter the sovereignty of Portuguese Timor.[83]

While certain Australian politicians, namely Percy Spender, pushed the line that Australia had certain rights in the region, that the wartime experience had proved the importance of Timor to Australia's defense, etc, the government, at least as revealed by Evatt's speech, had come 'round by early 1946 to a broader geopolitical view of the question commensurate with Australia's subordinate status within the new global realignment as underwritten by the Truman Doctrine, after the U.S. President of that name.

Sequels

The world has changed since the 1950s, and indeed since Hiroshima. Clearly the Azores bases have assumed a new importance in a nuclear world. As declassified Defense Department documents of the 1960-63 period reveal, owing to the relatively limited number of overseas U.S. bases, the installations in the Azores "play a major role in the defense of North America." Not only do the bases support strategic (nuclear) air operations, they are utilized for early warning operations and as an air transport link in support of the European command. Naval facilities support anti-submarine operations as well.[84]

Decolonization in the main had run its course by the mid-1960s. Old-style colonialism was seen even by the metropolitan countries as anachronistic. The Bandung Conference of 1955 hosted in the Indonesia of Sukarno signaled the emergence of the Non-Aligned bloc of nations of newly independent Afro-Asian states prepared even to stand up to neo-colonial arrangements devised by the old colonial powers.

But in Portugal, the poor man of Europe, the Salazar dictatorship held on. The Estada Novo embraced the Portuguese African and Asian colonies alike as integral provinces of the motherland. Indeed by 1960, at the time of the signing of a U.S.-Portugal arms production agreement, it had become increasingly clear that Salazar was prepared to fight for the retention of Portugal's colonies, especially in Africa. According to two students of Portugal's African wars, Humbaraci and

Muchnik, by 1961 the U.S. Congress was obliged to pass a resolution to keep up its military aid to Portugal, notwithstanding that country's breach of faith in using NATO arms in its colonies. While under the Kennedy Administration, U.S. aid to Portugal dropped away especially when the use of U.S. aid to Angola became public by 1962-63 American aid was on the increase. Again, Portugal played the Azores card, and a new treaty was signed by the U.S. Indeed, by 1963, the CIA had gone over to a strategy of backing the Angolan resistance movement of Holden R oberto.[85]

Ironically, while Portuguese Timor survived the blusters and tempests of the Sukarnoist era, it fared tragically at the hands of a U.S. ally, General Suharto. As José Ramos-Horta, the Fretilin delegate to the U.N. has written, a 1963 telegram sent from the U.S. Embassy in Jakarta to the U.S. Secretary of State summed up what would become the American position on the Timor question many years later. It argued that "Portuguese Timor (was) not economically viable," then went on to suggest that the "U.S. should urge Portugal to take steps in Timor now to cut its losses in a darkening future." This was a warning of a possible Sukarnoist intervention. Ramos-Horta notes that, then as now, U.S. relations with Indonesia overrode any consideration of the rights of the Timorese themselves. As Ramos-Horta also observes, (a theme that has emerged in our study), Salazar played the Azores card whenever it suited him to do so.[86]

It was not the death of the Portuguese dictator in July 1970 that brought Portugal out of its time warp—essentially the same policies were pursued by Salazar's successor Marcello Cataeno—but the unpopularity of the African wars among Portuguese youth.[87] Thus the leftward turn in Portuguese politics simultaneous with the emergence of the Young Officers Movement in 1974 proved especially portentous. The political opening in Lisbon, which lifted the lid on thirty years of dictatorship, lent stimulus not only to domestic political reform but served as a catalyst for burgeoning independence movements in the colonies.

For the U.S., as Harkavy has written, continued access to Lajes airbase in the Azores seemed to be jeopardized by the emergence and triumph of leftist forces in Lisbon. Indeed, certain Arab countries had offered substantial financial inducements to Portugal to eliminate that base as a staying facility on Israel's behalf. While some uncertainties remained, the subsequent rightward shift in Portuguese politics facilitated negotiations when they came up in 1970.[88]

In Timor, events in the metropolitan country gave rise to the first political organizations in 350 years of colonial domination. While the Portuguese role in withdrawing from Dili to Atauro in the face of an Indonesian campaign of political and military subversion throughout late 1974 and 1975 was not glorious, it was understandable, as was the Unilateral Declaration of Independence (UDI) on 28 November 1975 by the majority independence party, the Revolutionary Front for the Independence of East Timor (Fretilin). As it happened, some 15 to 30 percent of the population of Portuguese Timor (East Timor since the UDI) perished as a direct or indirect result of the Indonesian armed interventions of 1975-76.[89] Some twelve years after the Indonesian military invasion and occupation of the territory, main force units of the Indonesian Armed Forces (ABRI) are still harassed by the armed wing of Fretilin, the guerrilla units known as Falintil.[90] The irony should not be lost that it was access to Dili's arsenal of abandoned NATO-issue small arms that provided the wherewithal for Falintil's early military ascendancy.

Australia, the U.S. and Japan—the old protagonists in the struggle for the spoils of Timor that its strategic location offers, have quietly acquiesced—even facilitated—Indonesian goals on the island. On the U.N. stage Portugal remains the legal party charged with the decolonization process. Indonesia, having incorporated East Timor as its 27th province, fights rearguard actions in the world body and notably the Non-Aligned Movement over the issue. Indefatigable diplomatic efforts on the part of Fretilin coupled with a more recent expression of interest on the part of Portugal and the other Lusophone countries kept the Timor independence issue flickering.

Notes

1. This relates to the actions of the 400 members of the 2/2 Australian Independent Company who held down a force of some 20,000 Japanese in Timor. Before evacuation to Darwin in January 1942, the 2/2 Company had killed 1,500 of the enemy for a loss of 40. Aside from the official Australian War record, the legend of the 2/2 was cultivated by the wartime press, even captured on film by the "legendary" Australian War photographer Damien Parer. The legend has continued to grow with the publication of such participant accounts as:

Bernard Callinan, *Independent Company* (Heineman: Melbourne, 1953) and more recently, by the son of a participant: C.C.H. Wray, *Timor 1942*, (Hutchison: Sydney, 1987), but who well describes the action in "A breach of neutrality," pp. 22-32. But the tendency to mythologize has been perpetuated in such scholarly articles as: Peter Hastings, "The Timor Problem III: Some Australian Attitudes, 1941-1950," *Australian Outlook*, 29, 3, (1975): 323-334. Thus Hastings terms the Australian intervention of 17 December 1941 as an "arrival" (p. 325) and otherwise fails to come to terms with the broader moral and legal issues surrounding the invasion of a neutral.

2. "Portuguese Participation in Liberation of Timor," July 1945, State-War-Navy Coordinating Committee (SWNCC) #163, 112/1.

3. Ibid.

4. Robert E. Harkavy, *Great Power Competition for Overseas Bases: The Geopolitics of Access Diplomacy* (Pergamon Press: New York, 1982): 111.

5. Wray, *Timor 1942*: 8-10.

6. See document Australian Archives 2673 Vol.8 (1401 Agendum 270/1941–Supp. no.3, Portuguese Timor, War Cabinet Minutes, Melbourne (15 October 1941).

7. "The British Embassy to Department of State, Washington," 16 December 1941, *Foreign Relations*, 1941, Vol.V (1941): 385.

8. "The Minister in Portugal (Fish) to the Secretary of State," 19 December 1941, *Foreign Relations*, Vol V (1941): 383. This confusion is pointed up by an apparent agreement between London and Lisbon made at the end of 1941 that Portugal reinforce its

garrison in Timor to prevent occupation by Japan. According to Shute, Japan agreed but reinforcements sent from Lourenço Marques (Maputo) in Mozambique were refused safe conduct by the Japanese and were obliged to return to Africa (Neville Shute in Callinan, *Independent Company*, xix).

9. "Memo of conversation by Under Secretary of State Welles," 24 December 1941, *Foreign Relations*, Vol II (1941).

10. "Navy Department to State," Washington, 17 December 1941, *Foreign Relations*, Vol II (1941): 386.

11. Cf. "President Roosevelt to the Portuguese President of the Council of Ministers (Salazar)," Washington, 14 July 1941, *Foreign Relations*, Vol.II (1941).

12. Australian Archives A981, Timor Portuguese, 3 Part 1, Document 175, "Cablegram Governor of Portuguese Timor to Curtin," 17 December 1941, Dili (translation).

13. Australian Archives A981, Timor Portuguese 3 Part 1, "Evatt to Governor of Portuguese Timor," [via Ross], 18 December 1941].

14. His Majesties Consul, Batavia, 1 November 1938, *Public Record Office* (London), CO273/652.

15. "Grew to Secretary of State," Tokyo, 22 January, 1941, *Foreign Relations*, Vol V, (1941): 36.

16. Hudson Fysh, "Australia's Unknown Neighbour," *Walkabout*, (1 May 1941): 7-15. Fysh prophesied that Japan's ascendancy in Portuguese Timor was undoubtedly part of its southern drive; "a development that should be watched closely in Australia."

17. See *Guide to Archival Materials: Australian Archives*, nd. np. Ross, the Magic record reveals, was twice set on mission to persuade the Australians to surrender. As the local Japanese authority wryly noted of his failure to return on the second occasion, "He either fears the consequences of the failure of a second mission, or he just isn't coming back" (Magic, 18 July 1942). In fact Ross was evacuated to Australia on 10 July 1942.

18. Anon, *Sejarah Daerah Nusa Tengarah Timor: Departemen Pendidikan dan Kebudayaan* (Jakarta: Balai Pustaka, 1977/8). See Wray, *Timor: 1942*: 33-58 for a detailed account of the heroic four day fight of the 2/40 before surrender, in the face of overwhelming Japanese odds.

19. *War in the Pacific*, Vol.16, "The Southern Area (Part 1), Japanese Monograph No.45," (Garland, New York and London,

1980): 90.
20. *The Magic Documents: Summaries and Transcripts of the Top-Secret Diplomatic Communications of Japan: 1938-1945,* U.S. War Department (Magic), 9 October 1942.
21. Ibid. 19 October 1942.
22. Ibid. 30 May 1942.
23. Ibid. 8 June 1942.
24. Ibid. 10 June 1942.
25. Ibid. 15 September 1942.
26. Ibid. 18 December 1942.
27. Ibid. 18 September 1943.
28. Ibid. 15 October 1942.
29. James Dunn, *Timor: A People Betrayed,* (Brisbane: The Jacaranda Press, 1983): 23.
30. *The Magic Documents,* 17 October 1942.
31. Ibid. 4 November 1942.
The situation of the Portuguese community marginally improved after the Japanese facilitated the visit of an official Portuguese envoy, Costa, chief aide of the Governor of Macau, who arrived on 19 March 1944 and stayed one week (Magic, 3 April 1944).
32. Ibid. 1 December 1942, 9 February 1944 and 20 March 1942.
33. Ibid. 15 June 1942.
34. Ibid. 14 April 1943.
35. Callinan, *Independent Company:* 131.
36. *Sejarah Nusa Tengarah Timor.*
37. António O. Liberato, *Os Japoneses Estiveram em Timor,* (Lisboa: Empressa Nasional de Publicadade, 1951), preface.
38. *The Magic Documents,* 13 June 1942.
39. Ibid. 22 June 1942.
40. Ibid. 13 September 1942.
41. Ibid. 6 September 1943.
42. Ibid. 17 December 1943.
43. Ibid. 6 September 1943.
44   Ibid. 6 July 1944.
45   Ibid. 4 July 1944.
46. Ibid. 10 August 1944.
47. Ibid. 16 August 1944.
48. Ibid. 2 September 1944.
49. Ibid. 5 September 1944.

50.   Ibid. 22 August 1944.

51.   Ibid. 13 January 1945.

52.   Ibid. 9 February 1945.

53.   Ibid. 25 February 1945.

54.   Ibid. 6 May 1945.

55. SWNCC 163, "Memorandum, State Department, Col. John West," 11 June 1945.

56. SWNCC 163, "The Combined Chiefs of Staff: Memorandum for the Department of State: Foreign Office," 18 July 1945.

57. SWNCC 163, 20 July and 24 July 1945.

58. "Relations of the United States with Portugal: 20 October 1950: Policy Statement Prepared in the Department of State," in *Foreign Relations*, Vol. III, (1950): 1540-1547.

59. *The Magic Documents*, 29 September 1945.

60. "Editorial Note," *Foreign Relations*, VI, (1951): 1369-1370.

61. *The Magic Documents*, 16 March 1944 and 26 July 1944.

62. Ibid. 18 May 1945.

63. Ibid. 5 June 1945.

64. Ibid. 22 August 1945.

65. Ibid. 14 September 1945.

66. Ibid.

67. Ibid.

68. Ibid.

69. Ibid.

70.   W.D. Forsyth, "Timor II: The World of Dr Evatt," *New Guinea and Australia, the Pacific and Southeast Asia*, May/June 1975.

71.   Hastings, "The Timor Problem III."

72. *The Magic Documents*, 14 September 1945.

73. *Domei* in *The Mainichi* (Tokyo), 17 August 1945.

74.   Reuters (Lisbon), 11 September 1945 in "Magic," 14 September 1945.

75. *Sydney Morning Herald*, 14 September and 26 September 1945.

76. Forsyth, "Timor II," p. 34.

77. *Sydney Morning Herald*, 26 September 1945.

78. Hastings, "The Timor Problem III," p. 333.

79. N.K. Wallis, "Peace Comes to Dilli," *Walkabout*, February 1946.

80. Ibid.

81. Dunn, *Timor: A People Betrayed*: 27.

82. Hastings, "The Timor problem III."

83. *Hansard*, "Commonwealth of Australia: Parliamentary Debates," Session 1945-6, 20 March 1946.

84. "United States Department of Defense: Review of United States Overseas Military Bases," April 1960, Carrollton Press, #79/359C.

85. A. Humbaraci and N. Muchnik, *Portugal's African Wars* (Macmillan, London, 1974): 186-189.

86. José Ramos-Horta, *Funu: The Unfinished Saga of East Timor* (Trenton, N.J., The Red Sea Press, 1987): 89-90.

87. This fact would have been obvious to any visitor to Lisbon in the early 1970s. While this was the age of anti-Vietnam War protest in Western Europe, the graffiti in the Portuguese capital graphically registered the protest of Portuguese youth and erstwhile conscripts against the African wars. Discussions by the author on and off Lisbon University campus of 1970 revealed that the middle classes were likewise struck with the malaise.

88. Harkavy, *Great Power Competition*.

89. A respectable literature on the events of 1974-75 has emerged, regrettably, however, not matched by international action to seek redress for the Timorese people over the legal and human rights abuses occasioned by the Indonesian annexation. These works include:

Jill Jolliffe, *East Timor: Nationalism and Colonialism* (St. Lucia: University of Queensland Press, 1978).

Dunn, *Timor: A People Betrayed*.

Ramos-Horta, *Funu: The Unfinished Saga of East Timor*.

Roger S. Clark, "The Decolonization of East Timor and the U.N. Norms of Self-Determination and Aggression," *The Yale Journal of World Public Order*, 7, 1 (1980) for what is certainly the most precise analysis of the legal issues at stake.

90. See P. Wise, "More talks on Timor," *Far Eastern Economic Review*, 9 July 1987.

9. Language, Literacy, and Political Hegemony in East Timor

The roots: orality and literacy in East Timor

Racially and culturally the indigenous peoples of Timor reflect a division between Malay, physical characteristics and Austronesian languages towards the coast and non-Austronesian or Papuan languages in the interior. Anthropologists acknowledge that East Timor is far more linguistically complex than the western part of the island, with up to 31 separate languages (reflecting successive waves of Negrito, Melanesian, and proto-Malays) versus four or five linguistic groups in the west. But the largest ethnic and linguistic group on the island with speakers in both western and eastern Timor is Tetum.[1]

Clearly, the number of distinct languages spoken in East Timor will vary according to the way that language is designated. Even Tetum—the most widely understood language in East Timor—is subject to wide regional variations (eg, Tetum Terik and Tetum Belu in the east and Tetum-Los in the central-south coast). Only Tetum-Dili is spoken over all of East Timor. This dialect is a simplified version given currency by the Portuguese as a common tongue among all people. It also incorporates a number of Latinisms. But because of the existence of other important regional languages such as Makassai in the east and Mambai in the center-south, Tetum-Dili is spoken regionally with wide variation in pronunciation and vocabulary and influenced by a speaker's primary regional language.[2]

As British anthropologist David Hicks has written, social change in East Timor—especially since 1912—has had a differential effect on Timorese. The most affected have been the Tetum speakers. Although most missionaries were fluent in

Tetum, few were conversant in languages like Makassai and Mambai. Accordingly, the Tetum living in the easily accessible lowlands emerged as the most Christianized of the entire Timorese groups. Indeed, there was a close correlation between the spread of Christianity and the distribution of Tetum. As Hicks observed in the late 1960s: "Religion is the most sensitive index of the degree of acculturation of Portuguese Timor." To a certain extent, this still holds today under Indonesian domination. But where Hicks found that most young Tetum persons learn the creed through the medium of the Portuguese language, and many of the converts are reasonably literate, today Portuguese has been largely—although not entirely—replaced by Tetum and bahasa Indonesia as the language of faith, while bahasa Indonesia has entirely replaced Portuguese as the language of state. [3]

Work on translating catechism and prayer books into Tetum and other dialects as Galoli, Tokodebe, and Balkenu/Dawan commenced in 1875.[4] But before 1960, only 2 percent of Timorese children in a population of 517,000 received a primary education; there was only one high school for some 200 students. It was apparent that the rise in literacy in East Timor went hand in hand with missionization. In 1970 the Bishop of Dili set up a commission to translate *Rituale Romanum* and especially baptism and marriage sacraments into Tetum. This was a practical and realistic step. In any case, educational development in Portuguese Timor outside of Church auspices really only took off in the last decade of Portuguese rule. In this decade, expansion of primary and lower secondary technical education in the Portuguese medium sowed the roots of a Latinized culture, laid the basis of a metropolitan-looking urban bourgeoisie comprised of Timorese, African, Chinese, *mestiço* and other elements, and created the conditions for the emergence of a Lusophone intelligentsia, scion of the East Timorese nationalist revolution that today defines itself against Indonesian incorporation.

The Fretilin program for literacy

Among the political parties that emerged in East Timor in 1974 in the period after the Armed Forces Movement in Lisbon swept aside the fascist administration and placed the prospect of decolonization on the table, it was the radical-nationalist party, Fretilin, which squarely addressed the question of local culture and language. A reading of *Timor Leste Povo Mau Bere*, the bilingual Portuguese-Tetum Fretilin newspaper published during months of Fretilin's political ascendancy in East Timor (September-December 1975), is illustrative. After the "flower revolution" in Lisbon, such Fretilin leaders as Abilio de Araujo returned to Timor to work with Fretilin in a campaign to eradicate illiteracy. The alphabetization of Tetum was a priority. De Araujo then returned to Lisbon to prepare the printing literacy handbooks for use by Fretilin in Fretilin-supported schools throughout the countryside. While political literacy was uppermost, the method and inspiration was the *consciencialização* program of the controversial Brazilian educationalist Paulo Freire.[5]

This period also saw the flowering of an authentic East Timorese literature. The scion of this movement was the Fretilin poet Francisco Borja da Costa (killed and mutilated at age of 30 by Indonesian paratroopers). Like many of the Fretilin elite he received a Jesuit education in Dili and like such African nationalist writers as the Angolan Agostinho Neto, adopted the language of colonialism as his language. Another from this tradition, a contributor of revolutionary poetry in Portuguese to Timor Leste was José Xanana Gusmão, today the imprisoned leader of the East Timorese resistance to Indonesian occupation. But, as Jill Jolliffe has written, Borja da Costa's most valuable work was written in his native Tetum (the high or classical Tetum of the south coast). As such, he mixed "traditional form with modernist nationalist themes." Emblematic was his poem "Foho Ramaleu," later adopted as the Fretilin anthem. As with this anthem, it is significant that in this largely pre-literate society in 1975, most of the poems were meant to be spoken or sung.[6]

After the invasion

After the invasion of East Timor in December 1975, Indonesia moved quickly to politically, socially, and economically incorporate the territory as an Indonesian province. Central to this project was the Indonesianization of East Timor society under the auspices of Pancasila, the Indonesian state ideology, whereas the vehicle for this mass forced ideological rectification program was bahasa Indonesia.

Central to the Indonesian project of *integrasi* or integration in East Timor, as with the earlier incorporation of Irian Jaya (West Irian), has been education. Indeed, the construction of educational infrastructure has been one of the more impressive developments brought by Indonesia to East Timor. According to an Indonesian source, there were (in 1991) some 130,000 children enrolled in the school system. These were distributed through 580 primary schools, 94 middle schools, 44 higher middle schools. Additionally, scores of Timorese students secured places in Indonesian universities.[7] This means that within a decade or so Indonesia has fundamentally altered not only the mental horizons of a subject people but also the spatial hierarchy of the education system. For a generation of East Timorese, Jakarta, not Lisbon, is at the apex of the education hierarchy. Graduates of Indonesian universities return as administrative collaborators if they play the game. In a situation of widespread graduate unemployment in East Timor, not to play the game spells social and economic death.

No less vital in the campaign to Indonesianize East Timor has been the role of electronic and print media. Radio and television programming in East Timor is almost exclusively bahasa Indonesian. It goes without saying, then, that in the absence of other media sources, Timorese are obliged to relate to Indonesian media sources. With the obvious exception of short-wave radio broadcasts, it follows that all domestic and international news is mediated by the Indonesian state. To the extent that foreign languages figure, Portuguese has been displaced entirely by English and even French and German. Tetum is not the object of any serious programming. The press is no exception.

While during Portuguese times *A Voz de Timor* had been subject to official censorship, it also offered employment for two of East Timor's better known sons, José Ramos-Horta and Xanana Gusmão. As discussed above, under the Fretilin administration, *Timor Leste* played a special role as disseminator of Timorese language, culture, and history. Needless to say, in the post-1975 period, no Portuguese language successor paper, much less Tetum supplement, has been allowed to emerge. To the extent that a mass media exists in East Timor, the Indonesian authorities have substituted Indonesian media press for the Portuguese. This began in 1982 with the publication in Dili of the bahasa Indonesia medium *Dili Pos*, followed in 1985 by the *Suara Timor Timur*. The sole concession to Tetum in that paper is a postcard column. It is clear that the authorities in Jakarta would not be put out if Portuguese was entirely displaced as a second or third language in East Timor by English—just as Dutch stigmatized by its colonial associations in Indonesian—also lost rank to English.

Inside East Timor, the eradication of Portuguese language media has been almost total. The single Portuguese language publications on sale in Dili at the time of my visits in 1992-93 were those on display in the Ecclesiastical Bookshop. These included several ancient prayer books and religious tracts. The Dili Diocese Press then appeared to be the single exception to the Indonesian stranglehold on the media in East Timor. Besides publishing such offerings as Bishop Ximenes Belo's pastoral of 17 September 1991, on "The position of the Catholic Church as to the visit of the Portuguese delegation" and church histories,[8] it also keeps up the publication of *Seara* (*Boletim Ecclesiastico da Diocese de Dili - Timor Oriental*). This trilingual Portuguese, Tetum, bahasa Indonesia digest of church news was—intriguingly—the original forum for dissenting voices to Portuguese colonialism in the heady days of East Timorese nationalism in the pre-1975 period. Otherwise, publications in Portuguese to be found in East Timor are rare and treated as icons of the past.

The trial in 1993 of Xanana Gusmão is illustrative of the

tension between language nationalism and political freedom. Central to the Indonesian state case was that the plaintiff answer back in bahasa Indonesia. Just as axiomatic was the necessity of the rebel leader, living symbol of East Timorese nationalism—to reply in Portuguese, the language of the country deemed by the U.N. to be the legal administering power in East Timor. While these facts were reported in the international press, they were also made known to readers of *Suara Dili Dili* [9] —although not the heroic words, "Viva Timor Leste," uttered in reply to the sentence of life imprisonment by an Indonesian judge. One is reminded of the stand of certain Indonesian nationalists in the manner to which they replied to their own colonial oppressors.

How has the Church responded to Indonesianization? According to certain reports, when in 1981 the government tried to force the diocese to replace Portuguese with bahasa Indonesia in church services, the then Bishop of Dili, Mgr. da Costa Lopes, obtained permission from Rome for the liturgical use of Tetum.[10] Today mass is performed in churches in East Timor in either Tetum or bahasa Indonesia or Portuguese and in that order of frequency. In Dili, the only advertised mass in Portuguese is offered at the St. Antonio Motael church. In my enquiries in Dili, only church workers in the Motael church and at the Ecclesiastical bookshop actually initiated conversations in Portuguese or at least did not feel in the least restrained to speak Portuguese. But where the church was a bastion of conservatism in Portuguese times, today it is only the church which stands between the people and the foreign oppressors. Moreover, where the Indonesian state speaks to the people of East Timor in bahasa Indonesia—an alien and hitherto unfamiliar code—it is the church that is intimate in Tetum and Portuguese. As Indonesia specialist, Ben Anderson, has phrased the matter in an essay on nationalism in East Timor, Indonesian/Tetum corresponds in the 1990s to Dutch/Indonesian in the 1920s. In other words, the choice of Tetum as the language of liturgy has had "profoundly nationalizing effects" in East Timor.[11]

Visits to the few other bookshops in the capital were also instructive. Not only were these shops keyed to meeting the curriculum needs of local children obliged to attend Indonesian schools but their offerings were entirely foreign. With the possible exception of a thin Tetum-bahasa Indonesia wordbook and grammar, none of the Indonesian language books on sale spoke directly to East Timorese. Whereas an impressive array of social science translations of mainly American texts were available, including some of the more standard acceptable Western works on Indonesia, it is a pointed commentary on information control in East Timor that no Western works on East Timor have been translated into bahasa, nor were there any works in any language available in Dili on East Timor. The single exception are works on *"integrasi"* available in the government's information office. But then, such offerings came for free in the Hotel Turismo, where usually only money speaks.

The foregoing also relates to the recovery of Timorese history. While the Historic Archive of Goa, and the Macau archives remain extant, accessible, and celebrated under, respectively, Indian and essentially Chinese protection, the same cannot be said of the historical patrimony of the East Timorese under Indonesian occupation. Indeed, there is real fear that the record has been irretrievably lost, just as the state in Indonesia sought physically to eliminate some half-million members of the Indonesian Communist Party along with Sukarnoist camp followers as much as the historical memory surrounding that epoch, similarly in East Timor the occupier has sought to wipe clean the nationalist slate of the erstwhile enemy. Commencing from a new year zero, the history of integration effectively replaces national Timorese history. Thus the nineteenth century Javanese anti-Dutch Muslim rebel Diponogoro replaces Boaventura, the anti-Portuguese Timorese rebel leader, just as Suharto, the "Father of Development" replaces Xanana Gusmão, leader of the Maubere People's Resistance and, now, in incarceration; common criminal. This is the new received wisdom. Thus while the nationalist spirit of the East Timorese people has irredeemably proven that the oral tradition dies hard, the same cannot be said of the written record where it is either missing, or worse, manipulated.

Besides propagating an essentially Jakarta-centric worldview, it is important to note the function of bahasa

Indonesia as the carrier of an Indonesian cultural crusade. In replacing Portuguese, bahasa Indonesia thus becomes the print language of the Timorese as, in the main, the indigenous languages of Timor are untranscribed languages. Whereas some 67 percent of the population of Timor (1980 census) used only a local language (Tetum is predominant), and where 77 percent remain illiterate, the Indonesian project to expand primary education thus becomes the cutting edge in the battle for the hearts and minds of Timorese. Already a generation of school age Timorese has emerged, not only ignorant of Portugal and its mission, but linguistically competent in bahasa Indonesia. It follows that the Lusophone culture that linked Timor with its modern history has been expunged or is at least in the advanced process of eradication. Tetum and other languages in Timor have also become threatened as little cultures give way to the assimilationist thrust of the new cultural and political center.

Having criss-crossed East Timor by local transport—usually crowded country buses—this observer is struck with the way that bahasa Indonesia has emerged as a true lingua franca. First, many of the bus drivers appear to be native Indonesian speakers. The music played on local transport is never Timorese. Second, there are almost always Indonesian passengers on buses in East Timor. Third, there is almost invariably a sprinkling of East Timorese "collaborators" in any East Timorese crowd, identifiable by the paraphernalia of uniforms, that is to say East Timorese schooled in the Indonesian school system and obliged to work in some official or quasi-official position willy-nilly serving their masters as cultural brokers. Fourth, in line with classic counterinsurgency strategies, it has been along the roads and communication routes that the Indonesian armed forces first made their presence felt in East Timor. All over the Indonesian archipelago, it is the Indonesian Armed forces who serve as bearers (and enforcers) par excellence of bahasa Indonesia. Fifth, as in Indonesia itself, disparate dialect groups thrown together on public transport will "naturally" use bahasa Indonesia as the initial code of communication.

The matter is complex, however, as at home, in the market place, in the hills, among fisher folk and weavers—out of earshot of the ubiquitous military posts, military patrols, and system of spies—it is Tetum, Makassai and other dialects that hold sway. It has been this quintessential Maubere man and woman who has supplied the backbone of support to the albeit cosmopolitan Portuguese-Tetum speaking Fretilin guerrilla, of which Xanana Gusmão stood as exemplar. It has been the unlettered Timorese peasantry who has been the most impervious to the Indonesian cultural project, the most feared and the most beaten.

For the (bahasa Indonesia-speaking) visitor, conversation with school and college students in Dili comes as "natural" in bahasa Indonesia although depending upon the group some seek (hopelessly) to practice English. Few will respond (or none will publicly admit) to Portuguese. Among themselves the younger generation in Dili will chatter in Tetum. Just as Portuguese domiciled in East Timor made efforts to speak "Dili Tetum," so it appears that Indonesians or at least their offspring domiciled in East Timor have also gone some way in learning this older lingua franca. While Indonesia has made concerted efforts to Indonesianize the way Tetum is spoken (bahasa Indonesia terminology replacing Portuguese), one comes away with the impression that Tetum nationalism has been strengthened, not weakened, by the traumatic events of the past seventeen years which have seen a population loss of between one-quarter and one-third. But while the oral traditions of the Tetum world have held their own—no doubt strengthened by the embrace of the faith and use of the Tetum liturgy—the rise of Tetum as a print language as so actively encouraged by Fretilin has been actively and deliberately reversed by the occupier. Today of course it is not Tetum, much less Portuguese, which serves as the print language par excellence of East Timor, but bahasa Indonesia.

One concession to the past was the Externato De São José school, referred to by East Timorese as the "Portuguese school," established in 1964 under the auspices of the St Joseph Foundation. Although closed after East Timor's annexation by Indonesia, the school was reopened in 1983 under the patronage of Bishop Belo for the benefit of young Portuguese (who were left behind at least pending their eventual return to Portugal). But when most of the youths in this category returned to Portugal in 1987, the school continued to function, offering courses in Portuguese outside the national curriculum as well as in bahasa Indonesia, but only as a second language. Located about 100 m from the Santa Cruz cemetery, the site of the massacre in November 1991, the school was ordered to be shut down by the military authority in East Timor the following April. During the visit to East Timor by Pope John Paul in 1989, students from the school were implicated in the anti-Indonesian demonstration as well as in the Santa Cruz cemetery demonstration.[12] While there would be a large pool of latent Portuguese speakers scattered across East Timor among those schooled before 1975, today fewer and fewer Timorese would feel confident to initiate conversation in that language today for as much fear as fading memory. But for some, as I discovered on a secluded beach near Baucau at the eastern end of the island, a group of East Timorese nationalists sought to test my loyalty to their cause in Portuguese before allowing the conversation to revert to a resented—albeit mutually comprehended code—namely, bahasa Indonesia. Regrettably few outsiders—this writer included—speak Tetum.

Besides the network of primary and lower and upper secondary schools established by the Indonesian state in East Timor, the church has developed an impressive parallel network of schools, of which the Fatumaca Senior Technical school in the Baucau district is one of the best. Of the private Universiti Timor Timur (UNTIM) in Dili with 800 students and lecturers, and the Polytechnic at Hera, standards are said to be poor. But where facilities are lacking, exposure to the mores of the Indonesian state ideology, Pancasila, is not wanting. In the year 1989 alone, 39,730 junior and senior high school students were graduated through such courses.

One constraint in the full development and extension of the Indonesian educational project in East Timor, however, has been a chronic teacher shortage, in part complicated by the unwillingness of Indonesian teachers and Indonesian-trained East Timorese teachers alike to serve in East Timor. According to one Indonesian press report, East Timor was not only in need of an additional 2,500 teachers for its schools but also housing for teachers, books and other educational aids. A no less telling comment on the education crisis in the territory is the dearth of East Timorese in the teaching profession. For whatever reason, there is only one high school teacher of East Timorese origin in the whole of the place.[13] No doubt, self-esteem as much the system of offering employment priority to outsiders explains this abject situation.

Certain inferences may be read from this analysis for the fate of other little cultures and languages in such diverse parts of the sprawling archipelago such as Irian Jaya, where spirited resistance to hegemonic controls has also manifested itself in a variety of ways that also challenge Indonesian domination.

Notes

1. eg., see, H, G. Schulte Nordholt, *The Political System of the Atoni* (The Hague: Martinus Nijhoff, 1971).

2. Cliff Morris, *A Traveller's Dictionary in Tetun-English and English-Tetun from the Land of the Sleeping Crocodile: East Timor*, (Frankston: Baba Dook Books, 1992).

3. David Barry Hicks, "Eastern Timorese Society," (Ph.D. submitted to London University, 1971).

4. Notable are the pioneering works of Sebastião Maria Apericio da Silva, *Diccionario português-tetum* (1889) and, in turn, Raphael das Dores, *Diccionario teto-português* (1907). Dores found that over 1,000 Portuguese words had entered Tetum speech by 1873.

5. Jill Jolliffe (ed.), *Revolutionary Poems in the Struggle Against Colonialism: Timorese Nationalist Verse: Francisco Borja da Costa,* (Sydney: Wild and Woolly, Sydney, 1976).

6. Ibid.

7. *Tempo,* 23 November 1991 and see analysis on education in John J. Taylor, *Indonesia's Forgotten War: The Hidden History*, (London: Zed, 1991): 125-127.

8. *Posição da Igreja Catolica Perante a Visita da Delegação Parlamentar Portuguesa* (Dili: Imprensa da Diocese de Dili, September 1991).

9. "Berbahasa Porto, Xanana bisa kehilangan hak pembelaannya," *Suara Timor Timur,* 8 May 1993.

10. Geoffrey Hull, "East Timor: Just a Political Question?," Australian Catholic Social Justice Council Occasional Paper, No.11, p. 14.

11. Benedict Anderson, "Imagining East Timor," *Arena Magazine*, (April-May 1993): 23-27.

12. Paul Jacob, *Straits Times*, 31 March 1992.

13. "East Timor Needs More Teachers and Better Teaching Facilities," *The Jakarta Post*, 5 September 1992.

10 From Salazar to Suharto: Toponymy, Public Architecture, and Memory in the Making of East Timorese Identity

In its common-sense meaning, toponymy is the study of geographical place names, derived from the Greek words for *topo* meaning place and *onome* meaning name. Geographers confirm that place names can help us to locate features on the landscape and to provide insights into the history and culture of a region. Maps, new and old, are obviously a guide to such research. But even so, not all toponyms are recorded, many remain unwritten or part of verbatim speech or oral memory. Moreover, some ancient toponyms have faded away whereas others endure; moreover, others are imposed. Indeed, official toponymy, the state-imposed selection and imposition of place names, often ignores indigenous place names.

To offer an early example from the Timor-Flores trading zone first frequented by Portuguese traders and Dominican missionaries, the island of Timor was known in some writings as Santa Cruz, although obviously a name that achieved little currency. Rather, it was Timor (meaning "east" in Malay language), the ancient name applied to the island by Asian traders and navigators which came to be accepted by Timorese as "indigenous." On the other hand, Flores, also known to early navigators as Servite, Ilha Grande, Ende, Ende Grande, Solor Grande, Solor Novo, among other names superseded the indigenous name or names for that island (Leitão 1948: 65). An examination of Portugalized toponyms in Timor and the archipelago over time, and their survival and acceptance down to modern times, would be an interesting exercise, as would the counterpart exercise of identifying the origins of local toponyms ("oronyms" versus "hydronyms") against indigenous traditions such as researched by Portuguese anthropologist António de Almeida (1966; 1976). This chapter, however, is concerned with the official toponymy of Portuguese (East) Timor spanning the Salazar and Suharto eras, or what we might define as the contrived act by the state to officialize selected place names as part of a state-building or nation-building exercise.

But as state-building or nation-building is obviously not confined to the selection of names but typically embraces multiple elements and "inventions" ranging from school curricula to military service to the commemoration of public holidays, we wish in this paper to extend the definition of officialized toponyms to their three-dimensional analogues, namely political iconography in the form of statues, monuments, and even forms of public architecture. In any case, the link between the state-imposed selection of names and their visualization on maps, street signs, and the overt and covert messages encoded in political statuary (such as has been erected in Timor under Portuguese colonialism and under the Indonesian military occupation, should be all too apparent).

Political iconography

Still, from my observations during numerous visits to East Timor (most recently, August 1998) it is surprising, given the tempest-like or even locust-like occupation of the half-island by the Indonesian armed forces and camp followers, that a general desecration of these monuments of Portuguese colonialism did not occur (although there were exceptions). Today, certain of these historical sites are actually protected, in the sense of being inventoried and placed under the control of the Indonesian authority concerned with the protection of cultural relics and sites as part of a *warisan budaya nasional* or Indonesian national cultural inheritance (*Inventarisasi Kesenian* 1978). We may speculate about the reasons for the preservation or at least survival of these sites, but there is no question that their meaning and symbolism have been irremediably vitiated. We should add as well, neither has the armed resistance (Falintil) nor the urban, largely student-led *intifada* notably sought to deface or vandalize Indonesian symbols of state.

To be sure, as Anderson has written in a celebrated essay on political monuments in Indonesia, most monuments are meant to outlast their constructors "and so partly take on the aspect of a bequest or testament." In so doing, he continues, "monuments are really ways of mediating between particular types of pasts and futures" (Anderson 1978: 301). This is true, but what resonance do these relics of the colonial past hold for today's Timorese? Indeed, we might elaborate that, like the Pharaohs of Egypt, monument makers in Timor, from Salazar to Suharto, made the mistake of actually believing that their works were in perpetuity.

In any case, the Indonesian inventory offers a list of thirty "monuments" surviving from the Portuguese era, divided by *kabupaten* (regency), accordingly; namely, Aileu (1); Ainaro (9); Dili (5); Ermera (2); Liquica (4); Bobonaro (3); Viqueque (3); and Same (3). Even so, this attempt at categorization is somewhat deceptive as it includes the *tranqueira* (fortresses) of Ainaro, Liquica, Maubara, Balibo and Batugade (*Inventarisasi Kesenian*, 1978). It also excludes Oe-cusse, which boasts the surviving monument to the Portuguese "discovery" of Timor at Lifau.

Infante D. Henrique Monument: There is no question that the single or singular officialized monument of postwar Timor was that of Henry the Navigator or Infante D. Henrique (1394-1460), erected in Dili in 1960 as a "Homenagem de Timor" on the fifth centenary of his death. Prominently sited in the Largo or square of the same name fronting the Palácio do Governo, also known in colonial times as the Palácio das Repartições, there is no question that this edifice was meant to impress and to celebrate. While the meaning of the Portuguese inscription on one side of this monument may not have been entirely accessible even back in 1960, these famous words taken from Camões *(Lusiadas*, I.I), "Por Mares Nunca Dantes Navegados" [Over Seas Never Before Sailed], are nevertheless suggestive of imperium, omnipotence, and awe.

Still standing in a somewhat symbolically transformed Largo, fronting the now green-roofed Palácio turned "Kantor Governor" (Governor's Office), and, appropriately facing the *praia* and the Wetar sea, the monument, albeit somewhat weathered, retains its grandeur, just as it boldly displays its Santa Cruz emblem over official Portuguese symbols of state, the coat of arms of the Republic. Yet, one wonders, how is this monument apprehended today by Timorese, much less Indonesians? One clue as to official Indonesian understanding is contained in a publication of the public relations department of "Provincial Government of East Timor," which misleadingly describes Infante D. Henrique as a mere "Portuguese colonial ruler." In any case, unlike elsewhere in the world, including even Goa, the debate over the Columbus and Vasco da Gama quincentenaries appears to have washed over Indonesia (and Timor) in intellectual terms.

Today, the Largo serves as an Indonesian *medan* or parade ground, a miniaturized replica of the Medan Merdeka in Jakarta where all the symbols of state headed by the armed forces parade on such days as 17 August, the day that Suharto and Hatta proclaimed freedom of Indonesia from Dutch rule. Nevertheless, it cannot be said that even the function or symbolism of the Largo remains as it was in the past. Whereupon the tree-lined *praia* formerly served as space for relaxation, especially in the evenings, it is now derelict and mostly deserted, partly stripped of its trees, in any case paralleled by a busy road. Where not even Pombal achieved perfect symmetry in Lisbon, the surreptitious removal of a colonial edifice on the northeast corner of the Largo sometime between my visits of 1994-98 has achieved a new symmetry for this open space. Not imposing, the building which served as variously a Portuguese officer's mess and government tourism center was, nevertheless, one of the few buildings of old Dili that survived the Japanese invasion (Thomaz 1976).

The trend to demolish the old in Dili appears to have accelerated during these boom years, as symbolized by the construction of Jakarta-headquartered banks, intrusive symbols of New Order crony capitalism in Latin Dili, and otherwise distinctive for their unwelcoming air-conditioned blockhouse style, in a climate where common sense would favor the Dili-style veranda. Perhaps only military occupation (Portuguese, Japanese— as wartime headquarters—and today, Indonesian) of the adjoining barracks, turned museum in 1972, guarantees the survival of this edifice, the oldest in Dili and constructed by Governor José Maria Marques (1834-39) (Thomaz 1976), from predatory real estate operators. A Macassan restaurant somehow embedded into the fortress walls crowned with the still visible Portuguese state emblem adds an especially incongruous touch to this historic site. The sole, and laudable exception to the progressive demolition of old Dili appears to be the attempts to erect an annex to the Palacio/Kantor Governor in the original porticoed veranda style.

Maubisse: Por Portugal Contra O Invasor: One of the most bizarre monuments or at least relics of colonial rule in Timor surely must be the Pousada de Maubisse in the mountain town of that name. Arriving at the crossroads leading to the Pousada, one is confronted with an obviously colonial-era monument boldly displaying a Santa Cruz-like emblem embossed with the seal of the Portuguese Republic and flanked, in no unequivocal language, by the words "Por Portugal - Contra O Invasor." While appearing to defy the entrance of interlopers to this once intimate part of the world, the monument, at least at the time of the author's visit to Maubisse in August 1998, was in turn framed by a characteristic Indonesian New Order style triumphal arch cum signboard bearing the hybrid Portuguese-Indonesian inscription "Selamat Datang di Pousada Maubisse" or welcome to the Maubisse hotel. Presumably *pousada* along with *mercado* and some other Portuguese terms have now entered the Dewan Bahasa lexicon along with such seventeenth century incorporations as *metega, sekolah, jendela*, etc. Again I am uncertain as to how surviving Chinese shopkeepers or their Timorese counterparts who throng this street on market days apprehend these messages, but the search for meaning deepens as one traces the steep ascent along what appears to be the sole remaining *calcada* or cobblestone roads on Timor, albeit in bad repair, to reach the celebrated Pousada. Built on classic Portuguese colonial lines in 1937, featuring rich mahogany fittings and a Portuguese/Macau-style parquet floor, the Pousada was prudently abandoned by its Australian manager in 1974. Evidently stripped of its furniture by the "Invasor," the Pousada underwent some refit in 1996 (hence the triumphal arch) in the expectation of a surge in tourism. Alas, only strong imagination can recapture the Lusitanian ambience of this erstwhile "hill station" in miniature. The bar, the attached bakery, the plumbing, all lie in decay. Seized as Indonesian state property, the Pousada de Maubisse, along with its analogue, the Pousada de Baucau (sometime Hotel Flamboyant/sometime torture chamber) remain as degraded monuments of the invasion as much as cultivated affronts to would-be tourists of an erstwhile post-colonial age.

Tugu Pahlawan or Integration Statue: Sited in a triangular space between Dili harbor and the commercial center, the Tugu Pahlawan Integrasi or "Integration statue," officially opened by Indonesian Armed Forces Commander General M. Yusuf in 1978, stands atop a giant plinth partly veiled behind the spreading branches of trees. It is said that Timorese shun this enclosed space, and, in my numerous visits to Dili under Indonesian rule, I have seldom seen people other than grass cutters enter this fenced-off area.

Dwarfed by the towering rectangular plinth, the statue takes the form of a sword-wielding Timorese warrior defiantly spreading his arms wide to reveal his broken shackles. If we are to find an analogue of this piece of political iconography, actually commemorating the declared integration of East Timor as the 27th province of Indonesia on 17 July 1976, then it would be the Liberation of West Irian Monument on Lapangan Banteng in Jakarta. As with its Jakarta counterpart, the construction of the Dili monument closely follows in time the respective event it commemorates. In other words, as Anderson observes of the Jakarta monument, it is a monument created for a specific historical event (Anderson 1978: 303). As a "liberation" monument, Indonesia would no doubt wish it to be seen as a traditional monument in the sense that it is seen as a part of

Indonesian history in which (Anderson's observation) constructor and audience participated. This is interesting, and so are Anderson's ruminations as to the phallic symbolism of Jakarta's better-known public monuments, but the passage of years would tell us that neither Irianese nor Timorese shared this "liberation" project, hence the distance that Timorese feel towards this mediocre piece of masonry. But again, while the Irian monument located in the national capital might, at least by New Order stalwarts, be regarded as a national monument, the Integration monument sited in Dili is palpably perceived by large numbers of independence-seeking Timorese as something imposed from outside. In any case "integration" and the freedom suggested by the statue is an oxymoron in Timorese political consciousness.

The Cristo Rei Statue: Universally known in Timor by its Portugalized appellation Cristo Rei (Christ the Lord), the US$2 million Indonesian government-sponsored statue of Christ, is set athwart the dominating Fatocama cape overlooking a broad sweep of the Wetar sea (or at least the "female" sea as the northern sea is known in Tetum) and visible even from the hills surrounding Dili. Unveiled by former Indonesian president Suharto, the statue has been controversial since its conception, indeed the object of major international media and comment at the time. Indeed, the irony of the situation, namely the inauguration of the new monument in October 1996 four days after the award of the Nobel Peace prize to two sons of Timor, was not lost upon either the Indonesian people, the Nobel laureates, or the international media. Bishop Carlos Belo had already made it clear prior to the event by stating to the press: "What's the point of building a statue of Jesus if people are not going to be treated according to the gospel? It would be better to improve the situation rather than build statues." More than just a symbol of Christianity, it concerned some people that the statue was 27 metres high, fitting Indonesian political mythology that East Timor was happily integrated into the Indonesian Republic as 27th province or, in the words of one Western journalist, "clearly meant as a monumental display of faith in Timor's integration with the rest of Indonesia" (Cohen 1996).

It is not altogether clear to me how this statue is truly received today by ordinary Timorese, much less the church. One thing clear, however, it is not much visited, but then it is not that accessible. Some Timorese have commented upon its similarity to the Christ statue overlooking the Rio Tejo in Portugal; some journalists have compared it to its Rio de Janeiro analogue; some have likened it to the far smaller Christ statue atop the Balide church in Dili; while others are simply proud—or amazed—that it can be seen from a long distance. Some wags, albeit foreign, have commented that, anyway, it faces Mecca.

Timor toponymy

Not surprisingly, the town grid of Dili reflected Portugalized toponyms, as did the Luandas, the Maputos (Lourenço Marques) and a hundred other towns of the former Portuguese world. To be sure, unlike Macau today, not all these Avenidas, Ruas and Travessas in Dili are actually signboarded, a matter of municipal negligence, but still appear on current Indonesian tourist maps, etc, and still serve as postal addresses. Some bear the names of former Portuguese governors of Timor such as Avenida or Rua José Maria Marques (1834-39), J. Celestino da Silva (1894-1908); Rua Filomeno da Camara, after Filomeno de Camara Melo Cabral (1910-17), and (Fernando) Alves Aldeia (1972-74). One bears the name of the bishop of Timor and Macau (1885-97), Bispo Medeiros (D. António Joaquim de), also surviving as a street name in Macau today. Two, as explained, were towering figures of the Salazar dictatorship, namely Marechal (Oscar) Carmona (1869-1951) and Américo (Deus Rodrigues) Thomaz (1894-1987). In this sense it is illustrative that in the wake of the Portuguese revolution of 25 April 1974, Avenida Dr. Oliveira Salazar in Macau was changed by local authorities to the more neutral Avenida Amizade, just as Avenida Salazar in Dili (I am not sure of its location) no longer appears on current maps. Several other streets in Dili bear such sundry names, as Rua (Jalan) de Fernando and Rua (Jalan) Sebastião.

Very few street names in Dili actually commemorate Timorese. One is Rua dos Reis Noronha after D. Luis dos Reis

Noronha of Manatuto, and another is Rua D. Jeremias do Amaral, born in Luca in 1898 and murdered during the Second World War. D. Jeremias dos Reis Amaral is also commemorated by a monument in Viqueque. Other street names have a more local colonial connection. Such is Avenida Belarmino Lobo, Avenida Dr. Carvalho, and Rua Alf. Francisco Duarte Arbíru, 1862-1899.

Belarmino Lobo, the Goa-born, Bombay-trained doctor profiled by Manuel Teixeira in *Os Médicos em Macau* (1967:85-86) first distinguished himself in the attempt to combat a cholera outbreak in Damao (Portuguese India) before taking up his position as government medical officer in Dili in November 1880. Besides serving as medical officer in military operations in Lautem in 1899, he was also engaged in the work of stemming various epidemics in the colony. At times the only doctor in Dili, he was also the doctor of choice from Governor to lower officials, Chinese, Arabs, etc. He was also President of the Camara for fifteen years and engaged in various civic projects such as canalization of drinking water from Lahane to Dili, public education, the public library and the Vasco da Gama museum, and so on. He died in Dili in November 1914.

Rua do Dr. Carvalho is named after António da Costa Carvalho, born Barras (Coimbra) in 1862, graduate of the Faculty of Medicine of Coimbra University in 1888, prior to appointment as medical officer in Macau and Timor, where he served with great distinction for over three years (1890-93). Besides being appointed medical officer in the Maubara campaign of 1893, he was the key individual responsible for waging the campaign against the virulent cholera epidemic of the time and, tragically, was one of the victims. Amidst popular acclamation the Camara Municipal of Dili then named the street after him and, to honor his memory, erected a mausoleum in his name. This can be found near the entrance within Santa Cruz cemetery. "Aqui jaz o medico António da Costa Carvalho victima da dedicação profissional na epidemia de cholera em 1893...A memoria do heroe erigiu este monumento a Camara de Dilly em 1894." In 1911, to further honor his legacy, Governor Filomeno da Camara lent his support to renaming the (Castro) Lahane hospital in his honor (Ferreira 1957).

Others street names are more symbolic, such as Sá da Bandeira (now run together as Sada, as explained),   Rua Mousinho de Albuquerque (as explained); and Jacinto Candido, after Jacinto Candido da Silva, Minister and Secretary of State of Marine and Overseas Affairs, c.1897. That also holds for Jalan [sic] dos Martires do Patria. But others also signal place names such as in Farol,   Rua Mozambique, Rua (and Bairro) Formosa, as with its ancient Macau counterpart, probably bearing no relationship to the island also known as Taiwan, and Cidade ("Sidade") de Beja.

Where these toponyms have been set in marble, they remain as such; but more commonly the signboard has disappeared and been replaced with a tin counterpart adding the prefix *Jalan* (Jl) before the invariable *Avenida* or *Rua,* creating the hybrid *Jalan Avenida*! I found only one *Travessa* and one *Largo* in Dili still extant, both written in stone.

The exception to the practice of retaining Portuguese toponyms in Dili at least is where new streets have been created, such as in the new housing estate near Comoro (Kampong Merdeka?) not only a Javanese suburb in miniature, mostly inhabited by Indonesians, but replete with Javanized toponyms. Also, in some cases, Indonesian orthography has prevailed over Portuguese. Thus Comoro becomes Komoro; Becora (Bekora); Baucau (Bakau); Viqueque (Vikeke) (VKK) and so on.

One street not connected with a specific historical event either in Timor or in Portugal is "15 Oktober." This is deceptive, as 5 October was the day that the military movement in Portugal proclaimed the Republic and constitution of a provisional government. 15 October is, I believe, a day the Republic of Indonesia commemorates "Army Day"?

While there are of course many examples of Indonesian-imposed toponyms in Dili—"lapangan Pramuka" opposite the old Chinese school is one—the most celebrated and controversial example of toponymic manipulation must be the naming by Suharto during his visit to Dili in 1997 of Jalan Ibu Tien Soeharto, after his recently deceased wife, today flagged by a rather impermanent looking tin street sign, which, at this writing at least, has survived the ouster of the dictator. Linking the city center with the Comoro (Komoro) airport, Jalan Ibu Tien Soeharto terminates at a massive gleaming white marble monument, singular perhaps in the "Indonesian" world, perhaps more in place in some central European capital. Taking the form of a rotunda, the still unfinished work is distinguished by a circle of oversized cherubs blowing even more oversized trumpets. Just what these stone angels are heralding appears as bewildering to the Timorese as it does to me. But for visitors to Dili arriving by air, alongside diesel-spewing taxis and nipa hut villages, this is the first "sight."

But while the imposition of Indonesianized street markers might be explained as a "natural" development along with demographic changes brought about by the entry of large numbers of non-Timorese into East Timor, no such excuses can be made for the proliferation through East Timor of new Sanskritized symbols and codes that past and present units of ABRI have imposed upon the landscape. Aside from the Taman Pahlawan or Indonesian military cemeteries, these symbols range from the stylized, multi-colored, club-wielding Mahabarata figure that adorns the Dili headquarters of a Bali-based Udayana Military Command, to the grotesque spider insignia of a departed Indonesian Satgas or special forces battalion that graces a military-installed obelisk at a fork in the Areia Branca (now, Pasir Putih)-Hera road.

But otherwise it is difficult to identify the antiquity of Dili toponyms since its European settlement in 1769, or at least the Latinized versions. Of course, no such problem exists with Dili, an erstwhile indigenous toponym and Motael (after *mota ain* or mouth of the river), as in the well known Motael church, the key collaborating *regulo* or *reino* that made Portuguese occupation of the coastal plain of Dili possible. The first European toponym in Dili was plausibly the *fortalezas* of S. Francisco and Domingos which have long since disappeared. Bidau, still a *bairro* or suburb of Dili, took its name from the *moradores* or civilian military forces, a Christianized group arriving from Solor. Sica, also a very early place name in Dili— long since disappeared—took its name from the then Portugalized enclave of Sica on Flores. In any case, fires and earthquakes periodically wiped out the first *fortalezas* and churches along with their memory. It was not until streets were constructed during Governor Affonso de Castro's watch (1859-63) that toponyms became fixed, eg, the Lahane road to the Castro-Lahane hospital (later the Dr. Carvalho Hospital and today dubbed the Wira Usaha or Indonesian military Hospital). As mentioned, while the hospital was renamed, as indicated on a 1: 20,000 scale inset map in the 1927 1:100,000 Carta da Provincia de Timor, Castro-Lahane also denominated a mountain. Similarly, a plan of the port and city of Dilly (Dili) produced by Andrea and Machado in 1870 offers some of the first Portugalized toponyms: a fort, Nossa Senhora da Conceição (demolished in 1886); a *fortaleza* known as Carqueto; and a *ponte* known as D. Luiz I, all since disappeared. Even so, the Portugalized toponym Carqueto survived into the modern period as a *bairro* of Dili, located inland from the seaward Campo Mouro, although interestingly, the above-mentioned 1927 Carta indicates a Rio Carqueto entering the sea just east of Farol and a seafront cemetery (since disappeared) and the Casa do Regulo de Motael, also since disappeared, but doubtless near the site of the original fortress. A map of Dili port executed in 1892 by A. Heitor, the original of which is lodged in the Macau archives, signals the presence of substantial Chinese commercial houses located at the intersection of Rua do Commercio and Estrada de Lahane and Travessa das Figueiras—locus, no doubt, of the future Campo China. A Rua de S. Domingos connected the major thoroughfares with Rua da Praia Grande. All these toponyms have disappeared from usage and we cannot even assume that today's Praia stands on exactly the same ground as the old Praia Grande, owing to siltation and reclamation. In fact, however, it has been the postwar reclamation of Dili's notorious malarial *pantano* or swamps (cf. 1927 Carta) that has transformed the urban environment.

Most of the Portugalized toponyms found in Dili today, then, have their origins in this century. An exception is Santa Cruz, which probably takes its name from the cemetery allocated as a substitute to older cemeteries originally sited in Bidau and Motael and constructed at the urgings of the particularly intelligent and dynamic chief of health services, José Gomes da Silva, in the mid 1880s (*Boletim da Provincia de Macau e Timor*, XXXIII [5]: 31-32, 3 de fevereiro de 1887). But whether the Santa Cruz cemetery is that eulogized in Osório de Castro's 1909 *Flores de Coral* - "As casuarinas do cemiterio de Dili" remains unclear to me.

To return to the Salazarist theme, it is a matter of fact that in the immediate prewar period, a number of indigenous toponyms, including most of the smaller towns of the colony, came to be superseded on maps at least by Portuguese names, either as homage to individuals linked with the colony or as remembrance of towns and villages in Portugal. Nevertheless, Governor Duarte's 1930 book reveals only indigenous place names. Singular exceptions appear to be the names of *granjas* (farms) Eduardo Marques, Republica, etc., a practice dating from the time of Celestino da Silva. I am also struck in reading Osorio de Castro's *A Ilha Verde e Vermelha de Timor* (1909) by his mastery of indigenous toponyms and the absence of Portugalized names.

These included Vila General Carmona (Aileu); Nova Ourem (Atsabe); Vila Salazar (Baucau); Vila Eduardo Marques (Bazar-Tete); Vila Armindo Monteiro (Bobonaro); Boavista Calicai (Quelicai); Nova Nazare (Com); Nova Anadia (Fatu-Berlio); Nova Monchique (Fatu-Lulic); Oliveira (Fatu-Mean); Nova Gouveia (Fohorem); Vila de Avis (Fuiloro); Vila Celestino da Silva (Hatolia); Vila de Ourique (Laclubar); Vila Nova Malaca (Lautem); Nova Obidos (Lete-Foho); Mindelo (Maubesse); Belas (Ossu); Vila Tavaeira (Pante-Macassar); Nova Ancora (Raimoro); Vila Filomeno da Camara (Same); Nova Sagres (Tutuala); Viriato (Uato-Builaco); Leca (Uato-Lari); and Nova Luso (Uato-Udo). Cartographically, the new Portugalized *toponímia* is reproduced on the 1948 map entitled *Colonia de Timor, Esboço* (Escala 1:1,000,000).

Writing in 1956, Helio A. Esteves Felgas mused that while a change of nomenclature had merit in situations in which European colonists formed a nuclei and had brought about new developments, the endeavor to impose an imported name upon an age-old local feature was only a source of confusion and hardly convincing. For these reasons, he continues, the alteration was not successful. In any case only Vila Salazar endured (Felgas 1956: 348-350). Pretty much, this was confirmed by an American wartime intelligence report on Timor, which stated, "It is still customary on the island, however, to use the original native name, and this habit persists even amongst many of the Portuguese, the new name being used practically only in their official dealings. [Australian] Sparrow Force has always used the native names, and it is highly desirable that these names should be used for all maps, studies and reports" (*Area Study of Portuguese Timor* 1943: 79). To be sure, it is highly doubtful whether outside of official parlance these new names ever superseded indigenous names in indigenous consciousness. While the practice appears to have been retained into the postwar period, it must have soon lapsed. In any case, I never heard any name but Baucau applied to that town when I first visited in the 1960s.

It is uncertain as to how many monuments to Portugal were erected in Timor prior to the rude eruption of the Pacific war, but one which tells is that placed upon the summit of the otherwise sacred peak of Tata-Mai-Lau in 1938 by the Geographical and Geological Mission of Timor, the highest peak in the empire, namely "Portugal-Alto Império que o Sol logo em nascendo vê primeiro" (*Boletim Geral das Colónias* 15 (164): 105-106, Fevereiro 1939).

Again, while the Japanese were creative in inventing appropriate toponyms in occupied parts of Southeast Asia (eg, Shonan for Singapore), I have no evidence of this practice in Timor, although it could well have been an internal military practice. Neither did Japan appear to have left any monuments in occupied Timor such as the stone commemorating General Hideki Tojo's wartime stopover in Labuan (Malaysia), which still remains on public display in Victoria town.

On this thought, it is also possible that the Australian commando force invented toponyms for their own convenience, just as it is likely—even more certain—that ABRI invented their own counterpart bahasa Indonesia or Javanese synologues for various strategic features.

Not surprisingly, Indonesian maps of East Timor such as the 1:300,000 scale map entitled "Propinsi Timor Timur" produced by PT Karya Pembina Swajaya, a commercial house based in Surabaya, replaced all Portugalized identifiers with Indonesian, as in Tanjong for Cabo; Sungai for Ribeiro, Gunung for Monte; but also introducing new hybrids and oddities, such as Gunung Mundo Perdido while retaining the obscure Portugalized Tetum place markers Uma Lain de Cima and Uma Lain de Baixo (in Viqueque). But such license has also met with creative Timorese response. Surely, one of the more bizarre invented toponyms of recent times arising from the Indonesian occupation is the hushed Timorese reference to "Jakarta Jakarta," a notorious mountain cliff on the outskirts of Ainaro where captured Falintil or sympathizers have been pushed to their deaths.

Pacific war monuments

Even so, the Pacific war has bequeathed its share of monuments. Ten are listed in the Indonesian *Inventarisasi*. Two prominently sited monuments in Dili commemorate, respectively, Engenheiro Artur Canto Resende and Tenente Pires, both Portuguese victims of the war. Particularly noteworthy, however, is the striking monument-mausoleum to the massacre by the Japanese-backed Black Column of Portuguese administrators in Aileu on 31 August 1942 (cf. Vieira da Rocha 1996: 97-100). Rendered official with the Portuguese emblem, this quite massive walled and porticoed monument remains relatively well preserved under Indonesian custody, although signs of decay are showing through in part of the masonry, even between my 1994 and 1998 visits.

Another surviving reminder of the Japanese occupation is the less elaborate but no less compelling—even elegant— monument in Ainaro to Dom Aleixo Corte Real, the quintessential loyal Timorese chief killed by the Japanese in May 1943 (cf. Vieira da Rocha 1996: 109-112). Taking the form of a simple stone arch offering a large open window space into which a wrought-iron cross is placed, the monument is headed "Por Portugal" and, at the base, inscribed "A Memoria do Regulo D. Aleixo Corte Real, Morreu em 1943."

Yet, from an Australian War memorial photograph dated 24 January 1945 taken by K.B. Davis of Sparrow Force [Negative no. 125289], this monument was preceded by a sepulcher of the Royal family where the skulls of "King" Aleixo and his three "sons" or more likely *companeiros*, Alfonso, Francisco, and Aliveira, were on public (?) display, albeit arranged behind a crucifix.

A related Australian wartime photo [Negative no. 125374] offers what the caption describes without elaboration as a stone mosaic in the Ainaro town square bearing the inscription "Suro 1933." Alas, this singular art work in traditional Portuguese style no longer exists in Ainaro, nor to my knowledge was replicated elsewhere in Timor (although a great object of municipal pride in Macau today). Originally an interior kingdom, albeit stretching to the southern "male" sea (*contra costa*) and "pacified" in 1900, Suro (Suru) was enlarged by Governor Filomeno da Camara as a reward for standing firm during the campaign of 1911-12 against the "rebel" chief and Timorese hero Boaventura. However, in a blow to the prestige of Suro, the Comando Militar do Suro transformed the region into a military post subordinate to Manufahi. Only in 1933-4 did the seat of the kingdom return to Ainaro. This was Dom Aleixo's moment of triumph. Appropriately, this new and impressive monument inaugurated in *calcada* of 1933 was celebrated in song, or at least *tabedai* or war dance (Martinho 1947: 12).

Yet another war-related monument is that to the loyal *regulo* of Maubara. Located in what today is the playground of the Maubara primary school and therefore somewhat out of sight, the plaque on this monument bears the inscription: "Homenagem do Governo de Timor au seu mui fiel regulo de Maubara José Nunes (1874-1952)." At the time of my 1998 visit, neither the children who clambered over this monument nor some of their elders knew this figure, suggesting perhaps that history has to be actively remembered if it is to be remembered at all. It is therefore fortunate that a photograph of "King Nunis" of Maubara taken in 1946 exists in the Australian War Memorial Collection [Negative no. 125216] bearing the caption that he "organized anti fifth column campaign among his natives" and that he "remained loyal to the Portuguese."

On their part, Australian veterans have bequeathed their own monument, the Fatunaba monument, set against a pool of flowing water and erstwhile swimming pool for local children, in the hills above Dili—inscribed thus:

Ao Povo Portugues do Minho a Timor
OFERTA DO POVO AUSTRALIANO
COMO PROVA DE GRATIDAO
PELA AJUDA PRESTADA
AOS SEUS SOLDADOS
DURANTE OS ANOS DE 1939-1945
E MUITO PARTICULARMENTE AO
POVO DE TIMOR
PELOS HOMENS DO
COMANDO 2/2 (COMPANHIA INDEPENDENTE)
QUE AQUI COMBATERAM EM 1942

It is a statement of fact that many Timorese feel that this sentiment has been betrayed by the Canberra government's succor of the Suharto dictatorship and complicity in the misery of the Timorese people; Timorese, I am sure can distinguish between their good friends among Australian (and Japanese) veterans of this war and those who let them down. Erected in 1969, the plaque attached to this monument apparently disappeared after the Indonesian occupation (Wray 1987: 87), although I can confirm that a plaque (or a replica) is well in place.

It should be mentioned that just as Timor came to be mapped by various geographical surveys culminating in the Carta de Portugal: Provincia de Timor 1:50,000 Series, so the identification of toponyms, as much their nomenclature, attained a new fixity and currency. For example, *only* 2,824 toponyms are given to Timor in the 1:250,000 map of Timor published by the Serviço Cartografico do Exército in 1944, which in turn formed the basis of the Reportório Toponímico da Portugal published by the Ministério do Exército in 1966. But the proliferation of such geographical prefixes as *ponta, monte, ribeiro,* etc. suggests these maps were primarily for metropolitan consumption. Map literacy like print literacy of course was lost upon most Timorese in that age, at least outside of the military. There is reason to believe that—for good reason—Portuguese maps of Timor and even of Dili were treated as military intelligence.

Most of Dili's public buildings were destroyed by Allied bombs during the Pacific war, so we can assume the postwar period saw change in this area. In 1994, Hakka-speaking Chinese of Dili in charge of the Chinese temple told me that the temple building actually survived the war intact and retains its place name in received Hakka speech. I have not investigated the matter, but it is highly likely that, just as in Macau, speakers of Chinese dialects have acquired a store of local toponyms; although, unlike Macau, street signs in Timor were never bilingual. The exception to the absence of Chinese toponyms was the Chinese schools and the Chinese Commercial Association building on Dili waterfront. The Indonesian New Order, it should be recalled, proscribed not only Chinese schools but even the public display of Chinese characters.

To depart slightly from this text, it should be recalled that, dating from at least 1430, as revealed by the *Shun Feng Hsiang Sung* (Fair Winds for Escort), a Chinese nautical compendium, Chinese traders in sandalwood identified six toponyms on Timor, including Kupang and Maubara. Modern Chinese atlases also identify 13 toponyms specific to East Timor, including Dili.

Kampong Arab, also variously known as Kampong Islam or Kampong Alor, shared its Portugalized synonyms in Campo Mouro, Bairo Morros, Bairos Arabe or Morros Alor (simply marked "Mouro" on the Carta de Portugal: Provincia da Timor 1: 50,000 map). While the Arab quarter of Dili was originally sited in the Bidau quarter, my understanding is that, owing to the suspect loyalties of some members of this community during the Japanese occupation and at the time of the Indonesian revolution, the Portuguese administration sought to concentrate them in the present location. Thomaz states that they used to have their domicile in Colmera in a street called "dos árabes," but which cannot be located with precision (Thomaz 1976/77). Otherwise, very few Malayanized toponyms found acceptance in Portuguese Timor. Pulau Kambing (Atauro) was one, Batu

Gede (Batugade), perhaps, and most certainly, Pantai Macassar, the Buginese trading beach in Oe-cusse where these sea nomads traded seasonally. But, in the present period, while Chinese language and culture has lost rank in Timor, not so Islam, Islamic schools or even, occasionally, the public display of *huruf Arab* or Arabic script alongside (of course) romanized bahasa Indonesia. The book, *Islam di Timor Timur* (1995) offers the Arabized names of some hundred mosques and madrasahs (prayer-houses) erected in East Timor, with about two exceptions, all constructed since 1975.

The case of Alferes Francisco Duarte "O Arbíru" (1862-99)

Alferes (Sublieutenant) Francisco Duarte "O Arbíru" (the invincible) remains immortalized in the leafy Farol district of Dili in the form of a well-preserved street sign set against the manicured grass of a well-preserved colonial residence, now Indonesian military squat. But who was Duarte "O Arbíru"? Why was this figure memorialized by Portugal? Indeed, why has the memory of this man been preserved? Indeed are Portuguese, Timorese, and Indonesian remembrances of this figure at variance? Or, is his name just another icon left over from history? A Kemak legend retold to the author in trilingual Kemak/Portuguese/English) form by Snr. António Luís Mota goes as follows:

> Bui Cari atu Bui Cari
> Arbiru mate ara lolo
> Bui cari atu Bui Cari
> Arbiru tau tuli lolo
> Beu beu sala kahi sai
> Au eh dale tura kahi sai
> --
> Bui Cari rock Bui cari
> Arbiru (the invincible) was gunned down
> Bui Cari Bui Cari
> Arbiru lost his life

All of a sudden the evil was done
I meant to comfort him, but it was all over

Such was the reputation of this man, at least in Kemak lore, that it was believed that he could only be killed with a golden bullet, and such is how, in this story, he met his end.

In fact Duarte, the "Lawrence of Timor" in official Portuguese military writings, served more than one governor in at least five major military campaigns. Certainly his name became known in the Macau press at the time of the great Maubara rebellion of May-July 1893. According to Pélissier's reading of historical archives, Duarte was believed to have been the real instigator of this affair. Relieved of his position he nevertheless spearheaded subsequent suppression campaigns on the Balibo frontier, at Manufahi in 1895, albeit grievously wounded on October 7, only to recover to return to action in Cotubaba in July 1896 and Lamaquitos in 1897 (Pélissier 1996: 124-6, 129, 140-2, 144-9, 151-2, 154-8, 161-72, 175-7, 186-9, 210, 243). Died in combat on 17 July 1899, Francisco Duarte "O Arbíru" was laid to rest in Santa Cruz cemetery, where his mausoleum remains. Exactly forty years later on 17 July 1959, a stone was erected in his honour at the actual site of his death in Bobonaro. The monument is duly listed in the Indonesian inventory (*Inventarisasi Kesenian*, 1978), with Duarte duly recorded as a Portuguese "*pahlawan*" (hero), albeit obviously not of the Second World War as here stated. But for most Timorese *O Arbíru* was the name of the small Portuguese ship that tragically and mysteriously disappeared with much loss of life in the Flores Sea in May 1973 while on a mission to Bangkok to requisition rice supplies.

Sá de Bandeira should be something of a *double entendre* for Timorese—if they have read history, that is. The name either stands for the corvette *Sá de Bandeira* that visited Timor in 1869-70, first arriving at the height of a cholera epidemic and later in the wake of rebellion in Covalima, or more distantly stands for the nineteenth century Portuguese colonial politician, the Marquis of Sá da Bandeira, after whom the gunboat was named, and a figure known for what British Africanist Clarence-

Smith calls the "doubtful policy" of increasing customs revenues from the African colonies in order to develop the metropolis, along with expanding Portuguese control along the coasts of Africa (Clarence-Smith 1979: 12-13). In any case Sá da Bandeira is a familiar name in the Portuguese colonial world (Angola and elsewhere). Sá da Bandeira has even lent his name to a high school in Lisbon, and has been commemorated by a formidable marble statue and fountain in the same city. As observed by the author several summers past, this place offers a great swimming hole for local Afro-Portuguese children, or might we say, tongue-in-cheek, part of Sá de Bandeira's extended family.

Mousinho de Albuquerque: At this writing Rua Mousinho de Albuquerque survives as part street name and part stone plinth at a busy Dili intersection, albeit a rundown corner frequented by street vendors, not a few street urchins, and traffic police. There would be few alive in Dili today who could fathom the meaning of this icon set in marble, erected, according to an engraved message, in July 1972, in "Homenagem Da Arma De Cavalaria." As more than one Mousinho de Albuquerque exists in Portuguese historical imagination, I take it advisedly that the person referred to is Joaquim Mousinho de Albuquerque (1855-1902), Governor-General of Mozambique (March 1896-November 1897 and May 1898-July 1898), later received in Lisbon with extraordinary honors, and subsequently employed as tutor to the royal children of Dom Carlos. Death by suicide. While Mousinho de Albuquerque was commemorated in colonial times in Mozambique in the form of a statue, it is not altogether clear whether or not across the generations there was a Timor connection with this figure, aside from the possibility of a rotation of military command from Mozambique to Timor in 1972, or otherwise in remembrance of the role of soldiers from Mozambique in the Timor campaigns of 1912.

Marechal Carmona: Born in 1869, Marachel (Field Marshal) Oscar Carmona rose through the ranks as an officer of the cavalry taking the side of Salazar in the events of 1925-26, becoming the Minister of Foreign Affairs in the first government of the Estado Novo in May 1925 and, in 1928, stood as the sole candidate in the Presidential elections.

Américo Deus Rodrigues Tomás (1894-1987) was an Admiral who became President of the Republic (1958-74). Tomás was serving as Minister of the Navy when, at Salazar's prompting, he entered the presidential election against the main anti-Salazar candidate, General Humberto Delgado, and won, according to one source, due to electoral fraud (*Centro de Documentação, 25 de Abril*). Tomás was overthrown on 25 April 1974, a victim of the "Carnation Revolution." The question therefore remains as to why the Avenida Américo Tomás in Dili was not renamed by members of the Armed Forces Council dispatched to Timor in the wake of the restoration of democracy in Portugal?

Anthroponyms

But if this research has thrown into relief the ephemerality of imposed toponyms and the presumption of empire builders to impose their writ in stone for perpetuity, what has endured from the Lusophone inheritance on Timor and elsewhere in the archipelago are undoubtedly Portugalized anthronyms, or personal names. The modern process has been well studied by such Portuguese anthropologists as António de Almeida (1976). But such a practice goes back to the first conversions by the Dominican missions and the rise of the mixed race Larantuqueiros, also known as Topasses, whose scions, the da Costas and d'Hornays among others, have imprinted themselves on Timorese history. (Parenthetically, I observe two Portugalized toponyms surviving on the 1:300,000 tourist Indonesian map, both in the ancient enclave of Oe-cusse, namely Costa and Cunha). But it is interesting that just as early Portuguese governors conferred Portugalized titles on various *régulo*, for example, the rebel chief Boaventura and, in the modern period, hero of the resistance against Japan, Dom Aleixo Cortes Real (known as Nai-Sessu before his baptism in 1931), so the countertrend at the end of the colonial era to indigenize anthronyms. Most famously this practice was adopted by Fretilin as announced in its publication *Timor Leste: Journal do Povo Mau Bere*, one of whose contributors signed himself

as Sha Na Na (José "Xanana" Gusmão). Falintil of course
retains the practice of *nom de guerre* such as in Mau Huno
(António Gomes da Costa), among others. Last word on this
subject is a reflection that in most Christian cemeteries in East
Timor—filmmaker-journalist John Pilger's "land of crosses"—I
observe that epigraphs are invariably written in Portuguese.

Guided by ear in these times of political tumult when there
is greater opportunity to make conversational contact with
ordinary Timorese, it is clear that in Dili, at least, certain locales
have retained their Lusitanian place-maker identity. Those which
come to mind are Santa Cruz, Vila Verde, Bairro Pite, Mercado
Municipal, Liceu, Area Branca and "praia dos coqueiros."
Others take hybrid form, as in Mercado lama (old). Another
hybrid term is Escola China, a reference to the now defunct but
still extant Escola Chineza. Others get to be abbreviated in
common speech. For example, the postal address Jl. Travessa
de Lecidere would be simply glossed as Lecidere, as would the
largo of the same name. I suspect, however, the use of
Portugalized nomenclature depends upon generation and
education, as much as the speaker's repertoire of languages. More
familiarity with Dili, and more research would undoubtedly bring
to light a plethora of examples, especially as local forms of Tetum
and Tetum Praça and other languages and dialects take on or at
least appropriate the languages of struggle and common identity.

Memory

As a final word, it is inevitable that in an independent Timor
Loro Sae new and appropriate toponyms (and monuments) and
commemorations will take their place after Timorese heroes
and martyrs, but it is not for me to gainsay how Timorese will or
should remember their recent or even distant past. In fact, this
is already happening both inside and outside of Timor. For a
generation of Timorese the cemeteries and the ubiquitous
crosses are the single defining monuments of their lives.
Consider this single example, the prayer service to mark the
fourth anniversary of the massacre at Santa Cruz cemetery on
12 November 1991 by a non-Timorese, Reverend Max B.

Surjadinata of the (U.S.) National Council of Churches East Timor Working Group. "The role of memory," he suggested, "has always been crucial in the life of believing communities everywhere. Remembrance is a religious and spiritual act that brings vitality and hope to believers everywhere as the past is brought into the present for the future. Therefore it is more than a mere recalling of an objective memory image, but a way of presently entering into what went on before. Through the act of remembrance, faithful believers recall the past in the present as a challenge and a hope, as our commitment to struggle and to pray for the dawning of a transformative future" (http://www.indo.news.com/98/9844/ Friday/8217259.shtml). I write as historian, not preacher, but these words are eloquent of the complex ways that historical memory or collective memory of a people is brought into play; indeed part of the healing process necessary for the building and rebuilding of collective Timorese identity, just as the symbols of the past, toponyms and monuments, are to lesser and greater degrees reminders of this past.

Notes

As acknowledged, special thanks for information used in the research and writing of this paper to Kevin Sherlock of Darwin and Snr António Luís Mota of Macau.

Almeida, António de, "Antropónimos em nomes de Lugares do Timor Português," *Memórias da Academia das Ciências de Lisboa*, Classe de Ciências, XVIII (1976): 57-77.

Almeida, António de, "Contribution à l'étude de l'onomastique de l'Ile d'Atauro (Timor Portugais)," *Proceedings of the Ninth International Congress of Onomastic Sciences*, University College, London, July 3-8, 1966, International Centre of Onomastics, Blijde-Inkomststraat 5, Louvain, pp. 95-104.

Anderson, Benedict R. O'G., "Cartoons and Monuments: The Evolution of Political Communication under the New Order," in Karl D. Jackson and Lucian W. Pye, *Political Power and Communications in Indonesia* (Berkeley: University of California Press, 1978): 282-321.

Area Study of Portuguese Timor, Terrain Study No.50, Allied Geographical Section, Directorate of Intelligence, A.A.F., Southwest Pacific Area, 27 February 1943.

Australian War Memorial Database, http://www.agm.gov.au

Bazhar, Ambarak A., *Islam di Timor Timur* (Jakarta: Gema Insani, 1995).

Centro de Documentação 25 de Abril, http://www.civic.pt/Cd25a/25ahomeh.html

Colónia de Timor: Ebosço (Escala 1: 1000,000), in *Atlas de Portugal Ultramarino e das grandes viagens portuguesas de descobrimentos e expansão*, Lisboa, Junta das Missões, Geográficas e de Investigações Colonais, 1948, mapa 103.

Clarence-Smith, W.G., *Slaves, Peasants and Capitalists in Southern Angola 1840-1926* (Cambridge: Cambridge University Press, 1979).

Cohen, Margot, "Nobel Calling," *Far Eastern Economic Review*, 24 October 1996.

Dicionário Prático Ilustrado, (Porto: Lello & Irmão, 1979).

Duarte, Teofilo, *Timor: Ante-Câmara do Inferno?!*, (Famalição, 1930).

Felgas, Hélio A. Esteves, *Timor Português*, (Lisboa: Agência Geral do Ultramar, 1956).

Ferreira, Manuel, "O Doutor António da Costa Carvalho e a Epidemia do Cólera em Timor (1893)," Anais do Instituto de Medicina Tropical, XIV, 3-4 (Septembro-Dezembro de 1957): 547-575.

Inventarisasi Kesenian Propinsi Timor Timur, Proyek Pembinaan Pendidikan, Kebudayaan Nasional da Pembinaan Generasi Muda Timor Timur, (1978).

Leitão, Humberto, *Os Portugueses em Solor e Timor de 1515 a 1702*, (Lisboa, 1948).

Martinho, José Simões, *Vida e Morte do Régulo Timorense D. Aleixo*, (Lisboa: Pelo Império, 1947).

Pélissier, René, *Timor en Guerre* (Orgeval, France, 1996).

Teixeira, Manuel, *Os Médicos em Macau* (Macau: Imprensa Nacional, 1967).

Teixeira, Manuel, *Toponímia de Macau*, 2 Vols. (Macau: Imprensa Nacional, 1979).

Thomaz, Luis Filipe Ferreira Reis, "O afluxo ao meio urbano no Timor Português," *Revista da Faculdade de Letras*, Lisboa, Série IV, 1 (1976-1977): 495-553.

Vieira da Rocha, Carlos, *Timor: Ocupação Japonesa Durante a Segunda Guerra Mundial* (Lisboa: Sociedade Histórica da Independência de Portugal, 1996).

Wray, Christopher C.H., *Timor: 1942* (Sydney: Hutchison, 1987).

11.   The Student Solidarity Council Movement in East Timor

Given its reputation as a Southeast Asian "killing field," a visitor to Dili (the author was one) the seaport capital of the Indonesian occupied half- island known locally as Timor Leste or Timor Loro Sae, in the summer of 1998 would not have been quite prepared for the deceptively relaxed atmosphere. Notwithstanding the pervasive presence of ABRI, youthful supporters of East Timorese independence were on the offensive. The slogans and the tactics of the past had changed. Not surprisingly, the political conjuncture stemming from Indonesia's economic collapse, the advent of the "reformist" government of B.J. Habibie, and widespread public disdain across the archipelago for the military, had made its impact felt in the distant occupied territory. One early harbinger of change was the release in early June of a number of political prisoners, including 20 East Timorese, although notably not including José (Xanana) Gusmão, the captured resistance fighter and acknowledged East Timorese leader, widely believed to be held as a bargaining chip in ongoing U.N. negotiations over the occupied territory. Importantly, incoming President B.J. Habibie told an international news agency that he would consider offering "special status" and wider autonomy to East Timor, albeit within the Republic of Indonesia. Meeting with 1996 Nobel Peace Prize co-winner Bishop Carlos Ximenes Belo on 24 June, Habibie pledged a gradual withdrawal of troops from East Timor, an act played out to foreign news teams in early August, although, as subsequently revealed by leaked documents, and as widely known inside East Timor, this was a public relations play that masked a troop buildup. Why then was Jakarta so hesitant to let go of the occupied territory? What possible international credibility could be gained from striking an intransigent position both inside East Timor and abroad, at a moment of economic penury, civil strife, and public disorder and with the image of the New Order regime discredited or, at least, gravely damaged at home and abroad?

The Jakarta crisis and the Dili Spring of 1998

To the extent that the East Timor issue entered the consciousness of newspaper-reading Indonesians, it was undoubtedly the controversial but high-profile actions of East Timorese students in breaking in to Western embassies in Jakarta in 1995-97 that brought the issue to mind, albeit not yet sympathetically. But in staging these actions we should not neglect the role of Renetil or the underground East Timor student organization in quietly preparing the ground, not only among the East Timorese students studying in Bali and Java, but even from within the Indonesian prison system. Reviewing the immediate weeks after the fall of Suharto (21 May), we see the East Timorese students under the banner of Frontpetil (East Timor National Youth Front) involved in a mass demonstration on 12 June outside the Indonesian Foreign Ministry in demand of a meeting with senior government officials around the slogans of "referendum towards a just solution," "Viva reform in Indonesia," "Viva the people of East Timor," "Viva the people of Indonesia who support a referendum for East Timor," and "A referendum for peaceful victory." For the first time the Falintil flag and other East Timor independence symbols were on public parade in Jakarta. Video of the demonstration and its heavy-handed repression by units of ABRI also reached viewers of television news in Japan and other countries. This action was followed by a 17 June protest at the Indonesian Justice Ministry and a 25 June call for a referendum in East Timor.

While the hallmark of the Dili Spring or East Timor student solidarity movement of 1998, as discussed below, was its homegrown character, the collapse of the Suharto dictatorship offered new opportunities arising out of the Indonesian *reformasi* for the East Timorese, encouraged by the linking of the Indonesian democracy movement with their own struggle and that of the Irianese and the Acehnese, together subjected to the worst abuses of the Suharto dictatorship. While such a linkage was tactical it was also a prudent development, given the vastly changed political situation in Jakarta. Foremost of the Jakarta-based political groups in support of East Timorese self-determination was Fortilas (Forum Solidaritas untuk Rakyat Timor Leste). Taking as its slogan "No Democracy for Indonesia without Freedom for East Timor, " Fortilas, in turn, linked itself with the radical (social-democratic) People's Democratic Party (PRD), whose activist ranks inside Indonesia had earlier been targeted by the Suharto government with severe repression. Another of the Indonesian solidarity groups then to surface was Solidimor or Solidaritas untuk Kedamaian Timor Timur (Solidarity for an East Timor Peace Settlement), a human rights and environmental group, linked with the activist student network, PIJAR.

The Indonesia-U.N. autonomy proposal

Of no less consequence for political action in East Timor was Habibie's bid in early July to seal the fate of the East Timor issue by offering what even Suharto had rejected, namely *"autonomi luas"* or wide-ranging autonomy for East Timor but linked to international recognition of the territory's incorporation into the Republic of Indonesia. As discussed below, the suggestion that East Timor be offered a status in some way analogous to that of Aceh, where local rebellion was brutally repressed by the units of ABRI, was viewed by pro-independence supporters inside and outside Timor as ludicrous and a subject for fear.

But in what way did such a diplomatic opening sit with the crux of the problem, Indonesia's bloody annexation and 23-year near-genocidal rule of East Timor in contravention of the rules of self-determination as defended by the U.N.? Indonesian Foreign Minister Ali Alatas countered that a referendum would be divisive and would raise the specter of "renewed civil war," a self-serving argument but one which denied demilitarization, the entry of international peacekeepers and NGOs, and the creation of a level playing field such as would be necessary for an internationally supervised consultation. By late 1998, Habibie was also drawing the wagons, blustering that Indonesia could live without East Timor, but East Timor could not live without Indonesia.

But what was the role of the U.N. in answering Jakarta in these circumstances? Even prior to the Indonesian economic crisis and the fall of Suharto, the incoming U.N. Secretary-General Kofi Annan had moved further and faster than his predecessor by appointing a special representative for East Timor, a Pakistani diplomat, Jamsheed Marker, assisted by the Eritrean diplomat Tamrat Samuel. The Secretary-General also moved up the pace of the tripartite talks between the Indonesian and Portuguese Foreign Ministers, chaired by Annan.[1] While the special representative had been particularly active in consulting all interested parties to the question in Lisbon, Jakarta, and inside East Timor, including discussions with Xanana Gusmão in prison, and Bishop Carlos Belo, among others, the logjam in negotiations really only broke with Marker taking up the Habibie autonomy proposal as one that could be parlayed without prejudice to the positions of Indonesia and Portugal.

At this point, the central role of Gusmão, as the acknowledged leader of the umbrella resistance organization, the National Council of the Timorese Resistance (CNRT), and the key Timorese intelocutor with the U.N., became apparent, as, from May 1998 onwards, he was constantly sought out in Cipinang prison in Jakarta by a string of European ambassadors and even concerned U.S. officials. Earlier, in Peniche in Portugal the broadest possible coalition of Timorese in the diaspora had confirmed Gusmão as supreme leader of the resistance while looking to the future in the drafting of an East Timorese Magna Carta.

Even so, the fact that a leaked U.N. document on the autonomy proposal turned up in Dili and elsewhere ahead of the May 1998 meeting lends credence to the view that the idea originated from within the U.N. bureaucracy rather than from Habibie. On July 3, the Associated Press first sounded the existence of the 5-page discussion paper in "U.N. Paper by Jamsheed Marker Raises Possibility of East Timor Autonomy," offering that Indonesia would, in the plan, maintain control over foreign affairs, defense, currency and finance. Then on 2 July Marker condemned the leak as a "deplorable breach of diplomatic confidentiality" while protesting to the Indonesian Minister of Foreign Affairs. At the same time he downplayed the significance of the documents (dated 23 April 1998) as "exploratory in nature."[2] The fact remained that while the Timorese leaders were not officially privy to the document, much less the U.N. discussions, except on the sidelines, they were *au fait* with its contents, and concerned as to the direction that autonomy proposals were going, short of referendum.

Importantly, both sides agreed in August 1998 to set aside the issue of the territory's final status in the interests of furthering U.N. discussions on the organization of free elections to form an autonomous government in Dili. On 12 November Marker revealed that this plan was based on the Indonesian autonomy proposals with the caveat, "But we have decided to go further and prepare a more substantial document which could be accepted by both countries, whatever the final decision on the territory's status."[3] The matter was fuzzy but Lisbon and CNRT leaders continued to view the U.N. plan as a transitional arrangement pending a internationally monitored popular vote or referendum. Indonesia, on its part, held to the view that the autonomy "concession" would only be offered if the international community accepted Indonesia's sovereignty over East Timor.

Marker later stated in an interview published in *Diario de Noticias* (4 December 1998),[4] ahead of the 19 December meeting in New York between the U.N. Secretary-General and the foreign ministers, that while the Timorese leaders were not directly involved in these negotiations, he had sought to canvass the views of leaders by means of a questionnaire, notably as to the eligibility question for voting in elections for the "autonomous government" especially relating to the participation of Timorese outside the territory (a proposal Marker endorses), leaving the question of self-determination in abeyance. In this plan, East Timor would have "complete jurisdiction" except in defense, diplomacy, and taxes. Even so, he allowed, all Timorese political parties, including pro-independence parties could participate in these elections. As to monitoring the elections, he asserted, while he had plans for a permanent U.N. representation in Timor, "we have not yet received an Indonesian response to this."

Inside East Timor

As *Time* magazine reported (13 July 1998), Dili began to replay the events in Jakarta during Suharto's last days, namely in the form of demonstrations between pro-independence and pro-integrationists for greater autonomy within Indonesia outside the local "parliament." The movement quickly moved from the streets to the main campus of East Timor University (UNTIM). According to *Time*, it was in these circumstances that on 8 June the young East Timorese student Antero Bendito da Silva launched the Student Council for Solidarity (SMPTT) "with the goal of building a bridge between the two groups by limiting the debate to seeking a referendum on Timor's future." Only the brutal army killing of an innocent Timorese farmer on 16 June disrupted the daily gatherings of students at the university.

While army-linked Ninja thugs had long sown discord in East Timor, the fall and flight of Suharto's son-in-law Prabowo had left certain of these groups bereft of money and patronage. In August Marcel de Almeida, head of the Gadapaksi (Garda Muda Penegak Integrasi) or youth movement to promote integration of East Timor with Indonesia, pleaded (*Suara Timor Timur*, 13 August 1998) for protection from reprisal in return for disbanding his discredited and now bankrupt organization. But by year's end, as discussed in the following chapter, it was clear that the current had turned and that the ABRI, via its military-intelligence wing, SGI, had gone over to an active strategy of reviving and even arming these elements to neutralize the pro-independence movement and sow the seeds of instability to make the prospect of referendum infeasible.

Whereas in the past Timorese had been too intimidated to speak openly with foreigners, I was somewhat at a loss for words when asked by a youth on Dili's waterfront whether or not I wished to contact Falintil or the armed guerrilla movement that had been fighting a defensive war against Indonesian invaders since 1975/76. Pleading *"perigo"* (danger), a Portuguese term well understood by my interlocutor, the conversation turned to the burgeoning student-led referendum movement of the towns of East Timor. I was told to expect an invitation. But in what capacity and in what role? The invitation came in the night in the form of a muddled telephone conversation in English, evidently the language of clandestine conversations with foreigners in East Timor. Somewhat confused, I was relieved the following morning to meet the voice embodied in the form of a very young and shy Timorese student and his friend crouching in the shrubbery of my hotel, this time pleading for me to visit Manatuto, a coastal town east of Dili and site of an intended student "dialogue" on the Timor question. As the student *estafetas* or messengers had made the arduous journey just to plead their case, I could hardly refuse. It was now clear that the students wanted a foreign witness. Any foreigner would do, apparently, never mind their identity.

According to Solidarity Council leader, Antero da Silva, in an interview with the Dili newspaper *Suara Timor Timur* (15 August 1998), it was Jamsheed Marker, special representative of the U.N. Secretary General for East Timor, who granted the Timorese students the mandate to set up regional dialogues to ascertain aspirations of the people. This apparently occurred in a meeting between Marker and student representatives on the occasion of his visit to Baucau, the second town in East Timor, on 6 June. According to da Silva, the meetings were to be held in all areas of Timor at the level of *camat* (local government district) in line with the slogan "reconciliation and democracy."

The Solidarity Council first gained major local and even international attention following its well-publicized "free speech" campaign of 2 June held on the campus of UNTIM, an event attended by some 4,000 students. Unprecedented in East Timor under Indonesian military rule, the students made patently clear at this event their demands for a referendum and their rejection of military occupation of East Timor. Obviously taking advantage of the new political space afforded by the downfall of the dictator

/kleptocrat Suharto and the advent of the apparently reformist albeit interim Habibie administration, the students, joined by high school students and other concerned citizens, kept up the momentum of the free speech campaign by staging another event, termed "dialogue" on 6 June, involving an extraordinary public meeting to discuss the future of East Timor and attended by the much chastized Indonesian-appointed Governor, Abilio Soares. With the military standing on the sidelines for the first time in 23 years, the UNTIM students repeated their demands at mass rallies held on campus on 10 June, 13 June and 15 June. On 17 June, around 10,000 citizens of Dili participated in a funeral march for the Timorese man slain by an Indonesian soldier. Again on 20 June, 2,000 students marched on the regional legislative building demanding a referendum. On 27 June, the arrival of three European Ambassadors from Jakarta on a fact-finding tour brought out what eyewitnesses describe as the largest ever protest in East Timor's history, involving 50,000 people, many trucked in from other towns, a visit which tragically led to the shooting of six people (two killed) by Indonesian military vigilantes after the ambassadors entered a cathedral in Baucau.

Needless to say, the politicization of the UNTIM campus evidently breached military tolerance, leading to the closure for several months of the erstwhile autonomous Catholic university, albeit reopened on 24 August. Meantime, however, the Solidarity Council moved ahead in the spirit of Marker's mandate, by initiating regional dialogues. The first was staged in the remote enclave of Oe-cusse (Ambeno) on 6 June, although this cannot be verified, in any case an event not witnessed by foreigners. The next planned meeting was at Los Palos in the extreme east of the half-island. Although cancelled owing to the obstruction of the pro-Indonesian *bupati* or head of the region, the event was eventually held under strict military invigilation in late September.[5] The next dialogue (witnessed by foreigners) was held in a sporting arena in Baucau, drawing in an audience of around 2,000 from many walks of life, not exclusively student. The next intended meeting was at Maliano, near the border with west Timor, albeit blocked by the military, as were intended meetings at Lautem in the east and in Aileu (5 August), a mountain town south of Dili. In the case of Aileu, the military [Muspida or Military Area leadership Conference] proclaimed to the students that they should settle for "wide-ranging autonomy"as proposed by Habibie, not by instability, as their dialogue allegedly threatened. To this bluster the students replied with a letter to Marker, in care of the U.N., complaining of obstruction on the part of the local military, demanding that Jakarta be apprised of this breach of faith, accordingly. As witnessed by Stephanie Coop, this meeting transpired in September with Falintil elements brazenly providing protection.[6]

No doubt alarmed at the pro-independence tenor of the dialogues, on 7 August, the Indonesian Military Resort Commander (Korem) in Dili declared that they had to be framed in the context of the national unity of the Republic of Indonesia. In other words, talk of a referendum under U.N. auspices possibly leading to independence was not something that ABRI could stomach. Then on 10 August, the Indonesian chief of police in East Timor declared that the students could continue their dialogues, without even requesting permission from the Indonesian-appointed Governor or the police. But, in a clear attempt to neutralize the political message of the dialogues, he ordered no display of banners or posters, the hallmark of the free-speech campaigns and dialogues.

The next meeting, held on 6 August at Viqueque in the central east, drew in a crowd of 2,000, followed two days later by a meeting at Ainaro, nestled on the slopes of the formidable Ramaleu mountain range, virtually in the Falintil or armed resistance heartland, and attended by 1,000. The next dialogue was held at Same in Manufahi, like Ainaro a mountainous zone, drawing in 1,000 but also, according to a foreign witness, involving a spectacular caravan of trucks that descended on the south-central coastal town of Betano, and spreading the pro-referendum/anti-integrationist message along the way. The next, witnessed by the author, was held on 21 August inside the *bupati*'s office at Manatuto, a strategically located town on the northern coastal littoral. This meeting was attended by about 250 people, although it was also understood that local military had turned back truckloads of visitors arriving from outlying areas.

Forbidden from using the UNTIM campus as a forum, a seminar was also staged in Dili on 22 August accompanied by impressive cultural performances reflecting pride in Timorese cultural traditions. For the first time at a public forum in East Timor, Indonesians sympathizers joined pro-independence East Timorese. The Indonesians included two PRD activists recently released from prison. According to a witness, these speakers were enthusiastically received by the audience, making it an "historic" event from a resistance perspective.[7]

As to the nature of the "dialogue" and the content of the meetings, it would be sufficient to take the Viqueque meeting as representative. In the language of Janeiro da Silva Belo, spokesperson for the Viqueque Solidarity Council, as told to *Suara Timor Timur* (6 August), the following claims were pressed: first, that Indonesia withdraw ABRI (armed forces) from Timor Loro Sae, so as to create the necessary preconditions for a referendum, second; that Jakarta annul Law No. 7 1976 relating to the integration of Timor Loro Sae into the Republic of Indonesia; third, that special autonomy as a final solution as proposed by President Habibie be strictly rejected; fourth, that Indonesia release all political prisoners, especially Xanana Gusmão, who must be included in future dialogues {a reference to the tripartite U.N.-hosted meetings between the U.N. Secretary-General and the foreign ministers of Portugal and Indonesia); fifth, that Indonesia, Portugal, and the U.N. speedily create a transitional government as a first step towards a referendum; and sixth, stage a referendum as a final step towards the settlement of the Timor problem but in a peaceful environment acceptable to all sides. Among other demands made at Viqueque were calls to bring to justice all Indonesian war criminals (Suharto and the military) involved in Timor Loro Sae to the International Court of Justice in The Hague; quickly normalize relations between Portugal and Indonesia to hasten discussions on the Timor question; calls upon the U.S., the European Union, Russia, China, and other countries to cease supplying Indonesia with military equipment, at least until the

Timor Leste question was settled; and calls upon the World Bank (IMF, WTO) to make all loans to Indonesia conditional on settlement of the Timor question.

As a hesitant invitee to the Manatuto dialogue (although for various reasons careful not to be seen as a participant), I can verify that all these key demands were floated at that meeting. Procedurally, the Manatuto meeting began with a prayer in Tetum. This was salutary, as the venue was located next to a military barracks and uniformed military kept a close eye upon proceedings albeit through binoculars and from the precincts of the barracks. Baton-wielding Timorese auxiliaries were relegated to crowd control and traffic duty. The irony of the sight of a *bupati's* office, still decked out in red-and-white bunting left over from the 17 August Indonesian independence day celebrations, occupied by stalwarts of Timorese independence could not have been lost upon these hapless Indonesian military observers, much discredited since the events of May in Jakarta, nor the juxtapositioning of banners bearing Xanana Gusmão's picture over the colors of the Republic of Indonesia. As a veritable town hall, the rather splendid forum of the two-storied *bupati's* office back-to-back with a Portuguese colonial era structure certainly gave some semblance to a town-hall meeting, American style. But there the resemblance stopped. One by one delegates rose from the floor introducing themselves and the region for which they spoke while outlining their demands. Some spoke in Tetum, some in bahasa Indonesia, some cleverly code switching in bahasa, Tetum, and Portuguese, but all spoke for withdrawal of the military, rejection of autonomy, release of Gusmão, and referendum. All these demands were greeted with wild applause, depending upon the verve with which the speaker (including one woman) addressed the issues.

Perhaps in all this there is some truth in the allegation made by the Indonesian-appointed governor of East Timor, Abilio José Soares, that the students were not undertaking a true dialogue. To be sure, while the slogans of the day were reconciliation and democracy and *cinta-kasih* (love), there were no dissenting voices, the sentiments were unanimous. It was also apparent that this movement was entirely home-grown, springing from the aspirations of the Timorese themselves, from their reading of the local media and world events, and, as far as I can establish, without external support or links. One caveat to this statement was the increasing interest taken in the East Timor referendum question by Jakarta-based personalities and pro-democracy activists, who, from that time, began their networking activities inside East Timor. As implied, the students appeared ignorant, perhaps even wary of any kind of global support movement. In any case, as Solidarity Council leader Antero da Silva answered back to Soares (*Suara Timor Timur*, 22 August), unlike the Suharto era, people were for the first time (theoretically) free from intimidation and pressure, hence the outpouring of long-suppressed sentiments of freedom.

There was then an anxiety for many Timorese that this breath of fresh air would not turn out to be some kind of Indonesian "hundred-flower movement," a reference to Mao Zedung's famous call to intellectuals to speak their minds, only to be followed by repression. Indeed, as the military commander of the Dili headquarters darkly warned on 11 August, while some combat troop withdrawals were made, that did not mean that Timor's status under Indonesian rule as special military region or DOM had been revoked, as had earlier transpired in Aceh. Far from it, going by appearances the military presence in East Timor at the time of the author's visit, were as ubiquitous as ever in the 23 years of Indonesian military occupation.

It then seemed imperative that Indonesia, Portugal, and the U.N. would somehow get the student's message before the window of opportunity in Jakarta slammed shut. Contrariwise, the students then held high expectations that the upcoming tripartite meeting in late September would, for once, act not procrastinate, the hallmark of U.N.-mediated talks on East Timor. Inclusion of Xanana Gusmão in these talks appeared to be a precondition for progress.

At the time the Solidarity Council kept up the pressure on Jakarta, just as outbreaks of military-initiated violence broke the temporary "truce" with Falintil. Notably, on 13 November, the students stormed a government building in Dili, demanding that Indonesian troops be replaced by UN peacekeepers. On 24

November, thousands of students under the Solidarity Council banner marched on Dili's parliament. As discussed in the following chapter, the "peace" was eventually broken, however, by a long-expected ABRI campaign in November 1998. The unprecedented leak of ABRI documents a month earlier convinced Western analysts that contrary to an announced drawdown of troops in the territory, the period had seen a commensurate increase in extent and depth of military and paramilitary penetration.

In a word, then, the actions of the Student Solidarity Council demonstrated unequivocally to the world that, notwithstanding overwhelming pressures and constraints, sentiment inside East Timor was to reject talk of autonomy and to seek independence through a referendum. But, as revealed in the following chapter, the Solidarity Council and its youthful members were to be driven underground by even darker forces.

Notes

The author is especially grateful to Nelson Santos for numerous introductions in East Timor aside from expert knowledge of the situation and guidance on the ground.

1. See author's *East Timor and the United Nations: The Case for Intervention*, (Trenton, N.J., Red Sea Press, 1997), for documents and analysis on the U.N. process.

2. U.N. Press Release SG/SM/6628, 2 July 1998.

3. AFP, 12 November 1999.

4. C. Albino and L. Ferreira, "Just a step forward: East Timor Jamsheed Marker," *Diario de Noticias*, 4 December 1998.

5. Very little of this story reached the outside world. Exceptional was Andrew Perrin, "Fear stifles voice of reform," *The Australian*, 24 September 1998.

6. Stepahnie Coop, "Hopes for Referendum: Defying Guns and Goons, East Timorese Speak Out," *Japan Times,* 23 October 1998.

7. Although the author witnessed preparations for this event, the seminar and most of the Solidarity Council meetings held in July-August were videotaped by Andrew McNaughton, some of which were used on Australian television, later released under the title "Viva Timor Leste."

12. East Timor and the U.N. Ballot of 1999

Meeting on 5 May 1999 in New York at U.N. headquarters, the foreign ministers of Portugal (Jaime Gama) and Indonesia (Ali Alatas) signed a "historic" agreement on the question of East Timor, along with two protocols pertaining to the modalities of a popular ballot slated for August 1999 as to whether or not the East Timorese would accept or reject autonomy within the Republic of Indonesia, and another pertaining to security arrangements during and after the vote. Annexed to the agreement was Indonesia's "constitutional framework for a special autonomy for East Timor," otherwise known as the autonomy package. This agreement, endorsed by the Security Council on 7 May (Resolution 1236 [1999]), was widely portrayed as the triumph of 16 years of U.N. diplomacy on the question. It was cautiously greeted by proponents of the East Timorese resistance, inasmuch as the document recalled key Security Council resolutions on East Timor and the fact that the document, the process, and the results of the ballot were to be referred to the Security Council for approval. The document was also historic in the sense of heralding the almost immediate arrival in East Timor of an advanced U.N. "assessment team" (4-15 May) as a prelude to a full-blown United Nations Assistance Mission in East Timor (UNAMET) budgeted at some US$53 million. Under the agreement, the U.N. Secretary-General, acting on the advice of the assessment team, had until 13 June 1999 to decide if conditions in the territory made the consultation possible. Nevertheless, as events proved, leaving Indonesia and its armed forces in control of overall security was a recipe for disaster.

Background to the New York agreement of 5 May 1999

Essentially stalemated by the Suharto regime since the East Timor question was referred by the U.N. in July 1983 to the Governments of Indonesia and Portugal, but revived, as mentioned, with U.N. Secretary-General Kofi Annan's appointment of a Special Representative for East Timor in 1997, by late 1998, despite an apparent deadlock at the foreign ministers' meeting in December, there was a sense that Portugal and Indonesia had reached a rapprochement on the way ahead. This was all the more so when, in early 1999, each country moved to open an interest section in each other's capital. Nevertheless, many questions remained to be answered as to Jakarta's sincerity on the issue, especially as elite opinion in Jakarta among certain opposition figures (Megawati), retired Generals, etc. was not encouraging. But Indonesian Foreign Minister Ali Alatas' abrupt statement on 27 January 1999 as to a "second option" for East Timor as free from Indonesia raised international expectations to an even higher level, as did the 12 February statement by President Habibie that, "From January 1, 2000, the East Timor question should be resolved. We don't want to be burdened .. We will concentrate on the other 26 provinces."

As invoked by the 5 May document, the principle of "special status based on wide-ranging autonomy...without prejudice to the positions of principle of the respective governments" had been determined at the earlier meeting on 5 August 1998. Long holding out the scenario of civil war should a referendum be held, it was only at a subsequent meeting in New York on 21-23 April that Indonesia finally conceded the principle of a direct ballot or plebiscite, allaying concerns as to a West Irian (Irian Jaya) "act of free choice" scenario, a reference to the sham U.N. monitored plebiscite of 1969 in that territory.

Notably, at the 21-23 April meeting, Indonesia formally presented for the first time its 60-point "autonomy package," as mentioned, first broached by Habibie in June 1998. It was then revealed that the U.N. was expected to supervise a vote or plebiscite, whereupon on 8 August the East Timorese would be consulted as to whether they rejected or accepted the

Indonesian "autonomy package." Two additional documents were presented to the delegations for the first time. These covered security arrangements for the "popular consultation" and the "modalities" of the consultation. As Jamsheed Marker, U.N. Special Representative for East Timor explained, while a U.N. presence would be involved on the ground, the shape or form was yet to be worked out, further revealing that he favored the "word and understanding of Indonesia" and "diplomatic process" over dispatching Blue Helmets or peacekeepers.

Clearly, the 5 May document offered that, should the proposed constitutional framework for special autonomy be acceptable to the East Timorese people, then Portugal would initiate the procedures necessary to remove East Timor from the list of Non-Self-Governing Territories and Indonesia would make its constitutional adjustments in line with the autonomy package. On the contrary, should the autonomy proposals be rejected, then Indonesia would terminate its links with East Timor and the territory would revert to its pre 17 July 1976 status (a reference to the Indonesian parliament's incorporation of East Timor) and authority in East Timor would be transferred to the U.N. pending a transfer of power to an independent East Timor state. Fatally, such language masked the pact with Jakarta that required the new Indonesian parliament elected in June 1999 to actually vote to release East Timor from the illegal 1976 annexation.

The international push

Guided by Portugal, the European Union countries maintained a resolute position in pressuring Indonesia to abide by its pledges on East Timor and, on 12 December in a landmark decision, backed calls for a referendum and a permanent U.N. presence. For some of the EU states this position has meant drawing a line between arms sales to Jakarta and a moral position on East Timor. While official U.S. policy on East Timor had always been guarded in the interests of preserving business and military ties with a "moderate" Muslim country, in a landmark decision on 28 October 1998, the U.S. Congress voted to ban the use of

U.S.-supplied weapons in East Timor and, for the first time, to support self-determination for East Timor. No doubt the mainstreaming of the East Timor question in Australian politics and media was important—first, in pushing Prime Minister John Howard to do what no previous Australian Prime Minister had done, namely to write a letter to the Indonesian President stating his concerns on East Timor. As made public on 12 January 1999 by Australian Foreign Minister Alexander Downer, Australia now supported holding an "act of self-determination." Howard's letter has been viewed both inside Indonesia and Australia as serving as a catalyst for change on the part of the Jakarta establishment.[1]

While Australian resolve to commit funds and resources along with a civilian and police presence in East Timor was a major factor in galvanizing international support, the Canberra government still did not depart from its fine-tuned position of recognition of Indonesian sovereignty over East Timor. The Australian Prime Minister also let it be known that his preferred outcome was that East Timor accept the Indonesian autonomy package. However promising, Australian diplomacy in early 1999 on creating a Cambodia-style "contact group" for East Timor met with only lukewarm response in Japan, the U.S., and ASEAN.

Still, Portugal, pro-independence East Timorese, resistance spokepersons, and support groups globally were unanimous that a very strong peace-keeping presence was required in East Timor to provide security for the vote. The offer by such countries as Ireland, Canada, Brazil, and New Zealand (belatedly, and conditionally joined by Australia on 25 April) to supply peacekeepers to a U.N. mission in East Timor was not, however, matched by resolve at the U.N. Although Brazil raised the East Timor question in the Security Council on 19 April, no action was taken on that initiative, as would have been necessary for the presence of armed peacekeepers, in any case refused by Indonesia.

Then Jakarta's understanding of an acceptable international presence in East Timor was finally revealed at a "historic summit" between Howard, Australian military brass, and their Indonesian counterparts, held in Bali on 27 April. Although this meeting was portrayed in Australian media as bravely standing up to Jakarta, it was also, ignominiously, the occasion on which the regime let it be known to the world ahead of the 5 May agreement in New York that it would only countenance unarmed U.N. "police advisors" in East Timor. The world—East Timorese support groups, in particular—could not but notice that Howard also fell short of obtaining crucial guarantees from Wiranto or Habibie as to a disarmament of the militia groups.

Covert warfare: ABRI and the rise of the militias

To astute observers, it was clear that Jakarta was playing a wily dual diplomatic and military strategy over East Timor, on the one hand snaring the U.N. into mounting a flawed ballot with Portugal's acquiescence, and on the other hand, setting the trap masterminded by ABRI. The Foreign Ministry role was clearly to drag out the discussions to win time for a strategy aimed at routing out the pro-independence supporters, while ABRI through its agents provoked terror and coercion to prepare a favorable outcome. Accordingly, in May 1999, having been duly briefed, Wiranto announced that only three regional CNRT organizations remained in East Timor, facts also drawn to Habibie's attention.

Behind this strategy on the ground was the tactic to create the myth of equivalence between the militias and Falintil otherwise represented as warring parties. Ipso facto, with this logic disarmament of the so-called two warring factions would involve not only the militias but also Falintil. ABRI, the invader and tormentor of the Timorese people was, accordingly, elevated to the status of keeper of security, while Falintil, the protector of the Timorese people over 23 years, became the equivalent of the murderous ABRI-sponsored militias of some three months.

While Falintil and ABRI had entered into a virtual ceasefire arrangement since the flight of Col. Prabowo in mid-1998, and while the Koppasus-supported "Ninja" militia's had apparently been deactivated, or at least bereft of financial support, darker scenarios were being plotted. As discussed in chapter 11, the first months of reformation in Indonesia offered a rare opening for peaceful demonstrations by East Timorese in support of independence. First, as now well documented, ABRI's showcase evacuation staged for the foreign media in August 1998 masked a troop buildup in the east preparatory to an encirclement and assault on Falintil in that quarter. In effect, the unofficial ceasefire between ABRI and Falintil was disrupted by ABRI killings in Alas on the remote south coast in November 1998, provoking the Portuguese to postpone an upcoming round of discussions with the Indonesians at New York and attracting a statement of concern from the Secretary-General. Jakarta's veiled-glove strategy was now reversed. Commencing in late 1998, new militia groups were brought into line. The reported arrival of a Koppasus unit in West Timor on 10 November was one omen, and the precipitous attacks and killings in January 1999 of citizens in Suai by a militia group called Mahudi signalled the unfolding of a plan to destabilize the border area of East and West Timor, bringing into play ethnically akin Belunese from West Timor. There was no question that the militias had been paid off from a specially appointed fund bankrolled by Jakarta.

It is clear then that in keeping with 23 years' bad faith on East Timor, Jakarta quietly began sowing the seeds of a devastating contra-type operation on the ground in East Timor, not only to Timorize the war, to create the illusion of a civil war situation that only ABRI could invigilate, but to neutralize pro-independence forces and wreck the peace necessary for any fair ballot. Writing in February 1999, Richard Tanter reasons that the ABRI game plan in East Timor could conceivably follow a "Nicaraguan model," whereby ABRI would (eventually) withdraw but leaving behind "politically reliable and well-equipped pro-Indonesian *contras* with orders to derail the peace process in the short term, and to use terror to destroy an independent Timor."[2]

The duplicity of Jakarta's dual diplomatic and military strategy could of course no longer be contained, especially after the gruesome Liquisa church massacres of 5 April, leading to scores of deaths including innocent women and children, and, with even more brazen demonstration, the militia amok or rampage in Dili on 17 April leading to the deaths of hundreds of citizens including pro-independence figures, along with the burning of houses, shops, and even the office of the local newspaper. While Western embassies and observers had been quick to denounce the actions of "rogue" militia and military elements, Western intelligence already had advance notice of a coordinated ABRI-planned destabilization mission in East Timor at least as far back as late 1998. Small solace for the East Timorese victims that the Western capitals began asking themselves as to who was calling the shots in Jakarta, Commander-in-chief Habibie or military supremo Wiranto, or retired generals of a shadowy conspiracy that linked Suharto, Prabowo-in-exile, and even retired General Murdani, architect of the 1976 invasion. On the ground, intelligence figures in Dili included General Zacky Anwar Makarin, recently retired from head of military intelligence, and Kiki Syahnakri, a former ABRI regional commander, while Habibie's Minister of Information, General Yunus Yosifiah, a key player in Jakarta's public relations war, spearheaded the invasion of East Timor at Balibo in 1975.

Writing of these paramilitary death squads, all of which came into being or were reactivated after Jakarta's announcement of a "second option" for East Timor, we can say that all are led by pro-integration figures, and all gain support from ABRI. All have advocated or used violence in recruitment, and all have subjected the Timorese people to cruel terror. ABRI, along with pro-integrationist forces, have been widely observed at inauguration ceremonies. Some have conducted joint operations with ABRI units. ABRI personnel have been widely observed as advising or participating in militia activities, and, moreover, ABRI has supplied their modern weapons. Led by 24-year-old Eurico Gutteres, a former member of the Kopassus-trained Garda Paksi and well known gambling syndicate boss, Aitarak was one of the most threatening militias in Dili, where it paraded on 16 April in front of the Governor's palace in the presence of the Indonesian-appointed Governor Abilio Soares and Indonesian military brass. Besi Merah Putih, established on 27 December 1998, and based in the Maubara district, is led by Manuel de Sousa, a former pro-Suharto figure from Liquisa, also distinguished by its random acts of terror both in recruitment and against civilians. Mahidi, under the leadership of Cancio Lopez da Carvalho, a former worker in the provincial justice office, was formed in late December in Cassa town on the pretense of protecting itself from Falintil. By early April this militia boasted 1,000 members and 37 automatic weapons. It operates in Ainaro and Suai. Carvalho has even admitted support from ABRI in front of foreign media (ABC 4 Corners). Other militias, according to geographic distribution, include, in the east, Saka, based in Quelicai (Baucau), Team Sera and Team Makikit; in the center, Garda Paksi, Commando Darah Merah and AHI; in the south, Tatarah, Team Ablai, Laksaur Merah Putih and Loromea; and in the west, Naga Merah and Halilintar, based in Atabae. In turn, the political arm of the militias, the Forum for Unity, Democracy and Justice (FPDK), was founded in January 1999 by Basilio Dias Araujo and José Tavares, son of Halilintar strongman, João Tavares. Not only had the militias terrorized Timorese civilians, displacing up to 5 percent of the population and holding many thousands as virtual hostage in Liquisa, but, by targeting foreign aid workers, journalists, and Australian nationals, had forced a virtual evacuation of international humanitarian workers and eyewitnesses prior to the entry of the first U.N. officials.

By the time of the Liquisa massacres, ABRI denials of links with the militia began to ring hollow, as did Wiranto's disavowal of support, especially as ABRI took no actions against them. Indeed, Wirnato provided the militias with an alibi and a rationale, saying that Ratih or official militia groups were there to help the police maintain order. Nevertheless, the nationwide policy of arming militia with sticks was easily transmuted inside East Timor into the distribution of guns. Wiranto's much publicized visit to Dili on 20 April in the wake of the militia amok and the act of staging a peace pact between the militias and CNRT, in the company of the two bishops and local civilian and military authorities, was widely believed as a public relations ploy, es- pecially as the militias continued their terror, although it also revealed ABRI's ability to take orders. But, if taken seriously, the peace pact should have been the cue for the U.N. to dispatch its peace enforcers. Within days of the signing of the New York agreement, it seemed that militia violence in part aimed at derailing the prospects for an election was, to Indonesia's concern, strengthening international calls for the peacekeepers.

UNAMET on the ground

Simultaneous with the New York meeting of 21-23 April 1999, a U.N. interagency "humanitarian mission" visited East Timor to assess humanitarian and development needs. It reported "critical gaps in the delivery of basic services, particularly health and education." This assessment would not surprise many people, Timorese included—especially as a humanitarian disaster had been reimplanted by the destabilizing actions of the militias— but it is significant that for the first time in 24 years the U.N. had moved to even make an on-the-ground assessment in this area. The first members of the U.N. "assessment team" in advance of the full blown UNAMET mission arrived in Dili on 3 May, just ahead of U.N. discussions. This was a four-member team from the U.N. Political Affairs Department tasked to evaluate the needs of the future U.N. monitoring force. On 8 May, Om Rather, the top U.N. police advisor flew to Dili to assess the situation, offering that a force of between 250 and 300 U.N. police would be required and would start to arrive in June. While the important Security Council resolution unlocked U.N. funds to support the U.N. mission, still the potential donor countries were slow in announcing commitments, doubtless also deterred by the dubious security situation. Indeed, the U.N. imposed conditionality upon the process, requiring a positive assessment of the security situation to be constantly reported back to the U.N. Secretary-General, in turn to be reported to the Security Council in mid-June, which would, in turn, determine whether the registration process could proceed. By early July, according to U.N. spokespersons, all groups were required to "lay down their weapons," clearly a formula short of disarmament and a timetable comfortable for the militias to finish off their bloodthirsty work.

As set down in the Agreement on the modalities of popular

consultation, the runup to polling day on 8 August was to be in line with a strict timetable. The first stage was that of "operational planning/deployment" (10 May-15 June); followed by "public information programme/voter education" (10 May-5 August); "preparation and registration" (13 June-17 July); "exhibition of lists and challenges" (18 July-23 July); "political campaign" (20 July-5 August); and "cooling-off period" (6 August-7 August). Voter registration was to take place over 20 days in 200 centers inside Timor as well as in a number of Indonesian cities and in such centers where the diaspora formed communities as Macau, Lisboa, and Darwin. The campaign ahead of the vote was to be in line with a Code of Conduct. International observers were allowed. International civilian police were to be present in East Timor to "advise" the Indonesian police and to "supervise the escort of ballot papers." In this exercise, the voters were asked to accept or reject the Indonesian autonomy package. Within days of the agreement, the U.N. announced that alongside international civilian police, there would be over 600 international staff, including 400 registration and polling officers, as well as some 4,000 local staff. In fact, the ballot was twice delayed by the U.N. Secretary-General on the grounds that the conditions for security had not been met although, imprudently, the vote was allowed to proceed on 30 August.

Security guarantees

As the security protocol of the May 5 agreement outlined, a prerequisite for the vote was a "secure environment devoid of violence or other forms of intimidation." Such would be salutary for the East Timorese at the hands of the militias and ABRI, although the major contradiction of the agreement was, as feared by independence supporters, that "the maintenance of law and order rested with the appropriate Indonesian security authorities." Still the "absolute neutrality" of ABRI was demanded. But this was a matter of faith, as Kofi Annan explained in a press conference. One curiosity was that a hastily contrived "Commission of Peace and Stability" established in

Dili on 21 April was advised to become operational and to cooperate with the U.N. to "ensure the laying down of arms and take the necessary steps to achieve disarmament." Details on security were also outlined in an unsigned memorandum presented by the Secretary-General. This was presented to convey to Portugal and Indonesia that certain security conditions had to be met for the operational phase (or start-up) of the process. Primary was the need to bring armed civilian groups under strict control, a ban on armed rallies, the arrest and prosecution of those threatening to use violence, the "redeployment" of Indonesian military, and a "laying down of arms." Such sentiments were salutary but fell short of Indonesian military drawdown and disarmament.

In any case, the security question was to be subject to a number of tests, the first accounting of which was registered by the advance mission in its report to the UN Secretary-General, in turn submitted to the Security Council on 22 May (S/1999/595). In this, Kofi Annan declared, "Despite repeated assurances that measures would be taken by the Indonesian authorities to ensure security in East Timor and curtail the illegal activities of the armed militias, I regret to inform the Security Council that credible reports continue to be received of political violence, including intimidations and killings, by armed militias against unarmed pro-independence civilians...there are indications that the militias, believed by many observers to be operating with the acquiescence of elements of the army, have not only in recent weeks begun to attack pro-independence groups, but are beginning to threaten moderate pro-integration supporters as well." In identifying 24 militia groups across the territory, the Secretary-General also raised for the first time the possibility of assigning military liaison officers to assist UNAMET.

Assessment

From the outset, as elements of the UNAMET mission arrived in East Timor, analysts were cautious, even guarded, as to a peaceful outcome of the ballot, especially as the militia death squads were still operating with impunity. As some Western media concluded, this was a flawed U.N. agreement from both a security perspective, and also from an international legal perspective. Leaving the Indonesian armed forces and its adjunct police forces in control of security during the conduct of a U.N. supervised ballot was undoubtedly a precedent-setting strategy on the part of the world body, but one that bent over backwards to accommodate Indonesian face. As Francis Vendrall, Head of the U.N. Political Affairs Department, disarmingly clarified on the envisaged role of U.N. "police advisors," "advice cannot be forced upon the Indonesian police." Moreover, no timetable was entertained in the pact for the cantonment and withdrawal of ABRI, the invading force condemned in two UN Security Council resolutions. Neither did the call for "laying down of arms" on the part of the militias (and Falintil) strike the right chord, at least alongside resistance demands for an internationally supervised disarmament.

Neither did the Indonesian parliamentary veto on the outcome of the ballot bode well for what amounted for the East Timorese as a once-and-for-all vote on their destiny. Neither was Xanana Gusmão allowed his freedom to enter the campaign, notwithstanding a mounting chorus of international voices for his release. Almost from the outset a duty-bound UNAMET were obliged to defend themselves from Indonesian allegations of victim bias for having the temerity to expose a militia "training class" conducted by ABRI. Only faith in the agreement and the mandate held by the Secretary-General, and through him, the Security Council and General Assembly, to cancel, suspend, and/or pass judgment on the ballot, offered hope for a just outcome.

Notes

1. On Australian policy, see James Cotton (ed), *East Timor and Australia*, (Canberra: Australia Defence Studies Centre/Australian Institute of International Affairs, Canberra, 1999).
2. Richard Tanter, "Tomorrow, in Timor Lorosae," *Inside Indonesia*, (April-June 1999): 12-13.

Envoi

On 14 September, two weeks after the U.N.-sponsored ballot on East Timor's future, a beleaguered UNAMET evacuated to northern Australia, leaving behind a handful of officials in the dubious security of the Australian consulate. Within hours of their departure, the UNAMET compound was looted. Over the preceding two weeks, much of Dili had been systematically reduced to ashes, with most of its population forcibly removed. Decomposed bodies lay in the streets. Having long harassed and intimidated foreign observers, aid-workers, journalists, and even UNAMET, and having tasted blood with the pre-ballot assault on pro-independence campaigners, the devil licked its chops, and, scarcely awaiting the announcement of the ballot result on 4 September, began the wholesale slaughter of Timorese in the capital and in isolated towns and hamlets across the half-island. Especially targetted were males and those who voted for independence. But the unthinkable in Timor also happened; the Church was attacked, sparing neither priests, or nuns, while the Bishop of Dili made a narrow escape. The numbers killed or "disappeared" in this wicked display of medievalism are incalculable but undoubtedly run into the thousands, possibly tens of thousands. Who, then, committed this atrocity, bordering upon genocide? Precisely those entrusted by the U.N. to ensure the peaceful conduct of the ballot, the TNI, and their militias.

The few dazed citizens visible to departing UNAMET staff could be seen searching for food in the smoldering ruins of already looted shops. Water, power, and telecommunications services had been systematically destroyed. To the extent that governmental function existed it was in the hands of automatic-weapon-bearing black-clad militias and military, some driving looted UNAMET-marked jeeps. The U.N. Human Rights Commissioner, Mary Robinson, had just declared the necessity to create a commission leading to a Rwanda-style tribunal to prosecute crimes against humanity. The international community expressed outrage, as Jakarta went into denial mode and anti-foreign nationalism surged across Indonesia. With President

B.J. Habibie increasingly captive to the military, the world entered a breathless week of diplomatic brinkmanship. Undoubtedly only the threat of a war crimes tribunal along with the imposition of economic and military sanctions on Jakarta by the U.S. and EU countries, in tandem with the U.S. President's evident conversion on the Timor horror, persuaded Wiranto and Habibie—to the collective relief of the world—to agree on 12 September to invite the U.N. to dispatch an international force. Among the major economies Japan alone worked to preserve the Indonesian government's face. Still with the sword of Damocles hanging over the heads of the Timorese, the U.N. procrastinated on the terms of its mission until 15 September. On this day the Security Council unanimously passed resolution 1264 (1999) paving the way for the immediate entry into East Timor of a U.N.-mandated multinational "peace-enforcement" force pending the arrival of a full-fledged U.N.-commanded "blue helmet" or peacekeeping force in a later period. Mandated under Chapter VII of the U.N. charter, the Australian-led International Force for East Timor (Interfet) was authorized to deploy force and to take in hand the humanitarian crisis. Nevertheless, much ambiguity remained in the wording of the resolution over the withdrawal of the remaining 26,000 Indonesian security forces in East Timor. Neither were powers of arrest granted Interfet in the case of capture of militias.

But also the clock was ticking on the lives of some 300,000 to 500,000 internal refugees who fled the torched and devastated urban centers of East Timor for the mountains as food supplies dwindled and vindictive militia and military closed in. The fate of an additional 200,000 terrorized East Timorese pushed out of the cities and towns across the border to concentration-style camps in West Timor raised many questions as to rebuilding East Timor, especially as militias and Kopassus elements from within the military began to retreat to West Timor and even to Jakarta. Such fears were also carried in the report by a Security Council mission that visited Jakarta and Dili between 8 and 12 September drawing attention to the "systematic implementation of a 'scorched-earth' policy" by the Indonesian military, selective executions of East Timorese students, intellectuals and others, massive population displacements to West Timor and permanent displacements of East Timorese around Indonesia (S/1999/976).

As the *Independent* newspaper of London wrote on 15 September, "Quite apart from the blow to its institutional pride, UNAMET leaves the people it set out to help in an immeasurably worse state than when it arrived." Needless to say, recriminations over UNAMET's failure continued to circulate in media and diplomatic circles alike. Still, even this paper conceded that UNAMET fulfiled its mandate in the narrow sense of successfully conducting the ballot. Having been twice postponed, the ballot was duly held on 30 August with over 98 percent of the 451,792 registered actually voting. Despite the absence of a level playing field, as even UNAMET admitted, the result was an overwhelming victory for independence and a rejection of "special autonomy." To be precise, 78.5 percent voted to break with Indonesia while 21.5 percent chose the Indonesian autonomy package. The high voter turn-out and relative calm of the ballot was seen by UNAMET as a vindication of its mission, notwithstanding—as witnessed by the author, along with many hundreds of international observers—the concerted, illegal, and murderous drive by the Indonesian military-backed militia, in tandem with the central organs of the Indonesian information and foreign ministries, to intimidate or sway the minds of pro-independence voters.

An independent East Timor now seemed politically assured, but at what unconscionable human cost?

Credits

Earlier versions of the following chapters appeared in the following books or journals:

Chapter 1 originally appeared as, "Ideology and the Concept of Government in the Indonesian New Order," *Asian Survey*, XIX, 8, (August 1979): 751-769. Reproduced with permission of the Regents of the University of California.

Chapter 2, "Tan Malaka in Indonesian History," from *Tan Malaka's Naar de Republiek Indonesia: A Translation and Commentary*, (Nagasaki University, Faculty of Economics, Southeast Asia Research Center Monograph No. 29, 1996): 1-31.

Chapter 3, "The Garuda and the Dragon: Indonesian-Chinese Relations," *Asia Pacific Review*, (Summer 1987): 17-31.

Chapter 4, "Radical Islam in Southeast Asia: Rhetoric and Reality in the Middle Eastern Connection," *Journal of Contemporary Asia*, 16, 1 (1986): 30-54. Reproduced with permission.

Chapter 5, "Death and the State in Malaysia," *Arena* (Melbourne), 76 (1986): 116-127. Reproduced with permission.

Chapter 6, "The Image of Brunei in Western Literature," in Tan Pek Leng, G.C. Gunn, B.A. Hussainmiya and Iik Ariffin Mansurnoor, (eds.), *Essays on Modern Brunei History*, (Brunei: Department of History, Universiti Brunei Darussalam, 1992): 1-52.

Chapter 7, "Rentier Capitalism in Negara Brunei Darussalam," in Kevin Hewison, Richard Robison and Garry Rodan (eds.), *Southeast Asia in the 1990s: Authoritarianism, Democracy and Capitalism*, (Sydney: Allen and Unwin, 1993): 111-132.

Chapter 8, "Wartime Portuguese Timor: The Azores Connection," (Centre of Southeast Asian Studies, Working Paper No. 50, Monash University, 1988).

Chapter 9, "Language, Literacy and Political Hegemony in "East Timor," in David Myers (ed.), *The Politics of Multiculturalism in the Asia/Pacific* (Darwin: Northern Territory University Press, 1996): 117-123.

Chapter 10, "From Salazar to Suharto: Toponymy, Public Architecture and Memory in the Making of East Timorese Identity," paper delivered to International Conference on East Timor "History and Conflict Resolution," Osaka University of Foreign Studies and the University of Aveiro (Portugal), 5-6 December 1998.